John Dawson
Appalachian State University

STUDY GUIDE

to accompany

Modern Principles:
MACROECONOMICS

second edition

Tyler Cowen ▲ Alex Tabarrok

WORTH PUBLISHERS

Study Guide
by John Dawson
to accompany
Cowen/Tabarrok: *Modern Principles: Macroeconomics, Second Edition*

ISBN 13: 978-1-4292-9286-3
ISBN 10: 1-4292-9286-5

First Printing 2012

Printed in the United States of America

Worth Publishers
41 Madison Avenue
New York, NY 10010
www.worthpublishers.com
www.wortheconomics.com

Contents

Key to Corresponding Chapter Numbers

	Microeconomics	**Economics**	**Macroeconomics**
The Big Ideas	Chapter 1	Chapter 1	Chapter 1
The Power of Trade and Comparative Advantage	Chapter 2	Chapter 2	Chapter 2
Supply and Demand	Chapter 3	Chapter 3	Chapter 3
Equilibrium: How Supply and Demand Determine Prices	Chapter 4	Chapter 4	Chapter 4
Elasticity and its Applications	Chapter 5	Chapter 5	
Taxes and Subsidies	Chapter 6	Chapter 6	
The Price System: Signals, Speculation and Prediction	Chapter 7	Chapter 7	
Price Ceilings and Price Floors	Chapter 8	Chapter 8	Chapter 5
International Trade	Chapter 9	Chapter 9	Chapter 19
Externalities: When Prices Send the Wrong Signals	Chapter 10	Chapter 10	
Costs and Profit Maximization Under Competition	Chapter 11	Chapter 11	
Competition and the Invisible Hand	Chapter 12	Chapter 12	
Monopoly	Chapter 13	Chapter 13	
Price Discrimination	Chapter 14	Chapter 14	
Cartels, Oligopolies, and Monopolistic Competition	Chapter 15	Chapter 15	
Competing for Monopoly: The Economics of Network Goods	Chapter 16	Chapter 16	
Labor Markets	Chapter 17	Chapter 17	
Public Goods and the Tragedy of the Commons	Chapter 18	Chapter 18	
Political Economy and Public Choice	Chapter 19	Chapter 19	Chapter 21
Economics, Ethics and Public Policy	Chapter 20	Chapter 20	
Managing Incentives	Chapter 21	Chapter 21	
Stock Markets and Personal Finance	Chapter 22	Chapter 22	Chapter 10

	Microeconomics	Economics	Macroeconomics
Consumer Choice	Chapter 23	Chapter 23	
GDP and the Measurement of Progress		Chapter 24	Chapter 6
The Wealth of Nations and Economic Growth		Chapter 25	Chapter 7
Growth, Capital Accumulation and the Economics of Ideas: Catching Up vs. The Cutting Edge		Chapter 26	Chapter 8
Saving, Investment, and the Financial System		Chapter 27	Chapter 9
Unemployment and Labor Force Participation		Chapter 28	Chapter 11
Inflation and the Quantity Theory of Money		Chapter 29	Chapter 12
Business Fluctuations: Aggregate Demand and Supply		Chapter 30	Chapter 13
Transmission and Amplification Mechanisms		Chapter 31	Chapter 14
The Federal Reserve System and Open Market Operations		Chapter 32	Chapter 15
Monetary Policy		Chapter 33	Chapter 16
The Federal Budget: Taxes and Spending		Chapter 34	Chapter 17
Fiscal Policy		Chapter 35	Chapter 18
International Finance		Chapter 36	Chapter 20

Preface

This **Study Guide** is designed for use with the second edition of **Modern Principles: Macroeconomics** by Tyler Cowen and Alex Tabarrok. Economics is not just an interesting subject for study, but is an integral part of life used in everything from shopping at the local grocery store to buying a house to understanding national economic performance. To help you reach your goal of understanding economics, this study guide includes information and exercises that reinfoce key concepts and provide self-testing and repetition. Together, these activities will enhance your learning of text material and will help you to evaluate your understanding of important concepts.

Have you ever taken a test thinking you were well prepared only to discover that you really didn't understand a particular concept? Ideally, working through each study guide chapter will enable you to actively learn the text chapter's contents while also discovering and focusing on material you thought you had mastered but had not.

Learning Objectives, Summary and Key Terms

Each chapter begins by setting out learning objectives from the textbook chapter. These learning objectives are immediately followed by a chapter summary containing the essential points of the chapter, including references to important tables and graphs from the text. To make the material easier for you to digest, the summary is deliberately brief and straightforward. Reading the summary does not replace reading the text. Instead, the summary is designed to be a supplement to help solidify your understanding of the text material.

For your convenience, the key terms in the text chapter are listed separately and defined again.

Traps, Hints, and Reminders

These short sections first identify concepts that from experience we have found can be difficult for students. Helpful hints for understanding that material are provided. This section also includes information to reinforce concepts that we think are among the most important.

Self-Practice Questions and Homework Quiz

When you have finished studying the contents of each chapter, you can test and reinforce your understanding of key concepts by completing the self-practice questions. For a self-test of the chapter's material, about 20 multiple-choice questions are provided. The answers to all of these questions are provided at the end of the chapter along with references to relevant sections in the text.

Each study guide chapter also contains a separate homework quiz composed of multiple-choice questions. Your instructor has the correct answers to these questions. This self-test is yet another opportunity for active learning.

Acknowledgements

Tyler Cowen and Alex Tabarrok have written a truly revolutionary text for the Principles of Economics course. It is fresh. It is modern. It is not encyclopedic. And it has been a hit among both students and instructors. My work with the text began in the first edition as a reviewer and I am honored to be a part of the team that made this text possible—if only a small part. I am therefore thankful, first, to Tyler and Alex for writing a brilliant and insightful book. In addition, Alex took the time on several occasions to work with me one-on-one to convey the spirit of the macroeconomics in the text. This collaboration made this *Study Guide* a better product, and for that I am especially grateful.

I am also especially grateful to Tom Acox, who worked with me in developing the initial concept of this *Study Guide*. He did not miss a beat in seeing the project to its end. I would also like to thank Sarah Dorger and Paul Shensa at Worth for their faith in me and encouragement throughout the course of my work on this project. Their commitment has been tireless. The production team of Edgar Bonilla and Stacey Alexander helped to always keep the work flow moving. Additionally, there are numerous individuals at Worth—the accuracy checkers and others whose names and faces I never knew—that provided excellent support at various stages of the project. You all have a hand in making the final product as good as it is. Finally, I would also like to thank my students at Appalachian State University and other places over the years for teaching me much about teaching economics. The ideas that appear in this book are testament to that.

Last, but not least, much of my thinking and writing on this project took place during the summer of 2011. I am grateful to my family and friends who tolerated my random blank stares during those times when I could not take my mind off of work. You all make everything better.

J.W.D.
Boone, NC
December, 2011

STUDY GUIDE

1

The Big Ideas

Learning Objectives

The objective of this chapter is for you to learn about a number of big ideas of economics that are the overarching ideas that occur and reoccur throughout the book. The big ideas include:

> Incentives Matter
> Good Institutions Align Self-Interest with the Social Interest
> Trade-offs Are Everywhere
> Thinking on the Margin
> The Power of Trade
> The Importance of Wealth and Economic Growth
> Institutions Matter
> Economic Booms and Busts Cannot Be Avoided But They Can Be Moderated
> Prices Rise When the Government Prints Too Much Money
> Central Banking Is a Hard Job
> The Biggest Idea of All: Economics Is Fun

Summary

Incentives are rewards and penalties that motivate behavior, and they matter. For example, if you pay unemployed people longer, then the unemployment rate will remain higher than it otherwise would be. Good institutions align self-interest with the social interest. The market often does this in a manner for which Adam Smith coined the term, "the invisible hand." The farmer works hard on his farm, the trucker takes food from farm to market, the grocer takes risks and opens a store. All these people do these things in their own self-interest (to make money for themselves), not to make sure that you do not starve. Yet you and society benefit from their self-interest. Put more crudely, greed is often good.

Trade-offs are everywhere. You cannot have your cake and eat it, too. You must make a choice. The value of a lost opportunity is the **opportunity cost** of a choice: If you eat your cake now, you must give up having it later; if you save the cake for later, you have to give up eating it now. In order to understand trade-offs, you need to think on the margin. Thinking on the margin is thinking in terms of small changes. Examples include marginal cost, which is the change in cost when a firm produces one more of its product, and marginal revenue, which is the change in revenue when the firm sells one less of its product.

The power of trade is that trade and specialization allow people to produce more than they could otherwise. Trade takes place when both parties expect to and usually do gain. It also allows people to consume more than they can produce. It can even take place between the highly productive and the not-very-productive because of the concept of comparative advantage, the ability to produce at a lower opportunity cost than your trading partner. Trade leads to economic growth and wealth, which in turn leads to better lives for people—economic growth and wealth are associated with a longer life expectancy and lower infant mortality.

Institutions matter and affect economic growth and wealth. Countries that are similar but have differing institutions can vary widely in wealth and economic growth. The institutions that support good incentives are property rights, political stability, honest government, a dependable legal system, and competitive and open markets.

Economic booms and busts cannot be avoided but they can be moderated. Some economic shocks, for example, earthquakes and bad weather, cannot be avoided. But other important shocks that have contributed to "busts," for example, the Great Depression of the 1930s, have been due to bad economic policy and could have been avoided. In the 1930s, however, economic fiscal and monetary policies were less well understood than they are today. The current better understanding of both types of policy can and should help moderate booms and busts.

Central banking is a hard job. The U.S. central bank is called the Federal Reserve, or, simply, the Fed. Central banks must deal with an uncertain future, calls for them to accomplish more than they actually can, make policy today that affects the economy with a time lag, and face conflicting goals. If the central bank puts too little money in circulation, the economy can go into recession. If the central bank errs on the other side and prints too much money, prices rise.

The biggest idea of all is that *economics is fun*. We are surrounded by economics. It can tell us why some countries are rich and some are poor. It can tell us about how to reduce crime, or how to manage a business, or how to set up good incentives for government.

Key Terms

incentives rewards and penalties that motivate behavior

opportunity cost cost of a choice is the value of the opportunities lost

inflation a general increase in prices

Traps, Hints, and Reminders

Opportunity cost is a trap for students because it includes both explicit, or out-of-pocket costs, and implicit costs, ones that are not actually paid out of pocket.

Remember, when it says "See the Invisible Hand" in the book's margins, the authors are referring to the big idea that good institutions align self-interest with the social interest.

Marginal analysis involves changing by small units. Many later chapters also discuss marginal analysis. The term "marginal" means incremental or small change.

Comparative advantage is the ability to produce at a lower opportunity cost than another producer can. This allows a less productive producer to still be able to trade with a highly productive one.

Trade takes place when both sides expect to gain, which is what usually happens. Despite what people sometimes seem to think, no one *has* to lose in a trade.

Economist Milton Friedman has pointed out that "inflation is always and everywhere a monetary phenomenon"; in other words, inflation happens when the central bank prints too much money.

Central banks cannot do everything. There are really only a limited number of things they can do, but they *can*, first and foremost, provide a stable price level for the economy.

Homework Quiz

1. Incentives are
   a. rewards and penalties that motivate behavior.
   b. what one gives to charity.
   c. behaviors that motivate rewards or penalties.
   d. the value of opportunities lost.

2. The idea that good institutions can align self-interest and social interest implies that
   a. the government should control the market.
   b. sometimes self-interest or greed is good.
   c. consumers need government help to choose what to buy.
   d. firms need government help to choose what to produce.

3. The phrase that Adam Smith used to describe a situation in which self-interest promotes social interest is
   a. "greed is good."
   b. "the cost of opportunity."
   c. "the invisible hand."
   d. "thinking on the margin."

4. Opportunity cost is
   a. the change in costs when output changes.
   b. the money you spend on a product.
   c. the value of the time you give up consuming a product.
   d. the value of the opportunities lost.

5. If for this term your tuition is $5,000, your books are $1,000, you pay $4,000 for room and board, and you work part time, making $5,000 rather than $10,000 for the term, your opportunity costs of attending college this term are
   a. $5,000.
   b. $10,000.
   c. $11,000.
   d. $15,000.

6. A trade-off associated with more testing of a drug before it can be sold is that
   a. the drug is safer for consumers.
   b. some people are harmed before the drug can be sold.
   c. some people are harmed after the drug can be sold.
   d. the drug is less safe for consumers.

7. If you go to an all-you-can-eat pizza buffet, pay $5 for the buffet, and then eat 5 slices of pizza, the marginal cost of the second slice of pizza is

    a. $0.

    b. $1.

    c. $2.

    d. $5.

8. Two people trade when they expect that

    a. the seller will be better off, while the buyer will be worse off.

    b. the buyer will be better off, while the seller will be worse off.

    c. each will be worse off.

    d. each will be better off.

9. Trade can benefit

    a. only the productive.

    b. only the rich.

    c. even those who are not particularly productive.

    d. only sellers.

10. According to the authors, wealth and economic growth are associated with

    a. lower infant mortality rates.

    b. higher church attendance.

    c. an increased prison population.

    d. All of the answers are correct.

11. Since 1950, South Korea has grown much more than North Korea has because

    a. South Korea was the richer country in 1950.

    b. capitalist countries are conspiring against North Korea.

    c. South Korea has institutions that provide incentives for innovation and investment.

    d. North Korea is too mountainous for companies to build factories.

12. According to your text, the Great Depression was

    a. prolonged by bad policy.

    b. a natural occurrence in a capitalist society.

    c. caused by a famine in India.

    d. caused by the beginning of World War II.

13. The central bank of the United States is called

    a. Bank of America.

    b. the National Bank of the United States.

    c. the Federal Reserve.

    d. Washington Mutual.

14. When the central bank prints too much money

    a. people cannot get paper anymore.

    b. inflation occurs.

    c. prices fall too fast.

    d. All of the answers are correct.

15. Central banking is a hard job because

    a. printing money is a complicated business.

    b. the future of the economy is unpredictable.

    c. the central bank has little influence over inflation.

    d. there are not enough challenges to make central banking interesting.

Self-Practice Questions

1. One incentive a business can offer a customer to buy its product is

    a. a lower price.

    b. a better product.

    c. better service.

    d. All of these are incentives.

2. Good institutions

    a. eliminate trade-offs.

    b. align self-interest with the social interest.

    c. eliminate incentives.

    d. eliminate self-interest.

3. The phrase "invisible hand" refers to

    a. opportunity costs.

    b. when self-interest promotes social interest.

    c. what is sacrificed for a choice.

    d. the central bank.

4. Opportunity cost is

    a. the reward for a behavior.

    b. one reason central banking is hard.

    c. the value of an opportunity lost.

    d. the invisible hand.

5. If this term your tuition is $20,000, your books cost $1,000, you pay $10,000 for room and board, and you work part time, making $5,000 rather than $10,000 this term, your opportunity costs of attending college this term are

a. $21,000.

b. $26,000.

c. $31,000.

d. $36,000.

6. A example of a marginal choice would be

a. whether to hire one more worker.

b. the value of opportunity lost.

c. the invisible hand.

d. whether to enter a business.

7. Trade can increase production by means of

a. getting the better of the other party.

b. specialization.

c. protection.

d. All of the answers are correct.

8. Countries become wealthy due to:

a. conquests.

b. government.

c. economic growth.

d. environmental controls.

9. Inflation is

a. economic growth.

b. an increase in wealth.

c. an increase in the price level.

d. an increase in employment.

10. According to your text, the Great Depression

a. could have been moderated by better economic policies.

b. was a natural occurrence in a capitalist society.

c. was caused by free trade.

d. was caused by the U.S. Civil War.

11. Booms and busts cannot be completely avoided because of

a. economic policy mistakes.

b. shocks to economies, like destructive weather or earthquakes.

c. international trade.

d. incentives.

12. The central bank has a hard job because

    a. of time lags between policy changes and effects in the economy.

    b. it is difficult to foresee the future.

    c. it often has conflicting goals.

    d. All of the answers are correct.

13. When prices are rising in general, such a rise is known as

    a. a boom.

    b. inflation.

    c. rationing.

    d. appreciation.

14. Among the most powerful institutions for supporting good incentives are

    a. property rights.

    b. protection.

    c. monopoly.

    d. government intervention in markets.

15. The principles of economics hold

    a. only for businesses.

    b. only in capitalist countries.

    c. only in western countries.

    d. everywhere.

Answers to Self-Practice Questions

1. d, Topic: Incentives Matter

2. b, Topic: Good Institutions Align Self-Interest with the Social Interest

3. b, Topic: Good Institutions Align Self-Interest with the Social Interest

4. c, Topic: Trade-offs Are Everywhere

5. b, Topic: Trade-offs Are Everywhere

6. a, Topic: Thinking on the Margin

7. b, Topic: The Power of Trade

8. c, Topic: The Importance of Wealth and Economic Growth

9. c, Topic: Prices Rise When the Government Prints Too Much Money

10. a, Topic: Economic Booms and Busts Cannot Be Avoided But They Can Be Moderated

11. b, Topic: Economic Booms and Busts Cannot Be Avoided But They Can Be Moderated

12. d, Topic: Central Banking Is a Hard Job

13. b, Topic: Prices Rise When the Government Prints Too Much Money

14. a, Topic: The Importance of Wealth and Economic Growth

15. d, Topic: The Biggest Idea of All: Economics Is Fun

2

The Power of Trade and Comparative Advantage

Learning Objectives

The objective of this chapter is for you to learn about comparative advantage and the power of trade. Topics covered include:

> Trade and Preferences

> Specialization, Productivity, and the Division of Knowledge

> Comparative Advantage

> Trade and Globalization

The purpose of this chapter is for you to learn about the gains from trade.

Summary

Trade makes people with different preferences better off. Trade transfers a good to the buyer, who values the good more than the money it costs; and trade transfers money back to the seller, who values the money more than the good he or she gave up.

Trade allows people to specialize in production and take advantage of a division of knowledge. People will only specialize in the production of a single good when they are confident that they can trade that good for the many other goods they want. Without trade, specialization would be impossible.

Division of knowledge is also important in allowing people to specialize—each individual would need only to know more about his or her one specific area of knowledge. The farmer needs only to know about farming, the attorney needs to only know about the law, and the chef needs only to know about cooking. Without specialization, a person running a restaurant would have to know enough about farming to grow crops, know enough about the law to set up his or her business enterprise, and know enough about food preparation to be the chef.

Absolute advantage is the ability to produce a good using fewer inputs. Absolute advantage, however, is not required for trade. **Comparative advantage** is the ability to produce at the lowest opportunity cost. Every individual will have a comparative advantage in something, even if he or she does not have an absolute advantage in any one good. This applies to people individually and to the people of a country. Exploiting comparative advantage can be summed up as: sell what costs you a low amount to make and buy what would cost you a lot to make.

Absolute and comparative advantage can be illustrated by using a **production possibilities frontier (PPF)**. A production possibilities frontier shows all the combinations of goods that can be produced given productivity and the supply of inputs or resources. Figure 2.1 shows the PPF for the production of shirts and computers in Mexico and the United States.

Figure 2.1

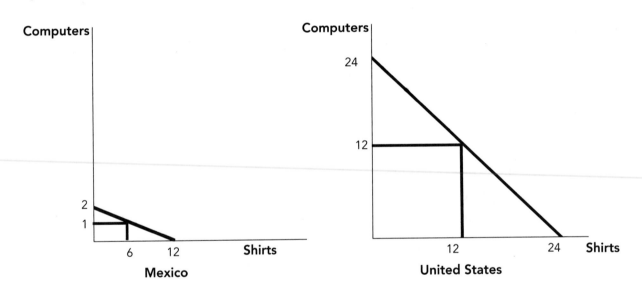

The graph on the left in Figure 2.1 shows that the Mexicans can produce either 2 computers and 0 shirts or 0 computers and 12 shirts. Thus, in Mexico, the opportunity cost of 1 computer is 6 shirts and the opportunity cost of 1 shirt is one-sixth of a computer. The graph on the right shows that Americans can produce 24 computers and 0 shirts or 0 computers and 24 shirts. Thus, in the United States the opportunity cost of 1 computer is 1 shirt or the opportunity cost of 1 shirt is 1 computer. These data are summarized in Table 2.1, in which the production columns summarize each country's situation if it produces only one of the two goods.

If there is no trade, both Mexico and the United States must consume what they each produce. Mexico could choose to produce and consume 1 computer and 6 shirts, while the United States could choose to produce and consume 12 computers and 12 shirts. That makes the total production and consumption of both countries 13 computers and 18 shirts. The no-trade position is summarized in Table 2.2.

Table 2.1 Opportunity Costs

Country	Production of Only Computers	Production of Only Shirts	Opportunity Cost of One Computer	Opportunity Cost of One Shirt
Mexico	2	12	6 shirts	1/6 computer
United States	24	24	1 shirt	1 computer

Table 2.2 Production 5 Consumption in Mexico and the United States (Specialization with No Trade)

	Production of Computers	Consumption of Computers	Production of Shirts	Consumption of Shirts
Mexico	1	1	6	6
United States	12	12	12	12
Total	13	13	18	18

Trade can improve the no-trade total result of 13 computers and 18 shirts. Mexico can shift its production to 0 computers and 12 shirts, while the United States can shift its production to 15 computers and 9 shirts. (Notice that both of these points are on the PPF of the respective countries in Table 2.1.) This makes the total production of Mexico and the United States 15 computers and 21 shirts, which is larger than the total production with no trade.

If the United States trades 2 computers to Mexico for 4 shirts, then Mexico consumes 2 computers and 8 shirts, while the United States consumes 13 computers and 14 shirts. Thus, with trade, Mexicans consume 1 more computer and 2 more shirts compared to with no trade, while Americans consume 1 more computer and 2 more shirts compared to with no trade. These results are summarized in Table 2.3.

Table 2.3 Production and Consumption in Mexico and the United States (Specialization and Trade)

	Production of Computers	Consumption of Computers	Production of Shirts	Consumption of Shirts
Mexico	0	2 (+1)	12	8 (+2)
United States	15	13 (+1)	9	13 (+1)
Total	15	15	21	21

As we have seen in the preceding table, both the United States and Mexico gained from trade. That is, they were able to consume at points outside their PPFs.

Key Terms

absolute advantage the ability to produce a good using fewer inputs than your trading partner.

comparative advantage the ability to produce a good at a lower opportunity cost than your trading partner

production possibilities frontier (PFF) what can be produced given productivity and the supply of inputs

Traps, Hints, and Reminders

Notice that both sides can gain from trade; that is, no one has to get the better of the other when trading. In fact, trade only takes place when both parties expect to gain, and both sides usually do gain.

Comparative advantage means that even if you are bad at everything you can still trade. There will be something you are the least worst at; that is, you will be able to produce that thing at the lowest opportunity cost.

Homework Quiz

1. If you can produce a good at the lowest opportunity costs, then you have

   a. an absolute advantage.

   b. a comparative advantage.

   c. an unfair advantage.

   d. All of the answers are correct.

2. You have an absolute advantage in producing goods that you can produce

   a. more of.

   b. at the lowest opportunity cost.

   c. using fewer resources.

   d. All of the answers are correct.

3. Everyone must necessarily have

   a. a comparative advantage.

   b. an absolute advantage.

   c. a tariff.

   d. All of the answers are correct.

Table 2.4

Country	Production of Only Cameras	Production of Only Computers	Opportunity Cost of Cameras	Opportunity Cost of One Computer
United States	3	5		
Japan	2	2		

4. According to the data in Table 2.4, the opportunity cost of a computer in the United States is

   a. 0.6 camera.

   b. 1 camera.

   c. 1.67 cameras.

   d. None of the answers is correct.

5. According to the data in Table 2.4, the opportunity cost of a camera in Japan is

   a. 0.6 computer.

   b. 1 computer.

   c. 1.67 computers.

   d. None of the answers is correct.

6. According to the data in Table 2.4, if both countries have the same resources, Japan has an absolute advantage in producing

   a. cameras.

   b. computers.

   c. both goods.

   d. neither good.

7. According to the data in Table 2.4, the United States has a comparative advantage in producing

   a. cameras.

   b. computers.

   c. both goods.

   d. neither good.

8. According to the data in Table 2.4, Japan has a comparative advantage in producing

   a. cameras.

   b. computers.

   c. both goods.

   d. neither good.

9. A production possibility frontier shows what the people of the area

   a. want to consume.

   b. can produce.

   c. want to produce.

   d. must produce.

Figure 2.2

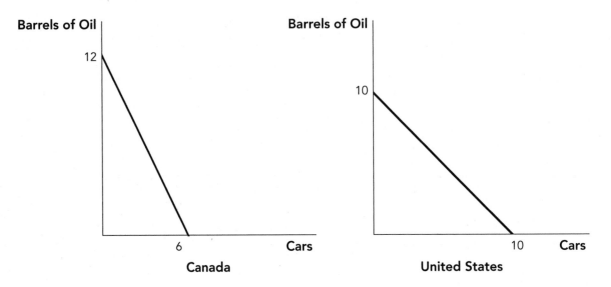

Canada   United States

10. In Figure 2.2, if both countries have the same resources, Canada has an absolute advantage in producing

    a. oil.

    b. cars.

    c. both oil and cars.

    d. neither oil nor cars.

11. In Figure 2.2, the opportunity cost of oil in Canada is

    a. 0.5 car.

    b. 1 car.

    c. 2 cars.

    d. 6 cars.

12. In Figure 2.2, the opportunity cost of cars in Canada is

    a. 0.5 barrel of oil.

    b. 1 barrel of oil.

    c. 2 barrels of oil.

    d. 10 barrels of oil.

13. In Figure 2.2, the opportunity cost of cars in the United States is

    a. 0.5 barrel of oil.   c. 2 barrels of oil.

    b. 1 barrel of oil.   d. 10 barrels of oil.

14. In Figure 2.2, Canada has a comparative advantage in producing
   a. oil.
   b. cars.
   c. both oil and cars.
   d. neither oil nor cars.

15. In Figure 2.2, the United States has a comparative advantage in producing
   a. oil.
   b. cars.
   c. both oil and cars.
   d. neither oil nor cars.

Self-Practice Questions

1. You have a comparative advantage in producing goods that you can produce
   a. more of.
   b. at the lowest opportunity cost.
   c. using fewer inputs.
   d. All of the answers are correct.

2. If you can produce a good using fewer resources, then you have
   a. an unfair advantage.
   b. a comparative advantage.
   c. an absolute advantage.
   d. All of the answers are correct.

3. To trade, you must at least have
   a. a wage advantage.
   b. an absolute advantage.
   c. a tariff.
   d. a comparative advantage.

Table 2.5

Country	Production of Only Cheese	Production of Only Computers	Opportunity Cost of One Cheese	Opportunity Cost of One Computer
United States	2	4		
France	3	1		

4. According to the data in Table 2.5, the opportunity cost of cheese in the United States is
   a. 0.33 computer.
   b. 0.5 computer.
   c. 2 computers.
   d. 3 computers.

5. According to the data in Table 2.5, the opportunity cost of cheese in France is
   a. 0.33 computer.
   b. 0.5 computer.
   c. 2 computers.
   d. 3 computers.

6. If both countries have the same resources, according to the data in Table 2.5, France has an absolute advantage in producing
   a. cheese.
   b. computers.
   c. both goods.
   d. neither good.

7. According to the data in Table 2.5, the United States has a comparative advantage in producing
   a. cheese.
   b. computers.
   c. both goods.
   d. neither good.

8. According to the data in Table 2.5, France has a comparative advantage in producing
   a. cheese.
   b. computers.
   c. both goods.
   d. neither good.

9. A production possibility frontier shows maximum production, given
   a. what people want to consume.
   b. rising productivity.
   c. government spending.
   d. the supply of inputs.

Figure 2.3

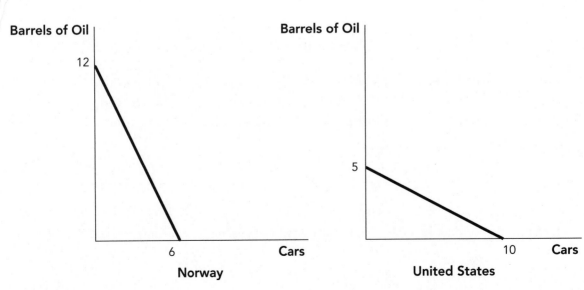

Norway   United States

10. In Figure 2.3, the United States has an absolute advantage in producing
   a. oil.
   b. cars.
   c. both oil and cars.
   d. neither oil nor cars.

11. In Figure 2.3, the opportunity cost of oil in Norway is
   a. 0.5 car.
   b. 1 car.
   c. 2 cars.
   d. 6 cars.

12. In Figure 2.3, the opportunity cost of cars in Norway is
   a. 0.5 barrel of oil.
   b. 1 barrel of oil.
   c. 2 barrels of oil.
   d. 10 barrels of oil.

13. In Figure 2.3, the opportunity cost of cars in the United States is
   a. 0.5 barrel of oil.
   b. 1 barrel of oil.
   c. 2 barrels of oil.
   d. 10 barrels of oil.

14. In Figure 2.3, Norway has a comparative advantage in producing
   a. oil.
   b. cars.
   c. both oil and cars.
   d. neither oil nor cars.

15. In Figure 2.3, the United States has a comparative advantage in producing
   a. oil.
   b. cars.
   c. both oil and cars.
   d. neither oil nor cars.

Answers to Self-Practice Questions

1. b, Topic: Trade and Preferences

2. c, Topic: Trade and Preferences

3. d, Topic: Specialization, Productivity, and Division of Knowledge

4. c, Topic: Comparative Advantage

5. a, Topic: Comparative Advantage

6. a, Topic: Comparative Advantage

7. b, Topic: Comparative Advantage

8. a, Topic: Comparative Advantage

9. d, Topic: Comparative Advantage

10. b, Topic: Comparative Advantage

11. a, Topic: Comparative Advantage

12. c, Topic: Comparative Advantage

13. a, Topic: Comparative Advantage

14. a, Topic: Comparative Advantage

15. b, Topic: Comparative Advantage

3

Supply and Demand

Learning Objectives

The objective of this chapter is to learn about demand and supply, using the market for oil as an example. Topics are:

> The Demand Curve for Oil

> The Supply Curve for Oil

According to the authors, as stated in the introduction to this chapter: "Even if you understand little else, you may rightly claim yourself economically literate if you understand these tools. Fail to understand these tools and you will understand little else."

Summary

This chapter covers supply and demand. A **demand curve** is a function that shows the quantity demanded at different prices. As shown in Figure 3.1, **quantity demanded** is the quantity buyers are willing and able to buy at a particular price.

Demand curves are typically downward sloping, implying that if the price falls, the quantity demanded increases. In Figure 3.1, if the price falls from $10 to $5, the quantity demanded increases from 100 units to 150 units. Similarly, if the price rises from $5 to $10, then the quantity demanded decreases from 150 units to 100 units.

Consumer surplus is the consumer's gain from exchange, or the difference between the maximum price a consumer is willing to pay for a certain good and the market price. For example, if you are willing to pay $1,000 for a Super Bowl ticket, and the market price is $480, then your consumer surplus is $520 = $1,000 − $480.

Figure 3.1

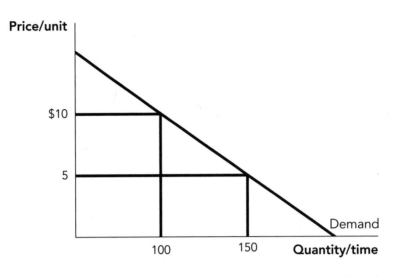

In Figure 3.2, the **total consumer surplus** is measured by the area beneath the demand curve and above the price.

Figure 3.2

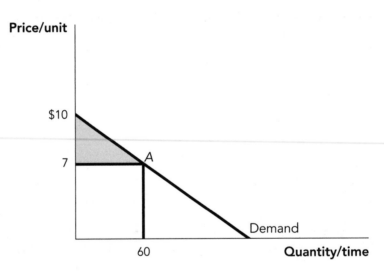

With a market price of $7, the total consumer surplus is the triangle determined by points $7, *A*, and $10, and it is shaded. The amount of this area can be calculated using the formula for the area of a triangle, which is (height × base)/2. In this example, the height is $3 = $10 − $7 and the base is $60. The height × base is $180 = $3 × $60. The total consumer surplus is $90 = $180/2.

It is important to understand what things cause demand to shift when they change. If, in Figure 3.3, the demand curve shifts from D_1 to D_3, then it is said that demand has increased. This means at every price the quantity of the good that people want to buy is larger. If, in Figure 3.3, the demand curve shifts from D_1 to D_2, it is said that demand has decreased. This means at every price the quantity of the good that people want to buy is smaller.

Among the important things that shift demand are changes in consumer income, population, the price of substitutes and complements, expectations, and tastes (how desirable a good is at a specific point in time).

For some goods, when consumer incomes rise, demand increases. These goods are called **normal goods**. For other goods, when consumer incomes rise, demand decreases. Such goods are called **inferior goods**.

Figure 3.3

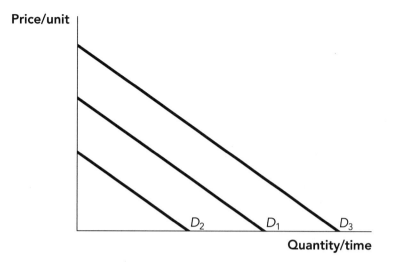

If, when the price of another good goes up and the demand for the original good rises, then the two goods are called **substitutes**. Consumers use one good instead of the other and buy more of the now relatively cheaper of the two goods. If, when the price of another good goes up and the demand for the original good falls, then the two goods are called **complements**. Consumers use the two goods together and buy less of both goods when the price of one of them rises.

If population, tastes (desire) for a good, and the expected future price of the good all increase at the same time, then the demand for the good will also increase. Again, that would be a shift like D_1 to D_3, as shown in Figure 3.3.

A **supply curve** is a function that shows the quantity supplied at different prices. In Figure 3.4, **quantity supplied** is the quantity that sellers are willing to sell at a particular price.

Supply curves are typically upward sloping, implying that if the price rises, then the quantity supplied also increases. In Figure 3.4, if the price rises from $5 to $15, then the quantity supplied increases from 50 units to 200 units. Similarly in Figure 3.4, if the price were to fall from $15 to $5, then the quantity supplied would decrease from 200 units to 50 units.

Figure 3.4

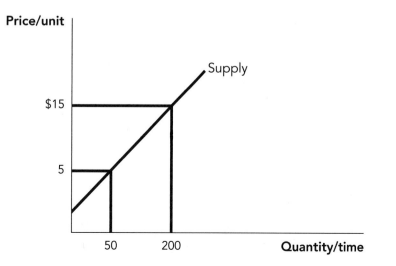

Producer surplus is the producer's gain from exchange, or the difference between the market price and the minimum price at which a producer would be willing to sell a certain quantity. For example, if you are willing to sell your car for $10,000 and the market price is $15,000, then your producer surplus would be $5,000 = $15,000 − $10,000 on that transaction.

Total producer surplus is measured by the area above the supply curve and below the price, as shown in Figure 3.5.

Figure 3.5

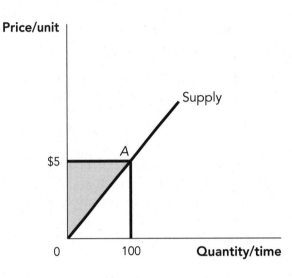

With a market price of $5, the total producer surplus is the triangle determined by points $5, *A*, and the origin 0,0. Again, the amount of this area can be calculated using the formula for the area of a triangle, which is (height × base)/2. In this example, the height is $5 and the base is 100. The height × base is $500 = $5 × 100. The total consumer surplus is $250 = $500/2.

As with demand, it is important to understand what things will cause supply to shift when they change. If, in Figure 3.6, the supply curve shifts from S_1 to S_3, it is said that supply has increased. This means at every price the quantity of the good that sellers

Figure 3.6

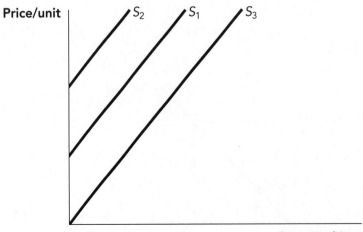

want to sell is larger. If, in Figure 3.6, the supply curve shifts from S_1 to S_2, it is said that supply has decreased. This means at every price the amount of the good that sellers want to sell is smaller.

Among the important things that shift supply are technological change, changes in the price of inputs in production, taxes and subsidies, changes in expectations, entry and exit of producers, and changes in opportunity costs.

If a technology involved in producing calculators improves, then the supply of calculators increases. Similarly, if the price of any input involved in producing calculators falls, then the supply of calculators increases.

If the government taxes the production of calculators, then the supply of calculators decreases. With the tax added, it costs the producer more money to supply calculators. A subsidy is the negative of a tax. If the government subsidizes the production of calculators, then the supply of calculators increases. With the subsidy factored in, it costs the producer less money to produce calculators.

When producers expect a higher price for the product tomorrow (future markets), they have less incentive to sell today (current markets). To the extent that producers can store their product, they will reduce supply today, so they can sell more in the future (when prices are expected to be higher).

An increase in the number of producers also increases supply. For any given amount of supply, if a new producer comes into the market, the supply is increased. Similarly, when any producer leaves the market, this causes a decrease in the amount supplied. In a similar manner, opportunity costs can affect supply. For example, if a self-employed glazier accepts a job installing air-conditioning units that pays more than a job of installing glass and mirrors, then the opportunity cost of installing glass and mirrors has increased. The glazier left the business of glass and mirror installation, thereby reducing supply in that market.

Key Terms

demand curve a function that shows the quantity demanded at different prices

quantity demanded the quantity that buyers are willing and able to buy at a particular price

consumer surplus the consumer's gain from exchange, or the difference between the maximum price a consumer is willing to pay for a certain good and the market price

total consumer surplus the area beneath the demand curve and above the price

normal good a good for which demand increases when income increases

inferior good a good for which demand decreases when income increases

substitutes two goods are substitutes if a decrease in the price of one good leads to a decrease in the demand for the other good

complements two goods are complements if a decrease in the price of one good leads to an increase in the demand for the other good

supply curve a function that shows the quantity supplied at different prices

quantity supplied the quantity that sellers are willing and able to sell at a particular price

producer surplus the producer's gain from exchange, or the difference between the market price and the minimum price at which a producer would be willing to sell a particular quantity

total producer surplus the area above the supply curve and below the price

Traps, Hints, and Reminders

Consumer surplus and producer surplus should not be confused with a surplus on a market. Though these terms have the word "surplus" in them, they are not related to surplus on a market or quantity supplied greater than quantity demanded.

Inferior goods are not necessarily substandard goods. They are simply goods that are negatively related to consumer income. If a person became rich enough, he or she might buy fewer small jets and more custom-fitted commercial jets. This implies that the small jet might be an inferior good to some people at a certain income level, but says nothing about its quality.

Whether goods are complements or substitutes is up to the consumer. To you, butter and margarine may be substitutes, but for the heart patient only margarine is acceptable, and for the pastry chef only butter is usable. You may think of peanut butter and grape jelly as complements; that is, you may only use them together on bread. However, someone else may think of them as substitutes; that is, he may put peanut butter on his toast and not jelly.

On a supply curve, any increase in supply is a shift to the right and down. This can be confusing. With supply or demand, "increase" or "decrease" describes the change along the quantity axis. Thus, an increase in supply is a shift to the right and down, because that moves supply to the right (that is, increasing quantities) along the quantity axis. Similarly, a decrease in supply is a shift up and to the left, because that moves supply to the left (that is, decreasing quantities) along the quantity axis.

A *subsidy* is a negative tax; that is, the government is giving someone money rather than taking it away. You could also think of a tax as a negative subsidy. So quite naturally, taxes and subsidies have opposite effects on supply. Thus, a tax on a product decreases supply, while a subsidy for a product increases supply.

The *area of a triangle* is one-half the height times the base. The area of a triangle can be calculated as (1/2) × height × base (or .5 × height × base).

Homework Quiz

1. If the price of oil rises, then

   a. the quantity of oil demanded falls.

   b. the demand for oil rises.

   c. the supply of oil rises.

   d. All of the answers are correct.

2. A demand curve shows

   a. the maximum willingness to pay for particular quantities.

   b. quantity demanded at different prices.

   c. different combinations of prices and quantities that consumers are able and willing to buy.

   d. All of the answers are correct.

3. If the most Tom is willing to pay for an ice cream cone is $5, and the market price is $2, then by purchasing an ice cream cone, Tom will get a consumer surplus of

   a. $2.

   b. $3.

   c. $5.

   d. $10.

Figure 3.7

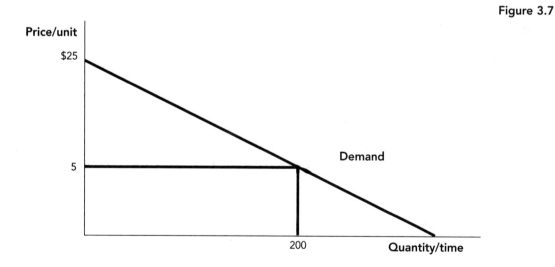

4. In Figure 3.7, if the market price is $5, then total consumer surplus is

   a. $25.

   b. $500.

   c. $1,000.

   d. $2,000.

5. If consumer incomes rise, then the demand for

a. inferior goods increases.

b. normal goods decreases.

c. inferior goods decreases.

d. complements decreases.

6. If peanut butter and jelly are complements, then an increase in the price of peanut butter will cause

a. an increase in the price of jelly.

b. a decrease in the demand for jelly.

c. an increase in the demand for peanut butter.

d. a decrease in the demand for peanut butter.

7. Inferior goods are

a. substandard.

b. those with expected future price decreases.

c. those that are negatively related to consumer income.

d. those that few people buy.

8. If people's taste for a good goes up due to a fad

a. the current price falls.

b. the good is a normal good.

c. the supply of the good decreases.

d. the demand for the good increases.

9. If the price of oil falls

a. the supply of oil decreases.

b. the quantity of oil demanded decreases.

c. the demand for oil increases.

d. the quantity of oil supplied decreases.

10. Quantity supplied is

a. negatively related to price.

b. the amount of a good that sellers are willing and able to sell at a particular price.

c. price without the willingness to sell.

d. All of the answers are correct.

11. The difference between the market price and the minimum price at which a producer would be willing to sell a particular quantity is

a. a demand curve.

b. a supply curve.

c. producer surplus.

d. consumer surplus.

12. In Figure 3.8, an increase in supply is

    a. a move from point A to point B on S_1.

    b. a move from point B to point A on S_1.

    c. a shift from S_2 to S_1.

    d. a shift from S_1 to S_2.

Figure 3.8

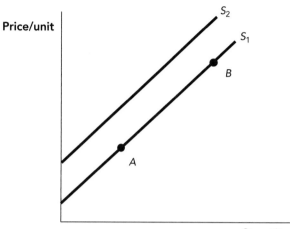

13. If technology increases, the

    a. supply curve decreases.

    b. demand curve decreases.

    c. supply curve increases.

    d. demand curve increases.

14. If firms expect the price of their product to increase in the future

    a. the demand today will decrease.

    b. the price today will decrease.

    c. the price in the future will decrease.

    d. the supply today will decrease.

15. If Al's Used Cars sells a car for a market price of $10,000, and the minimum that it would have sold for was $4,000, then the producer surplus of Al's Used Cars is

    a. $4,000.

    b. $6,000.

    c. $10,000.

    d. $40,000.

Self-Practice Questions

1. If the number of buyers of oil rise,
   a. the quantity of oil demanded rises.
   b. the demand for oil rises.
   c. the supply of oil rises.
   d. All of the answers are correct.

2. Different combinations of prices and quantities that consumers are able and willing to buy is called
   a. a demand curve.
   b. consumer surplus.
   c. a supply curve.
   d. producer surplus.

3. If the most Tom is willing to pay for an ice cream cone is $10, and the market price is $2, then by purchasing an ice cream cone, Tom will get a consumer surplus of
   a. $2.
   b. $8.
   c. $10.
   d. $20.

4. If consumer income falls, the demand for
   a. inferior goods decreases.
   b. normal goods decreases.
   c. normal goods increases.
   d. complements decreases.

5. If the price of a substitute for butter rises
   a. the demand for butter increases.
   b. the demand for butter decreases.
   c. the price of butter falls.
   d. the supply of the substitute decreases.

6. Normal goods are
   a. high quality.
   b. those with expected future price decreases.
   c. those that are positively related to consumer income.
   d. those that most people buy.

7. If the price of oil is expected to fall in the future, the
   a. demand for oil today decreases.
   b. demand for oil in the future decreases.
   c. supply of oil today decreases.
   d. supply of oil in the future increases.

8. If the price of oil rises, the
   a. supply of oil decreases.
   b. quantity of oil demanded increases.
   c. demand for oil increases.
   d. quantity of oil supplied increases.

9. Supply is
   a. negatively related to price.
   b. the amount of a good that sellers are willing and able to sell at a particular price.
   c. combinations of quantities and prices that producers are able and willing to sell and sell at, respectively.
   d. All of the answers are correct.

10. Producer surplus is
    a. the difference between the market price and the minimum price at which a producer would be willing to sell a particular quantity.
    b. the difference between the maximum price that a consumer would be willing to pay for a particular quantity and the market price.
    c. when the quantity supplied is greater than the quantity demanded.
    d. when the quantity demanded is greater than the quantity supplied.

Figure 3.9

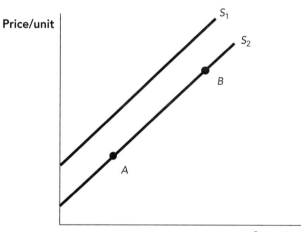

11. In Figure 3.9, a decrease in supply is
    a. a move from point A to point B on S_2.
    b. a move from point B to point A on S_2.
    c. a shift from S_2 to S_1.
    d. a shift from S_1 to S_2.

12. If the price of an input, such as wages of autoworkers, increases, the

a. supply of cars will decrease.

b. supply of cars will increase.

c. price of cars will decrease.

d. supply of autoworkers will decrease.

13. If a firm's opportunity cost of producing a product increases, the supply of that product will

a. increase as the number of firms in the industry grows.

b. decrease as the number of firms in the industry grows.

c. increase as the number of firms in the industry falls.

d. decrease as the number of firms in the industry falls.

Figure 3.10

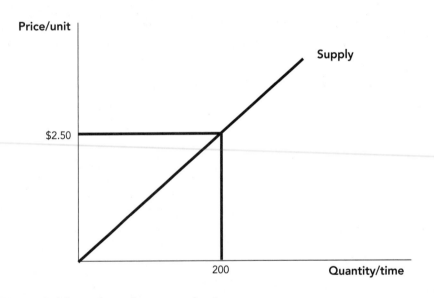

14. In Figure 3.10, total producer surplus is

a. $2.50.

b. $197.50.

c. $250.

d. $500.

15. If the least Tom is willing to sell his 1990 Civic for is $2,000, and the market price is $3,000, then by selling the car, Tom will get producer surplus of

a. $500.

b. $1,000.

c. $2,000.

d. $5,000.

Answers to Self-Practice Questions

1. b, Topic: The Demand Curve for Oil

2. a, Topic: The Demand Curve for Oil

3. b, Topic: Consumer Surplus

4. b, Topic: What Shifts the Demand Curve?

5. a, Topic: What Shifts the Demand Curve?

6. c, Topic: What Shifts the Demand Curve?

7. a, Topic: What Shifts the Demand Curve?

8. d, Topic: The Supply Curve for Oil

9. c, Topic: The Supply Curve for Oil

10. a, Topic: Producer Surplus

11. c, Topic: What Shifts the Supply Curve?

12. a, Topic: What Shifts the Supply Curve?

13. d, Topic: What Shifts the Supply Curve?

14. c, Topic: Producer Surplus

15. b, Topic: Producer Surplus

4

Equilibrium: How Supply and Demand Determine Prices

Learning Objectives

In this chapter, demand and supply are again discussed, this time in relation to market equilibrium. Topics included are:

> Equilibrium and the Adjustment Process

> Gains from Trade Are Maximized at the Equilibrium Price and Quantity

> Does the Model Work? Evidence from the Laboratory Shifting Demand and Supply Curves

> Terminology: Demand Compared to Quantity Demanded and Supply Compared to Quantity Supplied

> Understanding the Price of Oil

Summary

The interaction of supply and demand leads to a market equilibrium. As shown in Figure 4.1, market equilibrium occurs where supply and demand intersect.

Figure 4.1

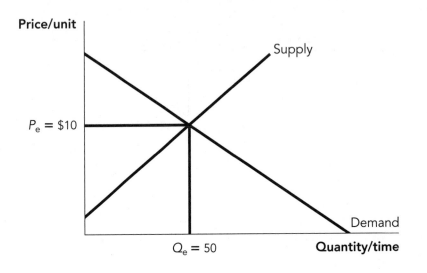

This intersection yields the **equilibrium price**, P_e = $10, and **equilibrium quantity**, Q_e = 50 units of the good.

The market equilibrium is stable, as shown in Figure 4.2, where the equilibrium is still at a price of $10 and a quantity of 50 units.

Figure 4.2

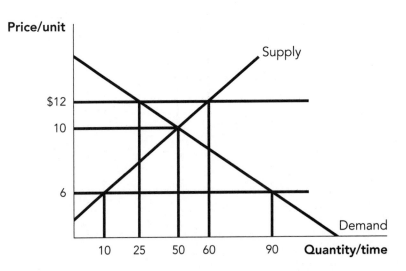

A price of $12 is above equilibrium. At $12, more of the product (60 units) is offered for sale than people want to purchase (25 units). Quantity supplied is greater than quantity demanded by 35 units, implying an excess quantity supplied, or **surplus**.

What will consumers and producers do about the excess quantity supplied? Producers who have rising inventories will start lowering prices below $12. Consumers who see that producers have extra product on hand will start offering prices below $12. Lower prices decrease quantity supplied and increase quantity demanded, moving the market toward equilibrium.

Similarly, a price of $6 is below the equilibrium price. At $6, consumers want to buy more of the product (90 units) than producers want to sell (10 units). This time, quantity demanded is greater than quantity supplied by 80 units, implying an excess quantity demanded, or **shortage**.

What will consumers and producers do about the excess quantity demanded? Consumers, many of whom cannot get the item, will start offering prices above $6. Producers, who see their product flying off the shelf, will start asking prices above $6. Higher prices increase quantity supplied and decrease quantity demanded, again moving the market toward equilibrium.

So whether the price is above or below equilibrium, competitive pressures move price and quantity toward the market equilibrium. Only at the equilibrium does quantity supplied equal quantity demanded, implying no pressure from either consumers or producers to change price.

Gains from trade are maximized at the market equilibrium. This can be seen in Figure 4.3, where the 26th unit is worth slightly less than $12, say $11.99, to the consumer and costs the producer only slightly more than $8, say $8.01.

Figure 4.3

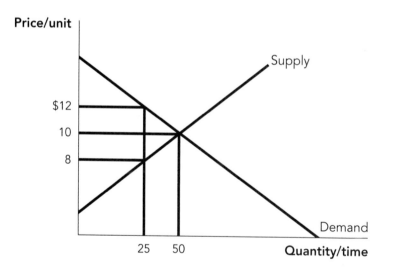

Any price between $11.99 and $8.01 makes both the buyer and seller better off. This is called an unexploited gain from trade. As long as the quantity is below the equilibrium quantity, there will be these unexploited gains from trade.

What if the quantity is above the market equilibrium of 50 units in Figure 4.3? In that case, the cost to producers of producing the unit is greater than what any consumer is willing to pay. So, while consumers are willing to consume the product at some specified price, that price is below the cost of producing the good. Producing such units would waste resources that would be better spent producing something consumers value more.

The free market's maximizing gains from trade means three closely related things. First, the supply of goods is bought by buyers with the highest willingness to pay. Second, the supply of goods is sold by sellers with the lowest costs. Third, between buyers and sellers there are no unexploited gains from trade, or any wasteful trades.

As shown in Figure 4.4, a change in demand causes a movement along the supply curve and a change in quantity supplied.

Figure 4.4

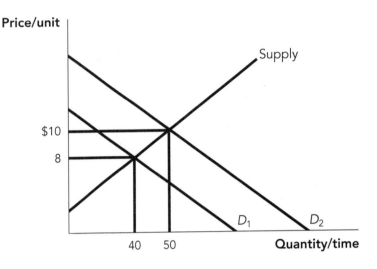

Originally with demand D_1, quantity supplied was 40 units. As demand increased to D_2, quantity moves along the supply curve and quantity supplied becomes 50 units.

For markets with upward-sloping supply curves and downward-sloping demand curves, an increase in demand increases equilibrium price and quantity. As shown in Figure 4.4, the movement of demand from D_1 to D_2 causes the equilibrium price to rise from $8 to $10 and the equilibrium quantity to rise from 40 to 50 units. If demand had decreased from D_2 to D_1, the reverse would have happened. The equilibrium price would have fallen from $10 to $8, and the equilibrium quantity would have fallen from 50 to 40 units.

Similarly, as shown in Figure 4.5, a decrease in supply causes a movement along the demand curve and a change in quantity demanded.

Originally with demand S_1, quantity demanded was 60 units. As supply decreased to D_2, quantity moves along the demand curve and quantity demanded becomes 35 units.

For markets with upward-sloping supply curves and downward-sloping demand curves, a decrease in supply increases equilibrium price and decreases equilibrium quantity. As shown in Figure 4.5, the movement of supply from S_1 to S_2 causes the equilibrium price to rise from $11 to $13 and the equilibrium quantity to fall from 60 to 35 units. If supply had increased from S_2 to S_1, the reverse would have happened. The equilibrium price would have fallen from $13 to $11, and the equilibrium quantity would have risen from 35 to 60 units.

Figure 4.5

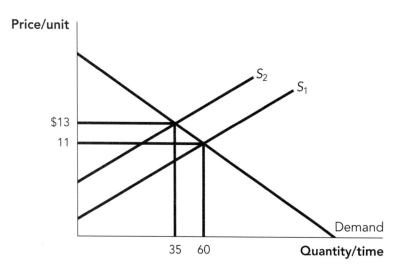

Key Terms

equilibrium price the price at which the quantity demanded is equal to the quantity supplied

equilibrium quantity the quantity at which the quantity demanded is equal to the quantity supplied

surplus a situation in which the quantity supplied is greater than the quantity demanded

shortage a situation in which the quantity demanded is greater than the quantity supplied

Traps, Hints, and Reminders

A surplus should not be confused with consumer or producer surplus, both of which were defined in Chapter 3. A surplus on a market is when quantity supplied is greater than quantity demanded. Consumer surplus is the maximum the consumer is willing to pay less market price. Producer surplus is market price less the minimum price at which the producer would sell.

A free market maximizes the gains from trade, or maximizes producer surplus plus consumer surplus.

A change in demand causes a movement along the supply curve and a change in quantity supplied. Similarly, a change in supply leads to a movement along the demand curve and a change in quantity demanded. The things that can cause changes in quantity demanded or supplied are different from the things that can cause demand and supply to change, as discussed in Chapter 3.

Also recall from Chapter 3 that changes in supply can be somewhat counterintuitive. An increase in supply is a shift to the right and down, while a decrease in supply is a shift up and to the left.

Homework Quiz

1. In an equilibrium market
   a. quantity demanded equals quantity supplied.
   b. total surplus is minimized.
   c. the market price is unstable.
   d. All of the answers are correct.

2. If price is above the equilibrium price, some
   a. consumers will offer to pay a higher price to be sure to get the product.
   b. consumers will offer to pay a lower price because the product is so available.
   c. producers will face excess demand and thus start raising the price.
   d. All of the answers are correct.

3. If price is below the equilibrium price, then
   a. every producer who wants to buy the product can do so.
   b. quantity supplied is greater than quantity demanded.
   c. there is a shortage of the product.
   d. All of the answers are correct.

Figure 4.6

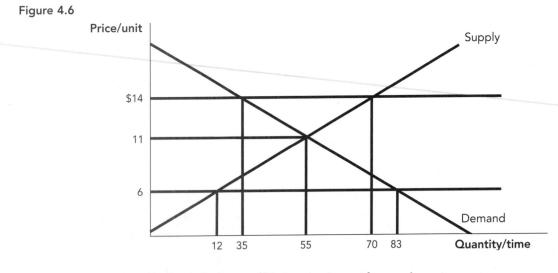

4. In Figure 4.6, the equilibrium price and quantity are
   a. $14 and 70 units.
   b. $11 and 55 units.
   c. $11 and 70 units.
   d. $6 and 12 units.

5. In Figure 4.6, at a price of $14, producers will want to sell
   a. 70 units.
   b. 55 units.
   c. 35 units.
   d. 12 units.

6. In Figure 4.6, at a price of $6, consumers will want to buy

   a. 12 units.

   b. 55 units.

   c. 70 units.

   d. 95 units.

7. In Figure 4.6, at a price of $14, there is an excess quantity

   a. demanded of 83 units.

   b. supplied of 83 units.

   c. demanded of 35 units.

   d. supplied of 35 units.

8. In Figure 4.6, at a price of $6, there is a

   a. shortage of 83 units.

   b. surplus of 83 units.

   c. shortage of 35 units.

   d. surplus of 35 units.

9. In a free market equilibrium,

   a. consumer plus producer surplus is maximized.

   b. gains from trade are maximized.

   c. no potential gains from trade are left unexploited.

   d. All of the answers are correct.

10. The free market's maximization of gains from trade implies that

   a. the supply of goods is bought by buyers with the lowest willingness to pay.

   b. the supply of goods is sold by sellers with the lowest costs.

   c. between buyers and sellers there are wasteful trades.

   d. All of the answers are correct.

11. The free market's maximization of gains from trade implies that

   a. the supply of goods is bought by buyers with the lowest willingness to pay.

   b. the supply of goods is sold by sellers with the highest costs.

   c. there are no unexploited gains from trade, or any wasteful trades, between buyers and sellers.

   d. All of the answers are correct.

Figure 4.7

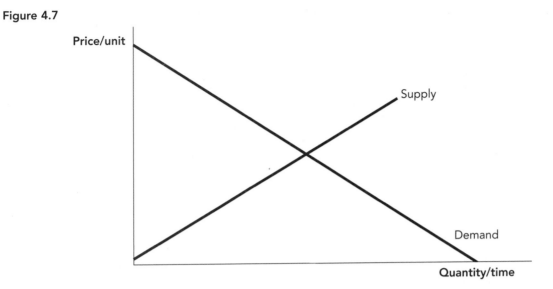

12. In Figure 4.7, if demand increases, then the equilibrium

    a. price and quantity fall.

    b. price and quantity rise.

    c. price falls and quantity rises.

    d. price rises and quantity falls.

13. In Figure 4.7, if supply decreases, then the equilibrium

    a. price and quantity fall.

    b. price and quantity rise.

    c. price falls and quantity rises.

    d. price rises and quantity falls.

14. In Figure 4.7, if the good is normal, and consumer income falls, then the equilibrium

    a. price and quantity fall.

    b. price and quantity rise.

    c. price falls and quantity rises.

    d. price rises and quantity falls.

15. In Figure 4.7, if technology improves production of this good, then the equilibrium

    a. price and quantity fall.

    b. price and quantity rise.

    c. price falls and quantity rises.

    d. price rises and quantity falls.

Self-Practice Questions

1. If price is above the equilibrium price, some
    a. consumers will offer to pay a higher price to get the product.
    b. producers will sell the product at a higher price.
    c. producers will have excess supplies and thus will start reducing price to get customers.
    d. All of the answers are correct.

2. If price is below the equilibrium price,
    a. every consumer who wants the product can get it.
    b. quantity supplied is greater than quantity demanded for the product.
    c. there is a shortage of the product.
    d. All of the answers are correct.

3. If price is above the equilibrium price,
    a. every producer who wants to sell the product can do so.
    b. quantity supplied is greater than quantity demanded.
    c. there is a shortage of the product.
    d. All of the answers are correct.

Figure 4.8

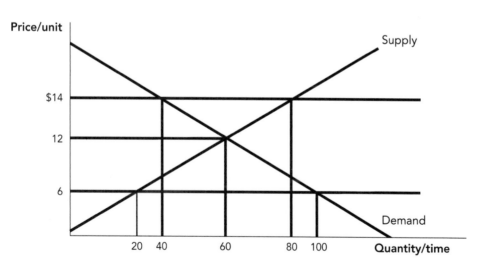

4. In Figure 4.8, the equilibrium price and quantity are
    a. $14 and 100 units.
    b. $12 and 60 units.
    c. $12 and 80 units.
    d. $6 and 40 units.

5. In Figure 4.8, at a price of $14, producers will want to sell
   a. 80 units.
   b. 60 units.
   c. 40 units.
   d. 20 units.

6. In Figure 4.8, at a price of $6, consumers will want to buy
   a. 20 units.
   b. 40 units.
   c. 60 units.
   d. 100 units.

7. In Figure 4.8, at a price of $6, an excess quantity is
   a. demanded of 80 units.
   b. supplied of 80 units.
   c. demanded of 40 units.
   d. supplied of 20 units.

8. In Figure 4.8, at a price of $14, there is a
   a. shortage of 80 units.
   b. surplus of 80 units.
   c. shortage of 40 units.
   d. surplus of 40 units.

9. The market will NOT produce a quantity greater than equilibrium because
   a. there are unexploited gains from trade still left.
   b. it is illegal.
   c. resources are wasted on production to the right of the equilibrium quantity.
   d. consumer plus producer surplus grows in that region.

10. The free market's maximization of gains from trade implies that
    a. the supply of goods is bought by buyers with the highest willingness to pay.
    b. the supply of goods is sold by sellers with the highest costs.
    c. between buyers and sellers there are unexploited gains from trade.
    d. All of the answers are correct.

Figure 4.9

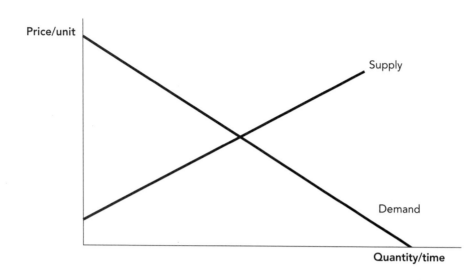

11. In Figure 4.9, if demand decreases, then the equilibrium

    a. price and quantity fall.

    b. price and quantity rise.

    c. price falls and quantity rises.

    d. price rises and quantity falls.

12. In Figure 4.9, if supply increases, then the equilibrium

    a. price and quantity fall.

    b. price and quantity rise.

    c. price falls and quantity rises.

    d. price rises and quantity falls.

13. In Figure 4.9, if the good becomes more popular, then the equilibrium

    a. price and quantity fall.

    b. price and quantity rise.

    c. price falls and quantity rises.

    d. price rises and quantity falls.

14. In Figure 4.9, if the wages of workers producing the good rises, then the equilibrium

    a. price and quantity fall.

    b. price and quantity rise.

    c. price falls and quantity rises.

    d. price rises and quantity falls.

15. In a free-market equilibrium,

    a. quantity demanded is less than quantity supplied.

    b. the sum of consumer and producer surplus is maximized.

    c. resources are wasted.

    d. there are no exploited gains from trade.

Answers to Self-Practice Questions

1. c, Topic: Equilibrium and the Adjustment Process

2. c, Topic: Equilibrium and the Adjustment Process

3. b, Topic: Equilibrium and the Adjustment Process

4. b, Topic: Equilibrium and the Adjustment Process

5. a, Topic: Equilibrium and the Adjustment Process

6. d, Topic: Equilibrium and the Adjustment Process

7. a, Topic: Equilibrium and the Adjustment Process

8. d, Topic: Gains from Trade Are Maximized at the Equilibrium

9. c, Topic: Shifting Demand and Supply

10. a, Topic: Shifting Demand and Supply

11. a, Topic: Shifting Demand and Supply

12. c, Topic: Shifting Demand and Supply

13. b, Topic: Shifting Demand and Supply

14. d, Topic: Shifting Demand and Supply

15. b, Topic: Terminology

5

Price Ceilings and Floors

Learning Objectives

This chapter discusses price ceilings and price floors and the effects of each on a market. The topics covered are:

> Price Ceilings
> Rent Control
> Arguments for Price Controls
> Universal Price Controls
> Price Floors

Summary

A **price ceiling** is a maximum price allowed by law. Most interesting are effective or binding price ceilings. To be effective, a price ceiling must be below the equilibrium price. If Congress passed a law stating that soft drinks could not sell for more than $100 each, such a price ceiling would not bind the market and, as such, it would have no effects in the current economy. Binding price ceilings create five important effects—shortages, reductions in product quality, wasteful waiting in line and other search costs, a loss of gains from trade, and a misallocation of resources.

That price ceilings cause shortages can be seen in Figure 5.1, where P_e and Q_e are the equilibrium price and quantity.

With the price ceiling below P_e, people want to buy Q_d of the good but producers want to sell Q_s of the good. Thus, there is a shortage of $Q_d - Q_s$ in the market.

Figure 5.1

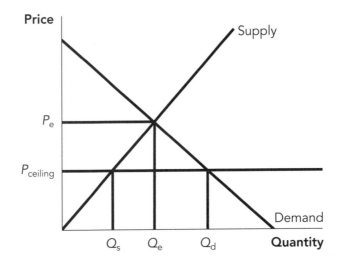

Sellers have more customers than goods they want to sell at the ceiling price. One way they can react is to give the customer less. Another way to do this is to reduce quality. Making their product cheaper is a way the producer can bring their costs more in line with the price ceiling. For example, reductions in quality can be less meat in a price-controlled sandwich. A reduction in service, such as having customers get their own drink is another way to lower quality and costs.

Since, with a price ceiling, there are more people who want to buy goods than there are goods being offered for sale, price is not allocating the good. Somehow the good must still be allocated. If no other allocation scheme is used, then a "first-come, first-served" scheme will be used. Since not everyone who wants to consume at the ceiling price will get the good, some customers will start arriving early to make sure that they get the good. Thus, we have people spending a valuable resource, that is, their time, to consume the product, yet the seller does not receive the value of that time. So that resource is wasted. In addition, since there is a shortage, customers will not be sure who has the product in stock. Thus, consumers will waste more resources in search of the product. The limit on these search costs is the point at which the price ceiling plus the search cost equals a consumer's willingness to pay.

There are also lost gains from trade, or deadweight losses, with a price ceiling. This can be seen in Figure 5.2, where the equilibrium price is $10 and the price ceiling is $5.

With the $5 price ceiling, quantity demanded is 100 units and quantity supplied is 50 units, so the shortage, $Q_d - Q_s$, is 50. There are 50 units sold. So for every unit between 50 and the market equilibrium of 75, there are unexploited gains from trade. Put another way, for each unit between 50 and 75, consumers are willing to pay more than it would take to get producers to supply that unit. Thus, area $A + B$ is the lost gains from trade, or **deadweight loss,** associated with the price ceiling of $5.

Finally, a price ceiling creates a misallocation of resources. With the price system, those who are willing to pay the market price get the item and those who are not willing to pay the market price forego the good. With the price ceiling, the buyer who

Figure 5.2

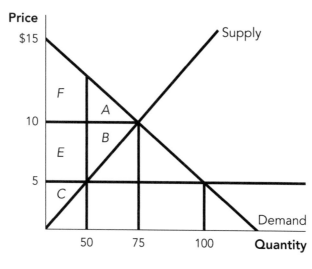

is willing to pay the most may or may not get to consume the good. A price ceiling therefore encourages bribery, for example, by selling to friends first or by bypassing the means to purchase the good (e.g., selling to someone "offline", when the only legal way the good can be purchased involves waiting in line).

If somehow, the consumers with the highest willingness to pay were able to get the good in Figure 5.2, then consumer surplus would be area $F + E$ and producer surplus would be area C. But if people arrive randomly, then the average value of ($5 + $15)/2, or $10, is the appropriate comparison and consumers only gain E rather than $F + E$. The loss of F is due to the misallocation of the good. An example of this would be people in a warm state heating their pool with price-controlled fuel, while people in a cold state not being able to buy enough fuel to heat their house.

Rent control is a regulation that prevents rents from rising to equilibrium levels. As with any other price ceiling, rent control creates a shortage. Rent control also leads to landlords not keeping up with the maintenance on their properties. Rent control leads as well to people wasting valuable resources searching for available properties. There are deadweight losses or lost gains from trade with rent control. Why? Because some people, those who are looking to rent, are willing to pay more than some landlords charge, yet, with rent control, these potential renters are not able to rent. Finally, with rent control, resources are misallocated, since fewer apartments are constructed and people often end up living in an apartment that is smaller or bigger than their optimal choice.

Rent controls and other price ceilings often start with a "freezing" of prices or rents due to public pressure against prices or rents rising too quickly. As we learned in Chapter 4, supply in a shorter time frame is relatively inelastic. So, at first there is not a huge impact on quantity supplied, and the shortage is therefore not huge. But over time, the shortage grows since the supply is more elastic over a longer time frame. Politicians who pass rent control or other price ceiling laws operate over short election cycles (from 2 to 6 years). So if they see "freezing" rents as a way to get reelected, then politicians may think that a price ceiling is worth implementing, even if the public does not support price ceilings or rent controls. A **price floor** is a minimum price allowed by law. The most interesting ones are effective or binding price floors. To be effective, a price floor must be above the equilibrium price. Binding price floors have four important effects—surpluses, a loss of gains from trade, wasteful increases in quality, and a misallocation of resources.

The effects of a price floor can be seen in Figure 5.3, where P_e and Q_e are the equilibrium price and quantity.

Figure 5.3

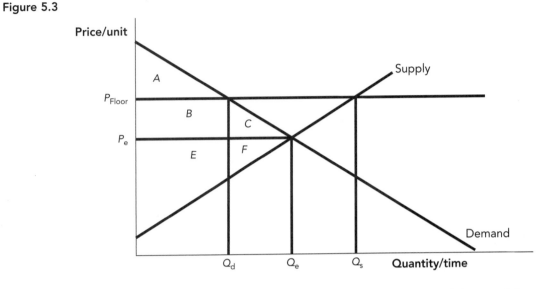

With the price floor above P_e, producers want to sell Q_s of the good, but consumers only want to buy Q_d. There is then a surplus of $Q_s > Q_d$ in the market.

Sellers have more of the good they want to sell at the price floor and not enough customers. Each firm is competing to attract customers, and a way they can attract them by giving them more. One way to do this is to raise quality. This is a waste in resources, however, since this higher quality is only used to attract customers who would be willing to buy at the current price and quality. The lost gains from trade, or deadweight losses, are area $C + F$. Finally, a price floor creates a misallocation of resources. With the price system, those who are willing to accept the market price get to sell the item, and those who are not willing to accept the market price forego selling the item. With the price ceiling, the sellers who are willing to sell at the lowest price may or may not get to sell the item.

Key Terms

price ceiling a maximum price allowed by law

deadweight loss the total of lost consumer and producer surplus when not all mutually profitable gains from trade are exploited. Price ceilings create a deadweight loss

rent control a price ceiling on rental housing

price floor a minimum price allowed by law

Traps, Hints, and Reminders

To be effective, a price ceiling must be below the equilibrium price.
To be effective, a price floor must be above the equilibrium price.
Rent control is a price ceiling on a particular type of good, such as rental housing units.
A deadweight loss is the same thing as a lost gain from trade.

Homework Quiz

1. A price floor is

  a. the maximum a consumer is willing to pay for a good.

  b. a maximum price allowed by law.

  c. the minimum a consumer is willing to pay for a good.

  d. a minimum price allowed by law.

2. A price floor causes

  a. surpluses.

  b. deadweight loss or lost gains from trade.

  c. misallocation of resources.

  d. All of the answers are correct.

3. An example of a price floor is

  a. gasoline price controls.

  b. the minimum wage.

  c. rent control.

  d. All of the answers are correct.

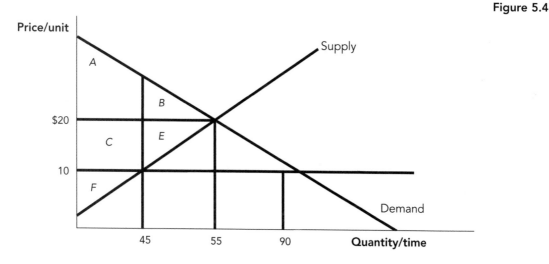

Figure 5.4

4. In Figure 5.4, a binding price ceiling would be

  a. $10.

  b. $20.

  c. $30.

  d. None of the answers is correct.

5. In Figure 5.4, the price ceiling quantity demanded is

  a. 40 units.

  b. 55 units.

  c. 90 units.

  d. None of the answers is correct.

6. In Figure 5.4, the price ceiling causes a shortage of
   a. 15 units.
   b. 35 units.
   c. 50 units.
   d. None of the answers is correct.

7. In Figure 5.4, if those with the highest value of the good get to consume, then the deadweight loss associated with the price ceiling is area
   a. $A + B$.
   b. $B + E$.
   c. F.
   d. $A + C$.

8. In Figure 5.4, the price ceiling producer surplus is area
   a. $A + B$.
   b. $B + E$.
   c. F.
   d. $A + C$.

9. In Figure 5.4, if those with the highest value of the good get to consume, then consumer surplus with the price ceiling is area
   a. $A + B$.
   b. C.
   c. F.
   d. $A + C$.

10. In Figure 5.4, if the product is randomly allocated so that it is consumed by consumers with an average value for the product, then consumer surplus is area
    a. $A + B$.
    b. C.
    c. F.
    d. $A + C$.

11. In Figure 5.4, if the product is randomly allocated, the most resources that consumers would waste standing in line and/or searching for the good is area
    a. A.
    b. $B + E$.
    c. C.
    d. F.

12. In Figure 5.4, the extra loss in surplus due to random allocation compared to allocation to those with the highest value for the good, is area
    a. *A.*
    b. *B + E.*
    c. *C.*
    d. *F.*

13. Rent controls
    a. cause shortages.
    b. create lost gains from trade.
    c. misallocate resources.
    d. All of the answers are correct.

14. A minimum wage
    a. increases unemployment of low-wage workers.
    b. creates extra gains from trade.
    c. creates a shortage of workers.
    d. All of the answers are correct.

15. A price floor
    a. causes wasteful increases in quality.
    b. creates a shortage.
    c. increases gains from trade.
    d. leads to a better allocation of resources.

Self-Practice Questions

1. A price ceiling is
    a. the maximum a consumer is willing to pay for a good.
    b. a maximum price allowed by law.
    c. the maximum value of all the inputs used to produce the good.
    d. All of the answers are correct.

2. A price ceiling causes
    a. a shortage.
    b. a surplus.
    c. pressure on the producer to lower the price.
    d. pressure on consumers to offer lower prices.

3. An example of a price ceiling is
    a. farm price supports.
    b. the minimum wage.
    c. rent control.
    d. All of the answers are correct.

4. Price ceilings lead to
  a. wasted resources.
  b. consumers searching for product availability.
  c. consumers waiting in line to buy the product.
  d. All of the answers are correct.

5. With a price ceiling, if nothing else is set up, the good will be allocated by
  a. income.
  b. price.
  c. a first–come, first–served scheme and by waiting in line.
  d. All of the answers are correct.

Figure 5.5

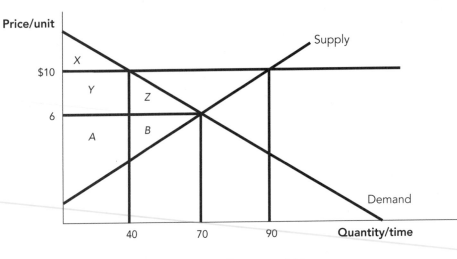

6. In Figure 5.5, a binding price floor would be
  a. $0.
  b. $6.
  c. $10.
  d. None of the answers is correct.

7. In Figure 5.5, with the price floor, quantity supplied is
  a. 40 units.
  b. 70 units.
  c. 90 units.
  d. None of the answers is correct.

8. In Figure 5.5, with the price floor, the amount of the surplus is
  a. 20 units.
  b. 50 units.
  c. 90 units.
  d. None of the answers is correct.

9. In Figure 5.5, with the price floor, consumer surplus is

    a. X.

    b. $Z + B$.

    c. $A + B$.

    d. Y.

10. In Figure 5.5, with the price floor, producer surplus is, at most

    a. X.

    b. $Z + B$.

    c. $Y + A$.

    d. Y.

11. In Figure 5.5, with the price floor, the deadweight losses from trade are at least area

    a. X.

    b. $Z + B$.

    c. $A + B$.

    d. Y.

12. The effects of rent controls are worse in the long run because

    a. the supply of rental units is more elastic in the long run.

    b. the supply of rental units is more inelastic in the long run.

    c. the demand for rental units is more elastic in the short run.

    d. the demand for rental units is unit-elastic in the long run.

13. With a price ceiling

    a. gains from trade are maximized.

    b. there are unexploited gains from trade.

    c. there are no trades made.

    d. the supply of goods is bought by the buyer with the highest willingness to pay.

14. With a price ceiling

    a. the quality of the good improves.

    b. there is a surplus on the market.

    c. resources are misallocated.

    d. All of the answers are correct.

15. With a price ceiling, goods may be allocated by all of the following EXCEPT

    a. bribery.

    b. publicly announced price alone.

    c. personal connections.

    d. a first-come, first-served scheme and by waiting in line.

Answers to Self-Practice Questions

1. b, Topic: Price Ceilings
2. a, Topic: Price Ceilings
3. c, Topic: Price Ceilings
4. d, Topic: Price Ceilings
5. c, Topic: Price Ceilings
6. c, Topic: Price Floors
7. c, Topic: Price Floors
8. b, Topic: Price Floors
9. a, Topic: Price Floors
10. c, Topic: Price Floors
11. b, Topic: Price Floors
12. a, Topic: Rent Control
13. b, Topic: Price Ceilings
14. c, Topic: Price Ceilings
15. b, Topic: Price Ceilings

6 (24)

GDP and the Measurement of Progress

Learning Objectives

In this chapter you will learn:

> What GDP measures
> What the *growth rate* of GDP measures
> How *nominal* and *real* GDP are different
> How GDP can be used to measure short-run volatility in the economy
> How GDP can be split into various components
> Some things that GDP does *not* measure

Summary

What GDP Measures

In a nutshell, this chapter introduces the key statistic economists use to measure national economic performance and explains how they use it. This statistic is called **Gross Domestic Product** or **GDP**. The chapter begins by providing the following definition of GDP:

GDP is the market value of all final goods and services produced within a country in a year.

Some key points of this definition are then discussed, including the following:

> GDP is a *market value*, meaning GDP is measured in dollar terms.
> GDP is a measure of *production*, meaning it counts what rolls out of the factories, offices, and other facilities in an economy.

> GDP counts *all* production across the entire economy.
> GDP counts production of both *goods* (tangible items such as computers or cars) and *services* (intangible production, such as haircuts or medical services).
> GDP counts only the production of *final* goods and services, meaning "intermediate" goods that are subsequently used in the production of other goods are not counted. (For example, a computer chip is an intermediate good and a computer is a final good. This prevents double-counting of intermediate goods since their value is included in final goods.)
> GDP measures production *within a country*, meaning GDP measures production that takes place within the borders of a nation. (Another measure called **GNP** is also discussed in the chapter, which includes production by domestic residents and domestically owned property, regardless of where the production takes place.)
> GDP figures measure the amount of production that occurs *in a year*, even though the U.S. and most other countries report GDP each quarter. (This means each quarter's figure is the amount of GDP that could be produced in a year if production continued at that quarter's rate for one year.)

As a measure of production, GDP provides a basic measure of how much economic activity occurs in a country. As such, we can compare the level of GDP across countries for a given year to determine which countries are experiencing the most economic activity. For example, Table 6.1 (24.1) in the text shows the 10 largest economies in the world according to GDP figures for 2007.

Another common way to use GDP figures is to report them on a per capita—or per person—basis. **GDP per capita** is just GDP divided by the population of a country. GDP per capita provides the level of GDP for the average person in a country. As such, it provides a measure of economic well-being for the typical person in a country. Table 6.1 (24.1) shows the level of GDP per capita in the world's 10 largest economies. Note that in many cases countries rank differently according to GDP and GDP per capita. For example, the United Kingdom has the world's sixth largest economy in terms of GDP, but the second highest GDP per capita.

GDP Growth Rates

If the *level* of GDP tells us how much a country produces in a given year, the *growth rate* of GDP tells us how much a country's production increases or decreases over time. The formula for calculating the growth rate of GDP is provided in the chapter. For example, to calculate the growth rate of GDP from 2004 to 2005, the formula is as follows:

$$\frac{GDP_{2005} - GDP_{2004}}{GDP_{2004}} \times 100 = \text{GDP growth rate for 2005}$$

This formula calculates the percentage change in GDP between 2004 and 2005. The years can be adjusted in the formula to calculate the growth rate over any desired period of time. All growth rates are expressed in percentage terms. Note that if GDP is falling over time, the growth rate will be a negative number. A worked-out example is provided in the chapter.

Since GDP *per capita* measures the well-being of the average person in a country, the *growth rate* of GDP per capita over time is used as a standard measure of economic progress in a nation.

Real vs. Nominal GDP

Another important issue discussed in this chapter relates to *how* GDP is calculated. Since GDP is a measure of production, the calculation of GDP statistics requires data on the *quantity* of output produced in a nation. But recall that GDP is measured in dollar terms. Dollars are used because we cannot simply add the production of cars, the production of computers, etc. without first converting to a common unit—namely dollars. To convert physical quantities of output to dollars, the *prices* of the goods and services are used. When *current* prices (prices from the year of production) are used in the calculation of GDP, the resulting GDP figure is called **nominal GDP**. For example, the calculations for 1995 and 2005 nominal GDP would be as follows:

$$1995 \text{ Nominal GDP} = 1995 \text{ Quantities} \times 1995 \text{ Prices}$$
$$2005 \text{ Nominal GDP} = 2005 \text{ Quantities} \times 2005 \text{ Prices}$$

Note that 1995 GDP uses 1995 prices and 2005 GDP uses 2005 prices.

A problem can arise, however, in the use of nominal GDP figures. When nominal GDP figures are compared over time—say from 1995 to 2005—it is unclear whether the change in the nominal GDP figure is from a change in the *quantities* or a change in the *prices* over time. If an increase in prices (called inflation) or decrease in prices (called deflation) has occurred from 1995 to 2005, this will influence the change in the nominal GDP figures over this time.

Since GDP is ultimately a measure of production, it is the quantities of output that are of primary interest. So, we need a GDP figure that reflects only the change in the quantities. To achieve this, another method of calculating GDP is used. Specifically, the calculation of GDP for *all* years is carried out using the prices from a *single* year. When *constant* prices are used in the calculation of GDP, the resulting GDP figure is called **real GDP**. For example, the calculations for 1995 and 2005 real GDP using 2005 prices would be as follows:

$$1995 \text{ Real GDP} = 1995 \text{ Quantities} \times 2005 \text{ Prices}$$
$$2005 \text{ Real GDP} = 2005 \text{ Quantities} \times 2005 \text{ Prices}$$

Note that 2005 prices are used in the calculation of both 1995 and 2005 GDP.

Since the prices are held constant in the calculation of real GDP, the change in the real GDP figure between 1995 and 2005 is attributable only to changes in the quantity of output produced over this period. Thus, real GDP figures provide a more accurate account of changes in production over time than nominal GDP figures.

Note that the use of the terms "nominal" and "real" to describe GDP before and after correcting for inflation is common in macroeconomics. In general, any **nominal variable** refers to one that has not been adjusted for price changes. Any **real variable** is one that has been corrected for price changes by using the same prices in all time periods. These terms will be used throughout the text. Other examples of nominal and real variables include nominal wages and real wages and nominal interest rates and real interest rates.

Measuring Short-Run Volatility in the Economy

Another important use of GDP growth rates is introduced in this chapter. Specifically, the growth rate of real GDP over short periods of time can be used to demonstrate the volatility—the ups and downs—in economic activity that occur over time. These short-run ups and downs are referred to as **business fluctuations** or **business cycles**. Figure 6.5 (24.5) in the text shows the quarterly growth rate of the U.S. economy since 1948. The figure clearly shows how the growth rate fluctuates above and below its long-run average of about 3.4 percent. Of particular interest are periods of decline in real GDP, which are called **recessions**. Periods of recession, shown by negative growth rates of real GDP, are shaded in Figure 6.5 (24.5).

Splitting GDP into Its Components

While GDP is defined as a measure of *production* early in the chapter, it is important to note that GDP can also be viewed as a measure of *spending* and as a measure of *income* in the economy. This is one of the more subtle aspects of understanding what GDP measures, but it is important to understand it. Intuitively, GDP is a measure of spending because everything that is produced is ultimately purchased by someone. Similarly, all of that spending ultimately lands in someone's pocket as income. Thus, for the economy as a whole, production, spending, and income are all equivalent concepts and GDP is a measure of them all.

Since GDP is a measure of spending, we can break GDP into its four spending components. Each spending component is based on who is buying the goods and services that make up GDP. These are **consumption** (spending by consumers), **investment** (spending by businesses), **government purchases**, and **net exports** (spending by foreigners on exports minus domestic spending on imports). This way of splitting GDP is known as the *national spending approach*: $Y = C + I + G + NX$, where $Y = $ GDP, $C = $ consumption, $I = $ investment, $G = $ government purchases, and $NX = $ net exports.

Since GDP is also a measure of income, we can break GDP into its four income components. Each income component is based on who receives the income from the purchase of the goods and services that make up GDP. These are wages (income by workers), rent (income by landlords), interest (income by capital owners), and profits (income by businesses). This way of splitting GDP is known as the *factor income approach*: $Y = $ wages $+$ rent $+$ interest $+$ profits, where $Y = $ GDP.

What GDP Does Not Measure

The chapter closes with a discussion of some things GDP does not measure. These include the following:

> GDP does not include the "underground" economy (illegal or otherwise "off-the-books" activity).

> GDP does not include "non-priced" production (such as the value of cutting your own grass or growing your own vegetables).

> GDP does not count leisure (the value of going fishing on your day off).

> GDP does not count "bads" (such as environmental costs of production).

> GDP does not measure the distribution of income (how equally income is spread across the population).

Key Terms

gross domestic product (GDP) the market value of all final goods and services produced within a country in a year

GDP per capita GDP divided by population

gross national product (GNP) the market value of all final goods and services produced by a country's permanent residents, wherever located, in a year

nominal variables variables such as nominal GDP that have not been adjusted for changes in prices

real variables variables such as real GDP that have been adjusted for changes in prices by using the same set of prices in all time periods

business fluctuations or **business cycles** the short-run movements in real GDP around its long-term trend

recession a significant, widespread decline in real income and employment

consumption spending private spending on final goods and services

investment spending private spending on tools, plant, and equipment used to produce future output

government purchases spending by all levels of government on final goods and services (transfers are not included in government purchases)

net exports the value of exports minus the value of imports

Traps, Hints, and Reminders

Remember that sales of used goods (such as a house or car) are not included in GDP, since nothing new has been produced. Any commissions or other fees associated with the sale of used goods, however, would be included in GDP as a service.

Purely financial transactions (such as the sale of stocks or bonds) are not included in GDP since they simply represent transfers of existing assets, not new production of goods and services. Any commissions or other fees associated with the sale of stocks and bonds, however, would be included in GDP as a service.

Make sure you know the difference between "intermediate" and "final" goods. Also, make sure you understand why counting intermediate goods in GDP would imply counting them twice (since the value of intermediate goods is included in final goods).

Remember that a positive GDP growth rate implies that GDP is rising over time, while a negative GDP growth rate implies that GDP is falling.

Make sure you know the difference between GDP and GNP, as the definitions are similar. Remember that what matters with GDP is *where* the production takes place (it must be within the borders of a nation to count in GDP). What matters for GNP is *who* is producing the good or service, regardless of where it is produced (it must be produced by domestically owned resources to count in GNP).

Remember that GDP is a measure of production, income, and spending, since all of these are equal for the entire economy. This means these terms can be used interchangeably when describing GDP.

Make sure you understand the difference between nominal GDP and real GDP. Real GDP has been corrected for price changes so that it only measures changes in the *quantity of production*. Nominal GDP includes changes in both prices and the *quantity* of production.

Nominal and real GDP data from a given year can be used to calculate a simple measure of inflation called the GDP Deflator. The formula for calculating the GDP Deflator is given in the text as follows:

$$\text{GDP Deflator} = \text{Nominal GDP}/\text{Real GDP} \times 100$$

For example, if nominal GDP for 2010 is $14.6 trillion and real GDP for 2010 is $13.3 trillion (in 2005 prices), the GDP Deflator is calculated as follows:

$$\text{GDP Deflator} = \$14.6 \text{ trillion}/\$13.3 \text{ trillion} \times 100 = 109.8$$

This means that prices in 2010 are $109.8 - 100 = 9.8\%$ higher than prices in 2005. When using the GDP Deflator to calculate inflation over a period of time, be sure to carefully calculate the inflation rate in percentage form. This may seem trivial in cases where prices are rising (inflation is occurring). For example, a GDP Deflator of 120 implies $120 - 100 = 20$ percent inflation. But, in cases where deflation is occurring, the calculation would be slightly different. For example, a GDP deflator of 0.9 would imply an inflation rate of $90 - 100 = -10$ percent. The negative sign indicates *deflation* of 10 percent since the base period.

Remember that the word "investment" has a very specific meaning in macroeconomics. Specifically, it is spending by businesses on new capital (tools, plant, and equipment used for production). The word "investment" should not be used to refer to some other common uses of the word, such as saving or buying stocks or bonds.

Remember that government transfer payments (such as social security payments) are not included in government purchases (and thus not included in GDP).

Self-Practice Questions

1. Calculate GDP for an economy that has consumer purchases of $6,000, investment purchases of $1,000, government purchases of $2,500, total exports of $1,000, and total imports of $500.

2. How are GDP, total output, total spending, and total income related in an economy? Explain.

3. What is a "recession," and how would a recession affect the level of real GDP and the growth rate of real GDP in a nation?

4. Calculate the annual growth rate of *nominal* GDP between the following years:
1969 GDP in billions: $948.6
1970 GDP in billions: $1012.2

5. What is the difference between *real* and *nominal* GDP? Which is the better measure of economic activity?

6. Imagine an economy that produces only pizza and pretzels. In 2010, the price of pizza was $20 and the price of pretzels was $1. In 2011, the price of pizza is $22 and the price of pretzels is $1.10. If 100,000 pizzas and 1,000,000 pretzels were produced in 2010, and 110,000 pizzas and 1,100,000 pretzels are produced in 2011, what is the nominal GDP and real GDP (using 2010 prices) for this economy in 2010 and 2011? Calculate the growth rate of real GDP for this economy during this period. Why is the growth rate of real GDP different than the growth rate of nominal GDP over this period? Can you use the GDP data to calculate the inflation rate from 2010 to 2011?

7. Would a significant decline in the economic activity of construction workers qualify as a recession?

8. Anuradha is a recent immigrant from India. She currently works as a software programmer in California's Silicon Valley. Are her earnings counted in India's GDP or America's GDP? What about GNP?

9. Jeff buys a used truck from a rental agency to make deliveries from his new furniture store. Would this purchase be included in GDP? If so, would it be consumption or investment spending?

Multiple-Choice Questions

1. Orrin mines iron ore, which he sells to Thorin, who turns iron ore into steel. The steel is sold to Gorin, who turns the steel into battle axes. The battle axes are sold by a merchant in the city to adventurers. Which of the following would be considered a final good?

   a. the iron ore

   b. the steel

   c. the battle axes sold to the merchant

   d. the battle axes sold to the adventurers

   e. All of these are final goods.

2. Imagine that Jack and Jill buy $500 worth of milk and $200 worth of crayons and coloring books each year for use in their day care business. Jack and Jill also hire a day care attendant at a salary of $14,000 per year. If Jack and Jill sell $100,000 worth of day care to parents each year, what is the contribution to GDP by Jack and Jill's Day Care?

   a. $100,000

   b. $700

   c. $100,700

   d. $114,700

3. Which of the following would be included in U.S. GDP?

   a. The purchase of stocks and bonds by a retiree living in Florida.

   b. Wages earned by an American working on an oil rig in Mexico.

   c. Cars produced in a Honda (a Japanese company) plant in Marysville, Ohio.

   d. Cars produced in a GM plant located in Canada.

4. Which of the following would be included in U.S. GNP?

a. The purchase of stocks and bonds by a retiree living in Florida.

b. Wages earned by an American working on an oil rig in Mexico.

c. Cars produced in a Honda (a Japanese company) plant in Marysville, Ohio.

d. Cars produced in a GM plant located in Canada.

e. Both b and d.

5. GDP is a measure of total _____ in an economy.

a. production

b. spending

c. income

d. All of the answers are correct.

6. Which of the following is considered investment according to the national spending approach?

a. depositing $1,000 into a savings account

b. buying $1,000 of stocks and bonds

c. spending $1,000 on college tuition

d. None of these is considered investment.

7. According to the national spending approach, which of the following is counted in investment?

a. A farmer buys some new land for growing corn.

b. An automobile rental company adds a new car to its fleet.

c. A college graduate builds a new house.

d. All of these are considered investment.

8. An economy has $10 trillion in consumption, $2.5 trillion in investment, $3 trillion in government purchases, $1 trillion in exports, and $1.5 trillion in imports. What is GDP in this economy?

a. $15 trillion

b. $15.5 trillion

c. $16.5 trillion

d. $18 trillion

9. Veronique is a Canadian citizen working in the United States as a welder for a Korean company. Her earnings are counted:

a. in U.S. GDP and Korean GNP.

b. in U.S. GNP and Canadian GDP.

c. in U.S. GNP and Korean GDP.

d. in U.S. GDP and Canadian GNP.

10. The largest spending component of GDP is:

   a. consumption.

   b. investment.

   c. government purchases.

   d. net exports.

11. If South Korea's GDP was $835 billion last year and is $885.1 billion this year, the growth rate of GDP this year will be:

   a. 106 percent.

   b. 6 percent.

   c. 5.66 percent.

   d. 0.06 percent.

12. Which of the following is NOT considered a government purchase?

   a. new rifles for the military

   b. unemployment checks

   c. salaries for public school teachers

   d. levees built by the Army Corps of Engineers

13. Real GDP:

   a. is calculated using the same prices in all years.

   b. includes both changes in quantities produced and changes in prices over time.

   c. has not been corrected for the effects of inflation over time.

   d. All of the answers are correct.

14. Which of the following is the best measure of how much living standards have changed in a country over time?

   a. real GDP

   b. real GDP per capita

   c. real GDP growth

   d. real GDP growth per capita

15. If a country is experiencing inflation, it would mean that:

   a. nominal and real GDP are growing at the same rate.

   b. nominal GDP is growing faster than real GDP.

   c. real GDP is growing faster than nominal GDP.

   d. nominal GDP is growing and real GDP is falling.

16. If nominal GDP is $12 trillion this year and real GDP is $10 trillion this year (in 2005 dollars), then inflation since 2005 must have been:

   a. 2 percent.

   b. 10 percent.

   c. 12 percent.

   d. 20 percent.

17. Which of the following is TRUE regarding the business cycle in the U.S. economy?

    a. Since 1948, 11 recessions have occurred.

    b. Since 1948, periods of expansion (booms) have generally lasted longer than periods of recession.

    c. The average annual real GDP growth rate has been 3.4 percent since 1948.

    d. All of the answers are correct.

18. Which of the following is likely to occur during an economic expansion (or boom)?

    a. Real income increases.

    b. Real GDP grows.

    c. Employment increases.

    d. All of the answers are correct.

19. Which of the following would indicate that an economy is in recession?

    a. Real GDP growth turns negative.

    b. Nominal GDP is falling but real income is rising.

    c. Nominal GDP is falling but employment is rising.

    d. Nominal GDP is falling but real GDP is rising.

20. Which of the following would most likely NOT be counted in GDP?

    a. Profit earned by Ford Motor Company.

    b. A cash payment to your neighbor's teenage son for cutting the grass while you are away on vacation.

    c. The legal sale of marijuana for medical purposes in the state of California.

    d. The cost of hiring an outside company to clean up a chemical spill at a local factory.

Homework Quiz

  1. Which of the following would be included in U.S. GDP?

    a. used books sold at a bookstore in the United States

    b. hip hop music made in the United States, but sold in Canada

    c. cars made in Germany at a General Motors factory

    d. the price paid by an American tourist for a hotel room in Mexico

2. Which of the following is TRUE for an economy?

    a. GDP = total income = total spending = total production

    b. GDP = consumption + investment + government purchases + net exports

    c. GDP = wages + interest + rent + profit

    d. All of the answers are correct

Use the following information to answer Questions 3–6:

Consider an economy that produces only DVD players and flat-screen TVs. In 2007, DVD players sold for $100 and flat-screen TVs sold for $500. In 2008, the price of DVD players was $90 and the price of flat-screen TVs was $400. In 2007, 5 million DVD players and 1 million flat-screen TVs were sold. In 2008, 5.5 million DVD players and 1.2 million flat-screen TVs were sold.

3. Nominal GDP in 2007 for this economy is:

    a. $850 million.

    b. $975 million.

    c. $1,000 million.

    d. $1,150 million.

4. Real GDP in 2008 (in 2007 dollars) for this economy is:

    a. $850 million.

    b. $975 million.

    c. $1,000 million.

    d. $1,150 million.

5. Real GDP growth from 2007 to 2008 is:

    a. −2.5 percent.

    b. 15 percent.

    c. 18 percent.

    d. 35 percent.

6. Inflation (or deflation) from 2007 to 2008 is:

    a. −2.5 percent.

    b. −10 percent.

    c. −15.2 percent.

    d. 17.6 percent.

7. Which of the following is TRUE regarding the difference between nominal GDP and real GDP?

    a. Nominal GDP is a better measure of economic activity than real GDP.

    b. Nominal GDP is influenced by price changes over time while real GDP is not.

    c. Nominal GDP has been corrected for inflation while real GDP has not.

    d. All of the answers are correct.

8. Which of the following is the best measure for comparing living standards across countries?

a. real GDP

b. real GDP per capita

c. real GDP growth

d. real GDP growth per capita

9. If real GDP is $15 trillion in 2011 and $15.6 trillion in 2012, then real GDP growth in 2012 is:

a. 3.8 percent.

b. 4 percent.

c. 6 percent.

d. None of the answers is correct.

10. Which of the following would NOT be included in GDP?

a. $100 of groceries purchased with unemployment benefits from the government

b. wages paid to a Mexican citizen working in the United States

c. tomatoes grown in your backyard that you use to make salsa

d. commission you pay for the purchase of a used car at a local dealership

Answer Key

Answers to Self-Practice Questions

1. $C + I + G + \text{(exports − imports)} = \$6,000 + \$1,000 + \$2,500 + (\$1,000 − \$500) = \$10,000$.

   Topic: What Is GDP?

2. Total output (production), total spending, and total income are all equal in an economy and GDP is a measure of all of these concepts. It is clear from the definition of GDP presented in the chapter that GDP is a measure of total production. Since all production is ultimately sold to someone, production must equal spending. Finally, since spending generates income to all those who had a hand in producing the output initially, income will equal spending and production. So, we can think of GDP as representing all of these concepts. Note that the national spending approach builds on the total spending interpretation by splitting GDP into four spending components: consumption, investment, government purchases, and net exports (exports minus imports). The factor income approach builds on the total income interpretation by splitting GDP into four income components: wages, rent, interest, and profit.

   Topic: The Many Ways of Splitting GDP

3. A recession is a significant, widespread decline in economic activity. Evidence of a recession will appear in a wide range of measures of economic activity—measures such as real income, consumer spending, employment, and real GDP. The level of real GDP will decline during periods of recession. This implies that the growth rate of real GDP will be negative during recessions, since a negative growth rate implies a declining level of GDP.

   Topic: Growth Rates; Cyclical and Short–Run Changes in GDP

4. $\dfrac{1,012.2 − 948.6}{948.6} \times 100 = 6.7\%$

   Topic: Growth Rates

5. Real GDP has been adjusted for price changes, while nominal GDP has not. As a result, real GDP measures only changes in the quantity of production, while nominal GDP measures both changes in the quantity of production and changes in prices. For this reason, real GDP is a better measure of economic activity.

   Topic: Nominal vs. Real GDP

6. To calculate nominal GDP for 2010, use 2010 quantities and 2010 prices:

	2010 Quantity	2010 Price	Market Value
Pizza	100,000	$20.00	$2,000,000
Pretzels	1,000,000	$1.00	$1,000,000
	2010 Nominal GDP =		$3,000,000

To calculate nominal GDP for 2011, use 2011 quantities and 2011 prices:

	2011 Quantity	**2011 Price**	**Market Value**
Pizza	110,000	$22.00	$2,420,000
Pretzels	1,100,000	$1.10	$1,210,000
	2011 Nominal GDP =		$3,630,000

To calculate real GDP using 2010 prices, 2010 prices will be used in the calculation of GDP for all years. For 2010, this would provide the same calculation as for 2010 nominal GDP shown. Thus, real GDP for 2010 (using 2010 prices) is $3,000,000.

To calculate real GDP for 2011 (using 2010 prices), use 2011 quantities and 2010 prices:

	2011 Quantity	**2010 Price**	**Market Value**
Pizza	110,000	$20.00	$2,200,000
Pretzels	1,100,000	$1.00	$1,100,000
	2011 Real GDP (in 2010 prices) =		$3,300,000

The growth rate of real GDP is calculated as follows:

$$\frac{3,300,000 - 3,000,000}{3,000,000} \times 100 = 10\%$$

The growth rate of real GDP is less than the growth rate of nominal GDP (which is 21 percent; check for yourself) because the growth rate of nominal GDP includes the increase in prices that occurred from 2010 to 2011 in addition to the increase in production (which is 10 percent as measured by real GDP growth).

Inflation from 2010 to 2011 can be calculated using the GDP Deflator as follows:

$$\text{GDP Deflator} = \frac{3,630,000}{3,300,000} \times 100 = 110$$

The GDP Deflator implies an inflation rate of $110 - 100 = 10\%$ between 2010 and 2011.

Topic: Nominal vs. Real GDP

7. A recession is defined as a significant, widespread decline in economic activity. So no, a decline of economic activity in the construction sector *alone* would not constitute a recession. But if the decline in construction is accompanied by declines in other sectors such as banking, retail, and manufacturing, this would meet the "widespread" criteria required for a recession.

Topic: Cyclical and Short-Run Changes in GDP

8. GNP counts the earnings of a country's citizens, so Anuradha's earnings are counted in India's GNP. But her earnings are counted in U.S. GDP because GDP measures what is created within a country's borders. Her earnings would not be counted in U.S. GNP or India's GDP.

   Topic: What Is GDP?

9. Since the truck is used, it would not be included in GDP. It is merely a transfer of an existing asset from one party to another with no new production. If the truck had been purchased new, it would be counted in GDP as investment spending.

   Topic: What Is GDP?; The National Spending Approach: $Y = C + I + G + NX$

Answers to Multiple-Choice Questions

1. d, Topic: What Is GDP?

2. a, Topic: What Is GDP?

3. c, Topic: What Is GDP?

4. e, Topic: What Is GDP?

5. d, Topic: What Is GDP?; The Many Ways of Splitting GDP

6. d, Topic: The Many Ways of Splitting GDP

7. d, Topic: The Many Ways of Splitting GDP

8. a, Topic: The Many Ways of Splitting GDP

9. d, Topic: What Is GDP?

10. a, Topic: The Many Ways of Splitting GDP

11. b, Topic: Growth Rates

12. b, Topic: The Many Ways of Splitting GDP

13. a, Topic: Nominal vs. Real GDP

14. d, Topic: Real GDP Growth per Capita

15. b, Topic: Nominal vs. Real GDP

16. d, Topic: The GDP Deflator

17. d, Topic: Cyclical and Short-Run Changes in GDP

18. d, Topic: Cyclical and Short-Run Changes in GDP

19. a, Topic: Cyclical and Short-Run Changes in GDP

20. b, Topic: The Many Ways of Splitting GDP; Problems with GDP as a Measure of Output and Welfare

7 (25)

The Wealth of Nations and Economic Growth

Learning Objectives

In this chapter, you will learn:

> What economists mean by "economic growth"

> Why economic growth is important

> Some basic facts about economic growth and living standards around the world

> What causes economic growth

> What "institutions" are and why they are important for growth

Summary

This chapter introduces the concept of economic growth. After presenting some basic facts about growth around the world and through history, it begins to consider what causes economic growth. A more advanced discussion of the causes of growth is found in Chapter 8.

What Is Economic Growth?

Before jumping into this chapter, it is important to understand exactly what economists mean by the term "economic growth." **Economic growth** refers to increases in living standards over long periods of time in an economy. Remember from Chapter 6 that living standards are best measured by the level of real GDP per capita. So, economic growth is measured by the growth rate of real GDP per capita.

Why Is Economic Growth Important?

Throughout this chapter, the importance of economic growth is emphasized. Since economic growth refers to increases in living standards in an economy, economic growth implies improvements in many aspects of the quality of life for the typical citizen in a country. This involves not only the material things we usually associate with prosperity—such as money, iPhones, swimming pools, and nice cars—but also more subtle things like better nutrition and health. Figure 7.1 (25.1) shows the close relationship between health and wealth, where countries with higher living standards (as measured by the level of real GDP per capita in 2000) are generally more healthy (as measured by childhood survival rates). Because of such far-reaching effects, economic growth is sometimes referred to as the greatest anti-poverty program in the world.

Some Basic Facts about Growth

It is also important to understand some basic facts about the growth experiences of countries around the world and over time. Three basic facts about growth are presented by three graphs early in the chapter. Fact one is that *GDP per capita varies enormously among nations around the world today*. This fact is demonstrated in Figure 7.2 (25.2). A couple of points are important: (1) there is a huge disparity between the richest and poorest nations in the world today (the richest have income per capita 20, 30, or 40 times higher than the poorest); and (2) the vast majority (80 percent) of the world's population lives below the *average* income level of $9,133 per person per year.

Fact two is that *everyone used to be poor*. This fact is demonstrated in Figure 7.3 (25.3). The figure shows the growth record of a number of countries over the last 2,000 years. It is important to note, however, that on the horizontal axis in this graph, the first 1,000 years are squeezed into a much smaller span than the last 1,000 years. If the first 1,000 years were stretched out, it would become more apparent that no visible growth occurred anywhere in the world until around 1500 A.D. Furthermore, most of the impressive growth of the richest countries in the world today has occurred in the last 50 years! So for most of the history of human civilization, everyone was poor. And the growth that has occurred has occurred very recently.

Fact three is that *there are growth miracles and growth disasters*. This fact is shown in Figure 7.4 (25.4). Some countries, like the United States, Japan, and South Korea, have grown tremendously in the last 50 years. Others, unfortunately, like Nigeria and Argentina, have remained stagnant with no growth at all. Explaining the differences between these experiences is a key goal of this chapter.

Growth experiences like those shown in Figure 7.4 (25.4) could be summarized by calculating each country's growth rate over the period shown (recall the formula for calculating growth rates from Chapter 6). Small differences in a country's growth rate can have a big impact over long periods of time (like 50 or 100 years). This point is demonstrated using the rule of 70. The rule of 70 is used to calculate how long it will take for a country growing at a given rate to double its living standard. The rule of 70 says that the time required to double living standards = $70/x$, where x is the country's growth rate. So, a country growing at 2 percent per year can double its living standard in $70/2 = 35$ years, while a country growing at 4 percent can double its living standard in just $70/4 = 17.5$ years.

What Causes Growth?

One of the most important points of this chapter is to answer the question "What causes growth?" It certainly makes sense to ask this question. If growth is so beneficial to so many people, how can we make it happen? Figure 7.5 (25.5) summarizes the key points of the growth process that is explained in this chapter to answer this question. It is important for you to study this figure and understand how the different parts of the growth process fit together.

In understanding Figure 7.5 (25.5), it is helpful to start at the bottom. At the bottom of the figure is real GDP per capita. This is the ultimate goal of growth: to increase real GDP per capita. The parts of the diagram explain how we can achieve this goal. Directly above the goal of growth are the *factors of production*. Factors of production are the resources that are used in an economy to produce goods and services. These include **physical capital**, **human capital**, and **technology**. (You can find definitions for these words in the key terms section that follows.) These factors of production must be organized in an efficient way to produce output in the economy. Simply put, countries that have abundant factors of production will produce more—and grow more—than countries with fewer resources. Because these factors of production are the closest to the ultimate goal of growth in the diagram, they are called the "proximate" causes of growth.

Above the factors of production in Figure 7.5 (25.5) are "incentives." To understand the role of incentives, ask yourself "Where do the factors of production come from?" Unfortunately, factors of production do not just fall from the sky. They must be produced just like any other good in an economy. So an economy will not have abundant factors of production unless it produces them. But why do some economies produce more factors of production than others? This is where "incentives" come into the picture. Incentives are penalties or rewards that influence human behavior. The incentives in an economy must be structured correctly to motivate economic players (humans) to build the factors of production an economy needs to grow.

For example, physical capital is created through *investment*. Remember that investment, introduced in Chapter 6, refers to purchases of new capital by businesses. Businesses will not invest in new capital unless there are proper incentives. Such an incentive is the opportunity to earn a profit using the capital. Similarly, human capital is created through *education and training*. Economic players will not engage in education and training to build human capital unless there are proper incentives to motivate that behavior. Such an incentive would be the opportunity to "profit" from the human capital by getting a better job and earning a higher income (after all, why are you in college?). The same is true of technology, which must be created through *research and development*. Businesses and individuals who discover new technology do so in response to incentives, namely the opportunity to profit from their discoveries.

So, to summarize, incentives are a necessary part of the process by which the factors of production are produced in an economy. Without the proper incentives, there will be insufficient factors of production. In thinking about this process, it may be useful to imagine inserting another step between incentives and the factors of production in Figure 7.5 (25.5). This in-between step would include the activities—investment, education and training, research and development—that produce the factors of production. These activities are driven by incentives and are a fundamental part of the growth process explained in this chapter.

Now that you understand why incentives are important, you might next ask "What determines the incentives in an economy?" This brings us to the top part of the growth process in Figure 7.5 (25.5): institutions. **Institutions** are the "rules of the game" that structure economic incentives. Institutions can be formal rules, such as laws or regulations, or informal rules, such as customs or traditions in an economy that structure incentives. Institutions are discussed at greater length later in the chapter. For now, it is important to recognize that without proper institutions the incentives in an economy will not generate growth. Since institutions and incentive are farther away from the ultimate goal of growth in Figure 7.5 (25.5), they are sometimes referred to as the "ultimate" causes of growth.

Institutions

The end of the chapter provides additional discussion of institutions. In particular, the institutions that economists believe are conducive to growth include:

> property rights
> honest government
> political stability
> a dependable legal system
> competitive and open markets

Property rights refer to the right of individuals to own and use a resource without the risk of having it taken from them. Property rights are important for growth because they can affect the ability of individuals to own and reap the rewards of their resources. To explain the importance of institutions, the chapter uses the story of communal farming in China following the Communist Revolution. In communal farming, workers did not own their property or the crops they grew on it, so payment was divorced from work effort. As a result, the incentive was for no one in the commune to work very hard in the fields, in hopes that everyone else would do the work (a problem known as **free riding**). This resulted in plummeting agricultural productivity and mass starvation in China. In an effort to overcome this dilemma, workers in the small village of Xiaogang formed a secret arrangement that assigned property rights to individual farmers. Each farmer could keep what they produced in their area (over and above the quota that was handed over to the government). This new arrangement provided the incentive for workers to work hard and produce more. Agricultural production skyrocketed under this new arrangement. Eventually, the Chinese government adopted the private ownership plan and this formed the basis for institutional changes that led to incredible growth in the Chinese economy in recent decades.

Honest government is an important institution because dishonest governments cannot be trusted to protect property rights or carry out the rule of law. For example, a government may say that property rights exist, but not enforce them. In effect, this is equivalent to having no property rights.

Political stability is an important institution for growth because a stable government creates an environment conducive for more investment in physical capital, education and training to build human capital, and research and development of new technology. All of these activities are carried out on the promise of pay-offs over long periods of time. If there is uncertainty about the political regime in a country in the future, there are few guarantees that one will be able to reap the rewards of their investment, education, or innovative activities. With fewer of these activities, there are fewer factors of production and less growth.

A dependable legal system is important for enforcing property rights and other laws effectively. Without an effective legal system, the property rights and laws might as well not exist.

Free and competitive markets are important because markets have been shown to be the most efficient way to allocate resources in an economy—far more efficient than government or central planning of resource use and economic activity. This is true because no person of group of people in government or elsewhere can possibly possess enough information to determine efficient resource use as well as markets can.

Key Terms

economic growth increases in living standards over long periods of time, as measured by the growth rate of real GDP per capita

physical capital the stock of tools, including machines, structures, and equipment, that businesses use to produce output

human capital the productive knowledge and skills that workers acquire through education, training, and experience

technological knowledge knowledge about how the world works that is used to produce goods and services

institutions the "rules of the game" that structure economic incentives

free rider someone who consumes a resource without working or contributing to the resource's upkeep

economies of scale the advantages of large-scale production that reduce average cost as quantity increases

Traps, Hints, and Reminders

In the discussion of economic growth in this chapter, do not confuse the use of growth rates (of real GDP per capita) over long periods of time with the use of growth rates over shorter periods of time to measure "business cycle" characteristics as discussed in Chapter 6. Economic growth generally refers to the longer-run phenomenon while business cycle effects refer to shorter-run performance.

The use of the word "institution" in this chapter is different from what many people might have in mind. They do not refer to large firms, banks, or government agencies. Instead, they are the formal and informal "rules of the game" that structure economic incentives.

Figure 7.5 (25.5) is crucially important in understanding the growth process explained in this chapter. Make sure you understand all of the parts of the process and how one part of the process leads to another.

In understanding the importance of incentives, make sure you recognize that incentives are what drive the creative activities—investment, education and training, and research and development—that lead to the production of the factors of production. These activities are not shown in Figure 7.5 (25.5), but are an important part of the growth process.

Self-Practice Questions

1. Why is it important to remember that all countries used to be poor, that some countries remain poor today while others are rich, and that the difference between the rich and poor today is vast?

2. Growing at rates in excess of 7 percent per year in recent decades, what has happened to the standard of living in China? Explain using the rule of 70.

3. How has the recent growth experience in China benefited the ordinary citizen in China?

4. In light of the recent growth that has occurred in China, how does its living standard compare to that of other developed countries in the world? Use Figure 7.2 (25.2) to explain.

5. List the causes of growth from the "ultimate" to the "proximate" causes.

6. What are "incentives" and why are they important in the growth process?

7. Investment, education, and development of new technology are usually mentioned as important factors in the growth process. Why are they important and where do they fit in the growth process shown in Figure 7.5 (25.5)?

8. Suppose two countries have similar factors of production. Would you expect them to grow at similar rates in the future? Explain why or why not. What example of this type of situation is provided in the text (hint: nighttime satellite view)?

9. List the institutions that are important for growth as discussed in this chapter.

10. Which important institution for growth is illustrated by the story of the village of Xiaogang in China? What does the story have to do with the free rider problem?

Multiple-Choice Questions

1. Low per capita GDP is likely to be associated with which of the following?
   a. high childhood mortality
   b. high literacy rates
   c. long life expectancy
   d. good nutrition

2. The average level of income per capita in the world is:
   a. about $4,000, similar to that in China.
   b. about $9,100, similar to that in Mexico.
   c. about $32,000, similar to that in the United States.
   d. about $50,000, similar to that in Luxembourg.

3. When economists talk about "economic growth" they mean:
   a. increasing the overall real GDP of a country.
   b. increasing the per capita real GDP of a country.
   c. increasing the geographic size of a country.
   d. increasing the population of a country.

4. If per capita GDP was $32,000 last year and is $34,000 this year, what was the economic growth rate?
   a. $2,000
   b. 8.25 percent
   c. 6.25 percent
   d. 5.88 percent

5. Which of the following is an example of a growth miracle and a growth disaster?
   a. Nigeria and Argentina
   b. The United States and Japan
   c. The United States and South Korea
   d. South Korea and Nigeria

6. Which of the following is TRUE about economic growth?
   a. All countries eventually grow rich.
   b. Once a country starts to grow, it will continue to grow.
   c. A country can grow and become wealthy, never grow, or grow and then begin to stagnate.
   d. Growth is a random process; in some years a country grows and in other years it doesn't.

7. Which of the following is a factor of production?

    a. physical capital

    b. human capital.

    c. technical knowledge

    d. All of the answers are correct.

8. Physical capital includes:

    a. knowledge and skills.

    b. people.

    c. factories and equipment.

    d. All of the answers are correct.

9. Human capital:

    a. refers to the physical strength of a worker.

    b. is acquired through education, training, and experience.

    c. refers to the skills a person is born with.

    d. is the same as technological knowledge.

10. When economists talk about "institutions" they mean:

    a. very big businesses.

    b. very old businesses.

    c. the rules of the game that structure economic incentives.

    d. large government agencies.

11. Which of the following is NOT included in the institutions of economic growth?

    a. property rights

    b. honest government

    c. competitive and open markets

    d. labor unions

12. Good institutions provide the incentive to:

    a. make as much money as you can as quickly as possible.

    b. take advantage of your neighbors.

    c. share everything with your neighbors.

    d. work hard and invest.

13. When China adopted communal farming, its agricultural output:

    a. increased exponentially.

    b. increased slightly.

    c. decreased dramatically.

    d. stayed about the same.

14. Free riding is a result of:

a. political instability.

b. a dishonest government.

c. poorly defined property rights.

d. All of the answers are correct.

15. Property rights:

a. are rules that let people profit from their own property.

b. are rules that split the profits from property equally among a group of people in a community.

c. are special courts for resolving property disputes.

d. are judges who oversee cases involving property disputes.

16. Which of the following is most important in determining the level of investment, education, and innovation in an economy?

a. institutions

b. factors of production

c. free riders

d. incentives

17. Which of the following is the most "proximate" cause of economic growth?

a. incentives

b. institutions

c. factors of production

d. property rights

18. Which factor best explains the different growth experiences of North Korea and South Korea since their division into two separate countries?

a. South Korea started with far greater resources than North Korea.

b. North Korea has had a less stable government than South Korea.

c. North Korea and South Korea adopted vastly different institutions following the division.

d. All of the answers are correct.

19. China increased its agricultural production by nearly 50 percent in five years from 1978–1983. What was the cause?

a. giving people the proper incentives to produce

b. using collective farming

c. a more stable government following the death of Mao Zedong

d. preventing bureaucrats from taking bribes

Homework Quiz

1. Which of the following countries would you expect to have the highest rate of childhood survival?

   a. Nigeria

   b. China

   c. Mexico

   d. South Korea

2. Which of the following has the highest level of per capita real GDP today?

   a. Nigeria

   b. Mexico

   c. Japan

   d. China

3. According to the "rule of 70," a country growing at 10 percent per year will double its standard of living in:

   a. 700 years.

   b. 10 years.

   c. 7 years.

   d. None of the answers is correct.

4. Which of the following provides the best measure of a country's standard of living?

   a. the level of real GDP

   b. the level of real GDP per capita

   c. growth in real GDP

   d. growth in real GDP per capita

5. Which of the following is a "factor of production"?

   a. human capital

   b. investment

   c. property rights

   d. incentives

6. Which of the following best describes the growth process from its ultimate to its proximate causes?

   a. incentives→institutions→factors of production→real GDP per capita

   b. institutions→incentives→factors of production→real GDP per capita

   c. factors of production→incentives→institutions→real GDP per capita

   d. factors of production→institutions→incentives→real GDP per capita

7. The key problem with China's collective farming system was:

   a. a corrupt government.

   b. political instability.

   c. the free rider problem.

   d. an ineffective legal system.

8. "Free riding" is a result of which of the following?

   a. too few factors of production

   b. free and competitive markets

   c. poorly defined property rights

   d. a dishonest government

9. Which of the following factors of production is created through research and development?

   a. technological knowledge

   b. human capital

   c. physical capital

   d. organization

10. If a country's real GDP per capital increases from $50,000 to $59,000, its rate of economic growth is:

    a. $9,000.

    b. 15.25 percent.

    c. 18 percent.

    d. None of the answers is correct.

Answer Key

Answers to Self-Practice Questions

1. These facts are important because there must be some explanation for the different growth experiences that have occurred in different countries over time. Understanding what causes some countries to remain poor while others grow rich is a key goal of this chapter.

Topic: Key Facts about the Wealth of Nations and Economic Growth

2. With growth in excess of 7 percent per year, the rule of 70 says that China is able to double its standard of living in less than $70/7 = 10$ years. Growing at these rates for several decades means China has been able to double its income several times over.

Topic: A Primer on Growth Rates

3. Economic growth has many benefits for the typical citizen in a country. Not only does it mean more material things are available with higher income levels, but it also means citizens will enjoy better nutrition, better health, longer life expectancy, and more opportunities for education, entertainment, recreation, and even leisure activities.

Topic: Introduction

4. Although China has experienced phenomenal growth in recent decades, it remains one of the poorest countries in the world. Figure 7.2 (25.2) shows that China's nearly 2 billion people have a standard of living that is about half of the world average. So while China has made great strides recently, it has a long way to go to catch up with the richest countries in the world.

Topic: Key Facts about the Wealth of Nations and Economic Growth

5. Institutions→Incentives→Factors of Production→Real GDP per capita

Topic: Understanding the Wealth of Nations

6. Incentives are rewards or penalties that motivate human behavior. Incentives are important for growth because they motivate (or deter) the activities necessary to create the factors of production in an economy. These activities include investment (to build physical capital), education and training (to build human capital), and research and development (to create new innovation and technology). Without proper incentives, these activities will not occur and the economy will not have sufficient factors of production for growth to occur.

Topic: Incentives and Institutions

7. Investment, education, and development of new technology are important because these are the activities that create the factors of production in an economy. In Figure 7.5 (25.5), these activities would occur between "incentives" and the "factors of production." See the answer to the previous question for more details.

Topic: Understanding the Wealth of Nations

8. Even if two countries have the same factors of production initially, they may grow at very different rates over time. This is because there is more to the growth process than just factors of production. Specifically, if the institutions and incentives are different in the two countries, they will likely have different growth experiences. The example discussed in the text is North Korea and South Korea. Their experience is unique because the two countries started with nearly identical resources when the North/South division occurred. Having vastly different institutions, South Korea's economy flourished while North Korea's languished.

   Topic: Incentives and Institutions

9. (1) property rights; (2) honest government; (3) political stability; (4) a dependable legal system; and (5) competitive and open markets.

   Topic: Incentives and Institutions

10. The story of the village of Xiaogang demonstrates the important role of property rights in an economy. Property rights are important because they provide the incentives necessary for work effort. The story demonstrates the free rider problem because without property rights, there is little incentive to work. Without an incentive to work, everyone laid back and waited on everyone else to do the work, but still consumed the fruits of the labor—which is what a free rider does. But if everyone is a free rider, no one works and nothing gets produced. This is exactly what happened during China's experiment with communal farming, as millions died of starvation.

    Topic: Incentives and Institutions

Answers to Multiple-Choice Questions

1. a, Topic: Introduction

2. b, Topic: Key Facts about the Wealth of Nations and Economic Growth

3. b, Topic: A Primer on Growth Rates

4. c, Topic: A Primer on Growth Rates

5. d, Topic: Key Facts about the Wealth of Nations and Economic Growth

6. c, Topic: Key Facts about the Wealth of Nations and Economic Growth

7. d, Topic: The Factors of Production

8. c, Topic: The Factors of Production

9. b, Topic: The Factors of Production

10. c, Topic: Incentives and Institutions

11. d, Topic: Incentives and Institutions

12. d, Topic: Incentives and Institutions

13. c, Topic: Institutions

14. c, Topic: Institutions

15. a, Topic: Institutions

16. d, Topic: The Factors of Production

17. c, Topic: Understanding the Wealth of Nations and Economic Growth

18. c, Topic: Institutions

19. a, Topic: Institutions

8 (26)

Growth, Capital Accumulation, and the Economics of Ideas: Catching Up vs. the Cutting Edge

Learning Objectives

In this chapter, you will learn:

> How to use production functions to graph the relationship between output and the factors of production in an economy

> What the law of diminishing returns implies for growth in an economy

> How capital accumulation depends on investment and depreciation

> What a "steady state" is in the Solow Model of economic growth

> Why "catching-up growth" cannot explain growth in the very long run

> How "cutting-edge growth" can explain growth in the very long run

> About the special nature of ideas and their role in economic growth

Summary

This chapter provides a more detailed look at economic growth (than was provided in the previous chapter) by presenting a model of growth in an economy. The model is called the Solow model—named after the economist Robert Solow, who invented the model in the 1950s. The Solow model explains how growth results from capital accumulation and the creation of new ideas in an economy.

Mastering the Solow model requires an understanding of the following topics:

1. Production functions and the law of diminishing returns
2. Capital accumulation and the concept of a "steady state"
3. Catching-up growth
4. Cutting-edge growth

Let's now take a closer look at each of these.

Production Functions and the Law of Diminishing Returns

A *production function* is a mathematical or graphical description of production in an economy. It describes the process of turning inputs (or factors of production) into output of goods and services (GDP). Consider the following mathematical production function:

$$Y = F(A, eL, K)$$

where Y is GDP, A represents the ideas or technology used in production, eL is labor adjusted for the level of skills or education, K is physical capital, and F represents a specific mathematical function for relating the factors of production to the quantity of GDP produced. If A and eL are held constant, we can simplify the production function as $Y = F(K)$. The specific example of a production function used in the text is:

$$Y = F(K) = \sqrt{K} .$$

Graphing this function provides the graphical production function shown in Figure 8.1 (26.1). It is important that you are familiar with this production function, since it is used throughout the chapter. This function shows that increases in capital (K) along the horizontal axis cause increases in output (Y) on the vertical axis.

The $Y = \sqrt{K}$ production function demonstrates another important characteristic of production functions, namely its concave shape. More specifically, at low levels of K the function is very steep, but as the level of K increases the function becomes flatter. This means that the first unit of K will provide a larger increase in Y than, say, the 16th unit of K (as shown in Figure 8.1 [26.1]). The increase in Y for each unit increase in K is called the **marginal product of capital**. As you can see, the marginal product diminishes as K increases (for example, the marginal product of the first unit of K is larger than the marginal product of the 16th unit of K).

This property of production functions is known as the *law of diminishing returns*. In words, the law of diminishing returns simply says that the first units of capital employed will be more productive than later units. Note that if the production function did not have this concave shape (for example, if it were a straight line), it would not exhibit diminishing returns.

Capital Accumulation and the Steady State

An important part of the Solow Model is the process of *capital accumulation*. Capital accumulation refers to the process by which the capital stock in an economy grows or declines. To understand capital accumulation, you must understand the forces that cause the capital stock to increase or decrease. Two such forces are discussed in the text:

1. investment increases the existing capital stock;
2. depreciation decreases the existing capital stock.

Remember from Chapter 6 that *investment* refers to purchases of new capital by firms. Such purchases of new capital will add new capital to the existing capital stock. *Depreciation*, on the other hand, is the wearing out of the existing capital stock as it is used for production. This wearing out of capital causes the capital stock to decline.

It is important to note that investment and depreciation have opposite effects on the capital stock. With one adding to the capital stock and the other subtracting from it, the net effect depends on the difference between the two forces. That is:

> > if investment > depreciation, then the capital stock will *grow*
> > if investment < depreciation, then the capital stock will *decline*
> > if investment = depreciation, then the capital stock will *remain constant*

The process of capital accumulation can be seen graphically by graphing investment and depreciation. Investment is shown in Figure 8.2 (26.2) in the text. In this graph, it is assumed that a constant share (30 percent) of GDP in the economy is used for investment. This provides an investment curve that lies below, but has the same shape as, the production function. Depreciation is shown in Figure 8.3 (26.3), where it is assumed that constant fraction (2 percent) of the existing capital stock wears out. The depreciation function is a straight line, since depreciation will increase uniformly with each unit increase in capital along the horizontal axis.

Putting these two curves together in the same graph, it is easy to see the point where the two curves intersect. This is shown in Figure 8.4 (26.4). Since the intersection of the two curves is where investment equals depreciation, this is the point where the capital stock remains constant over time. This important reference point is defined as the economy's **steady state**. The level of capital associated with the steady state is called the *steady-state capital stock*. At points to the left of the steady-state capital stock, investment > depreciation and the capital stock grows toward the steady state. At points to the right of the steady-state capital stock, investment < depreciation and the capital stock declines toward the steady state. Once the economy reaches its steady state, the capital stock remains constant.

Catching-Up Growth

With an understanding of the steady state in hand, we can demonstrate the first type of growth that can occur in the Solow model. Looking at the production function graph, you can see that increases in K along the horizontal axis cause Y to increase on the vertical axis. In other words, increases in K cause growth. So, if we imagine a country that starts at a level of K that is below its steady state, the capital accumulation that moves the economy toward its steady state will cause growth. This type of growth—growth caused by capital accumulation—is called *catching-up growth*. Figure 8.8 (26.8) in the text, which shows the production function along with the investment and depreciation curves, is a good graph to use to see how catching-up growth occurs.

An important characteristic of catching-up growth is that it cannot last forever. Once the economy reaches its steady state, capital accumulation and growth will stop. For this reason, catching-up growth cannot explain growth in an economy in the long run. Notice that the reason capital accumulation and catching-up growth eventually die out relates to the concave shape of the production function and investment curve. Remember that this concave shape results from the law of diminishing returns to capital. In other words, as capital accumulation occurs and more and more capital is used in the economy, the marginal product of capital declines. This means that increases in K due to investment will slow down and eventually equal depreciation, at which point capital accumulation stops and there is no more catching-up growth.

Cutting-Edge Growth

So far, the type of growth generated in our model cannot explain long-run growth in an economy. So where does long-run growth come from? To see, let's return to our production function. Remember when we first introduced the production function, we assumed A was constant. This (along with the assumption that eL was also constant) allowed us to simplify the production function as $Y = \sqrt{K}$. Now let's allow A to change, so that the production function becomes:

$$Y = A\sqrt{K}.$$

Remember that A represents the technology or "ideas" used in the production process, so an increase in A represents an improvement in technology or "new ideas." A is multiplied by the whole production function because better ideas increase the productivity of all inputs.

Figure 8.6 (26.6) in the text shows how an increase in A shifts the entire production function upward. This means that with better ideas more Y can be produced with the same level of K. If we imagine a continuous flow of new ideas, so that A is continuously increasing, the production function gradually shifts upward. This gives rise to continuous growth in Y even if the level of K remains constant. This type of growth—growth caused by new ideas—is called *cutting-edge growth*.

It is important to recognize that cutting-edge growth is fundamentally different from catching-up growth in several ways. First, catching-up growth requires capital accumulation, whereas cutting-edge growth can occur even if K stays constant. Second, since the development of new ideas is potentially unlimited, cutting-edge growth can go on forever. Therefore, cutting-edge growth can explain long-run growth in an economy. Recall that catching-up growth eventually dies out because of diminishing returns to capital.

Putting It All Together

We can combine what we have learned about growth from the Solow model into a single diagram. This is shown in Figure 8.12 (26.12) in the text. This graph looks complicated, but it's really not that bad. Starting at an initial steady state at point a, better ideas shift both the production function and the investment curve upward. We immediately see cutting-edge growth as output increases from point a' on the old production function to point b' on the new production function. But the shift of the investment curve also causes the steady state to move from point a to the intersection between the new investment curve and the depreciation line at point c. This causes capital accumulation to occur as the economy moves toward its new steady state. This capital accumulation causes catching-up growth to occur as output increases from point b' to point c'.

In conclusion, cutting-edge growth sets into motion a process whereby both cutting-edge growth and catching-up growth occur simultaneously. Although Figure 8.12 (26.12) is included in the optional "Details and Further Lessons" section of the chapter, it is an important graph since it brings the two types of growth together in a single diagram.

Details and Further Lessons (Optional Section)

An "optional" section in this chapter introduces two applications of the Solow model. The first demonstrates the effect of an *increase in the investment rate*. This is shown in Figure 8.9 (26.9). An increase in the investment rate shifts the investment curve upward and causes a new steady state (at the intersection of the new investment curve and the depreciation line). As the economy moves from its old steady state to the new steady state, catching-up growth occurs. Therefore, the Solow model predicts that countries with higher rates of investment will experience higher growth rates. Figure 8.10 (26.10) shows real-world evidence that supports this prediction.

The second "optional" application involves a concept known as *conditional convergence*. Conditional convergence can be illustrated in a graph like Figure 8.4 (26.4) in the text. Imagine that two similar countries have the same steady state at 225 units of K in this graph. Imagine further that both countries start out below their steady states: one at $K = 100$ (the poor country) and the other at $K = 200$ (the rich country). Since the poor country starts at a lower capital stock, its marginal product of capital is higher than the rich country's (remember diminishing returns says the marginal product is higher at lower levels of K). With its higher marginal product of capital, the poor country will initially grow faster than the rich country. This tendency—among countries with similar steady states—for poor countries to grow faster than rich countries as they converge to similar income levels is known as **conditional convergence**. Real-world evidence on conditional convergence among OECD countries is shown in Figure 8.11 (26.11).

The Economics of Ideas

Given the important role of new ideas in explaining long-run growth in the Solow model, this chapter closes with a discussion of the special properties of ideas. To summarize, the following properties of ideas are discussed:

1. Ideas are *similar* to other productive resources in that they must be created by profit-seeking firms and individuals, which means there must be sufficient incentives for the creation of new ideas. (See Chapter 7 for more discussion of incentives and their role in fostering R&D to create new ideas or technology.)

2. Ideas are *different* from most other productive resources in that they can be used by many people at once without decreasing the benefits to anyone. Because of this property, ideas are said to be **non-rivalrous**. Because ideas are non-rivalrous, there are potential benefits or *spillovers* from their widespread use—and the more widespread are their use, the greater are the spillovers. Because the potential social benefits of such spillovers are so large, too few ideas are created.

3. There is a conflict between the desire to have widespread use of ideas and the need to protect the incentives for the creation of new ideas. Because of this conflict, governments have a role in improving the production of ideas. *Patents*—which grant exclusive rights to all proceeds from the invention of an idea to the creator of the idea for a period of time—are one way governments can protect incentives. But patents essentially grant monopoly power to the creator of an idea and, thus, limit their availability. Governments can also encourage the creation of ideas by subsidizing firms or universities who engage in R&D to create new ideas.

Key Terms

marginal product of capital the increase in output caused by the addition of one more unit of capital. The marginal product of capital diminishes as more and more capital is added.

steady state when the capital stock is neither increasing nor decreasing

conditional convergence the tendency—among countries with similar steady state levels of output—for poorer countries to grow faster than richer countries, and, thus, for poor and rich countries to converge to similar income levels

non-rivalrous term used to describe a good that can be consumed by two or more people at the same time (such as ideas)

Traps, Hints, and Reminders

The graphs used in this chapter can be difficult for some students. Make sure you draw the graphs over and over until you become familiar with them. It may be helpful to use different colors. And draw them big! Graphing questions may appear on exams and quizzes, especially questions that involve shifts in curves. Always draw the graphs for these questions; never try to imagine them in your head.

Pay special attention to the law of diminishing returns and the terms related to it, such as the marginal product of capital. The law of diminishing returns says that the marginal product of capital declines as more and more capital is used. This concept is used throughout this chapter. Remember that the law of diminishing returns is what causes the concave shape of the production function. And since the investment curve has the same shape as the production function, the law of diminishing returns is responsible for its shape as well.

The steady state in the Solow model is similar to "equilibrium" in a market. It is a state of balance, so starting from any point away from the steady state will imply movement toward the steady state. Once the steady state is reached, the economy will remain there until something happens (a curve shifts or K changes) to create a new steady state or move the economy away from the existing steady state.

Remember that catching-up growth and cutting-edge growth come from different sources. The source of catching-up growth is capital accumulation, while the source of cutting-edge growth is new ideas.

The text discusses two examples of catching-up growth: (1) the rapid growth in modern-day China and (2) the rapid growth in the war-torn countries of Germany and Japan following World War II. It may be useful for you to familiarize yourself with these examples.

Two types of events can initiate catching-up growth (if you imagine an economy that is initially at its steady state). First, a shift in either the investment curve or the depreciation line in the steady state diagram (Figure 8.4 [26.4]) will cause the steady state to move. As the economy moves from the old to the new steady state, catching-up growth occurs. Second, if the economy is knocked away from its initial steady state to a lower level of K, the economy will gradually move back to its steady state (note that the steady state itself has not moved in this case). This movement back to the steady state is catching-up growth.

It is important to know what will shift the various curves in the graphs used in this chapter. The production function will shift when A changes (as shown in Figure 8.6 [26.6]). The investment curve will shift when either (1) the investment rate (denoted γ in the text) changes or (2) the production function shifts (see Figure 8.2 [26.2]). The depreciation line will shift when the depreciation rate (denoted δ in the text) changes (see Figure 8.3 [26.3]).

Even though the graphs for the Solow model shown in this chapter graph K on the horizontal axis, it is correct to think of this axis as measuring capital *per worker* (K/L). This was never an important issue in the chapter because the labor force was assumed to be constant. But by thinking in terms of capital *per worker* on the horizontal axis we can analyze changes in the labor force. For example, a sudden decrease in the labor force (L) will increase capital *per worker* and move the economy above its initial steady state. The capital stock will then decline as depreciation outpaces investment and the economy moves back toward its original steady-state capital stock (per worker). This decline in the capital stock will result in negative catching-up growth. Pay attention to this issue in Multiple-Choice Question #10.

Self-Practice Questions

1. Draw the graph for the Solow growth model showing the investment curve and the depreciation line. Identify the steady state in the graph. Label the steady-state capital stock. After identifying the steady state, add the production function and identify the steady-state level of output.

2. Draw the graph for the Solow model to show the effects of increasing the savings rate.

3. Draw the graph for the Solow model to show the effect of increasing technology.

4. Compare the output effects of increasing savings and technology from the previous two questions. Is there an advantage of increasing technology instead of increasing savings?

5. Draw a graph for the Solow model to show how a war that destroys half the capital stock in a nation will affect growth in that nation.

6. What are the positive and negative effects of patents on the creation of new ideas?

7. Imagine an economy where investment equals $.3\sqrt{K}$ and depreciation equals $.03K$. What is the steady state capital stock? If the production function is $Y = \sqrt{K}$, what is the level of output in the steady state?

8. Imagine an economy where investment equals $.4\sqrt{K}$ and depreciation equals $.02K$. What is the steady state capital stock? If the production function is $Y = 5\sqrt{K}$, what is the level of output in the steady state?

Multiple-Choice Questions

1. In the Solow growth model, if a country has capital such that the depreciation line is above the production function, then:

   a. the country should use more capital.

   b. the country has too much capital.

   c. the country has the optimal amount of capital.

   d. the answer cannot be determined from this information.

2. The additional output produced with an additional unit of capital is called:

   a. the marginal product of capital.

   b. the capital stock.

   c. the level of output.

   d. the steady state.

3. Diminishing returns to capital suggests:

   a. at some point there will be too much capital.

   b. using more and more capital brings smaller and smaller gains in output.

   c. countries can never have too much capital.

   d. the capital stock in an economy will approach infinity.

4. In the basic Solow growth model, everything is held constant in the production function EXCEPT:

   a. land.

   b. labor.

   c. capital.

   d. entrepreneurship.

5. If there are *constant* returns to capital in a country, then its production function would be:

   a. a straight line.

   b. concave.

   c. convex.

   d. downward sloping.

   Use the following graphs to answer question 6

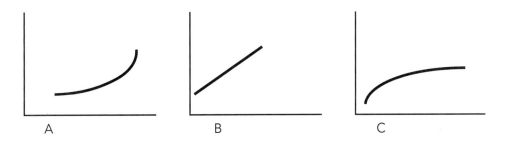

A   B   C

6. Which of the graphs shows the *y*-axis variable increasing at an increasing rate?

  a. A

  b. B

  c. C

  d. None of the answers is correct.

Use the following graphs to answer question 6.

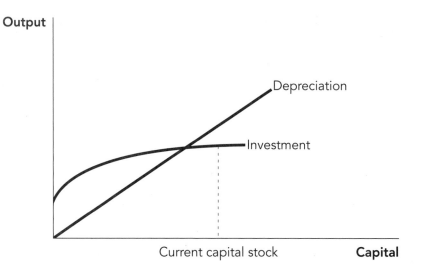

7. At the current capital stock shown in the graph the capital stock in this country would be:

  a. increasing.

  b. decreasing.

  c. remaining constant.

  d. None of the answers is correct.

8. If a country increases its savings rate, the:

  a. depreciation curve shifts upward.

  b. investment curve shifts upward.

  c. production function shifts upward.

  d. All of the answers are correct.

9. When a country increases its savings rate:

  a. catching-up growth occurs as the economy moves toward a new, higher steady-state capital stock.

  b. cutting-edge growth occurs following an upward shift in the production function.

  c. the capital stock will fall as the economy moves toward a new, lower steady-state capital stock.

  d. no growth will occur.

10. If a plague kills half the labor force in a country leaving it with much more capital *per worker* than before, then you would expect:

    a. the capital stock would begin to depreciate faster than it is replenished.

    b. capital would increase faster.

    c. the country would have negative growth.

    d. Both a and c are correct.

11. If a country invents or copies new technology:

    a. the investment curve shifts upward.

    b. the production function shifts upward.

    c. the steady-state capital stock increases.

    d. All of the answers are correct.

12. Cutting-edge growth:

    a. results from capital accumulation.

    b. results from new ideas or technology.

    c. cannot explain long-run economic growth in a country.

    d. All of the answers are correct.

13. The Solow model's prediction that poor countries should grow faster than rich countries:

    a. is a result of diminishing returns to capital.

    b. is known as "conditional convergence."

    c. occurs because the marginal product of capital is higher in poor countries who are starting out with less capital than rich countries.

    d. All of the answers are correct.

14. New ideas or technology in an economy cause:

    a. cutting-edge growth to occur.

    b. an increase in the steady-state capital stock and output level.

    c. catching-up growth to occur.

    d. All of the answers are correct.

15. If savings in a country decreases, what will happen?

    a. Steady-state output will decrease.

    b. Steady-state capital stock will decline.

    c. Negative growth will occur for a period of time until a new steady state is reached.

    d. All of the answers are correct.

16. Which of the following is TRUE about the creation of ideas?

a. Most new ideas are created by government.

b. Ideas created by government are the most beneficial ideas because they are nonrival.

c. Government can help promote the creation of ideas by issuing patents.

d. Ideas created by government are usually not useful because of spillovers.

17. The Solow model says that:

a. the further a country's capital stock is below its steady-state value, the faster it will grow.

b. the further a country's capital stock is above its steady-state value, the faster it will grow.

c. the further a country's capital stock is below its steady-state value, the slower it will grow.

d. None of the answers is correct.

18. When firms decide to engage in R&D, which of the following is important?

a. patents

b. potential spillovers to other rivals

c. government subsidies for scientists

d. market size

e. All of the answers are correct.

19. Which of the following goods are non-rivalrous?

a. an apple

b. a national park

c. the idea of penicillin

d. a dose of penicillin

20. In the Solow model, a decrease in the depreciation rate would:

a. cause catching-up growth to occur.

b. cause cutting-edge growth to occur.

c. cause both catching-up and cutting-edge growth to occur.

d. cause no growth to occur.

Homework Quiz

1. The law of diminishing returns to capital implies that the production function will be:

   a. concave.

   b. convex.

   c. a straight line.

   d. a rectangular hyperbola.

2. In the Solow model, a steady state occurs where:

   a. investment is at its highest level.

   b. depreciation is at its lowest level.

   c. investment equals depreciation.

   d. the economy's growth rate is at its highest level.

3. An economy in a steady state with no new idea (technology) creation will:

   a. grow due to capital accumulation.

   b. experience negative growth as the capital stock declines.

   c. enjoy continuous growth in its steady-state output level.

   d. not grow at all.

4. In the Solow model, long-run growth in an economy is best explained by:

   a. cutting-edge growth.

   b. catching-up growth.

   c. capital accumulation.

   d. nothing; no economy can grow forever.

5. According to the Solow model, a decrease in a country's saving rate will:

   a. shift its investment curve downward.

   b. shift its production function downward.

   c. increase growth since less saving means more spending.

   d. Both a and b are correct.

6. If an earthquake destroys half the capital stock in a country, the Solow model predicts:

   a. an increase in the country's growth rate in the years following the earthquake.

   b. a decrease in the country's growth rate in the years following the earthquake.

   c. a decrease in the country's steady-state capital stock.

   d. an increase in the country's steady-state output level.

7. Conditional convergence:
   a. implies that poor countries will grow faster than rich countries if they both have similar steady states.
   b. results from poor countries having a lower marginal product of capital than rich countries.
   c. results from poor countries' inability to create new ideas (technology).
   d. predicts that poor countries will experience negative growth rates and rich countries will experience positive growth rates.

8. Cutting-edge growth:
   a. results from new ideas (technology).
   b. can occur even without capital accumulation.
   c. causes catching-up growth to occur.
   d. All of the answers are correct.

9. In the discussion of new ideas, spillovers refer to:
   a. the widespread benefits to society from the use of new ideas.
   b. the negative aspects of new ideas, such as jobs lost from the widespread use of computers.
   c. the extra benefits patents bring to those who create new ideas.
   d. the cost of government supporting R&D to create new ideas.

10. In the Solow model, new ideas cause:
    a. the production function to shift upward.
    b. the investment curve to shift upward.
    c. a higher steady-state capital stock.
    d. All of the answers are correct.

Answer Key

Answers to Self-Practice Questions

This graph is the most important graph for understanding the Solow model. It is important that you are able to draw it correctly. The steps for drawing the graph are shown.

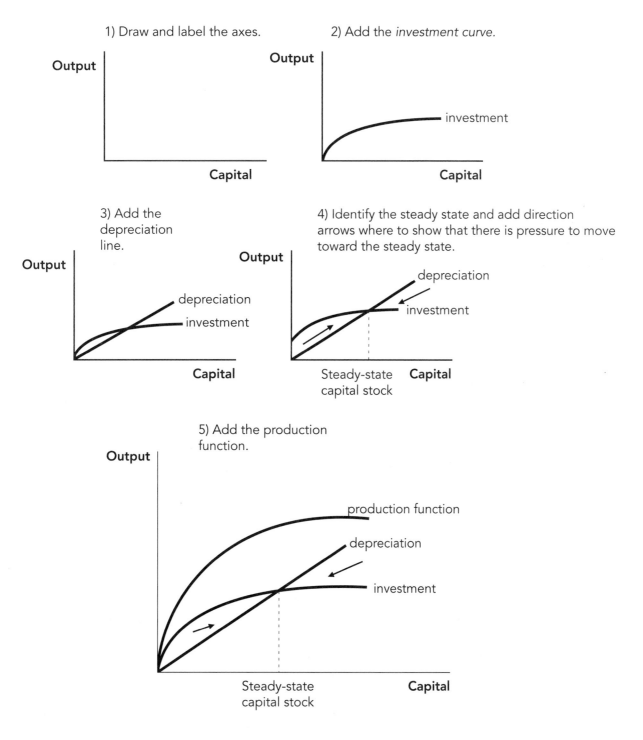

1) Draw and label the axes.

2) Add the *investment curve.*

3) Add the depreciation line.

4) Identify the steady state and add direction arrows where to show that there is pressure to move toward the steady state.

5) Add the production function.

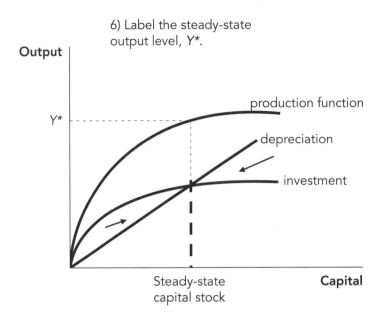

Topic: The Solow Model and Catch-Up Growth

2. Begin with a graph like the one you ended up with in Question #1. The increase in the saving rate will increase the rate of investment in the economy. This will cause the investment curve to shift upward. The shift in the investment curve will create a new steady state with a higher steady-state capital stock. Over time, growth in output will occur as the economy moves from the old to the new steady state. This is shown in the graph below. Since this growth is due to capital accumulation (as the economy moves from the old to the new steady state), this is "catching-up" growth.

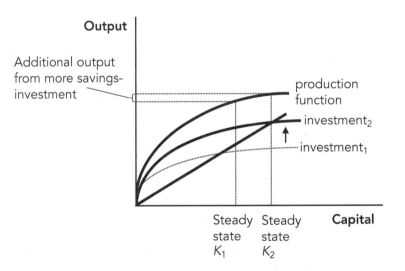

Topic: The Solow Model and an Increase in the Investment Rate

3. Once again, start with a graph like the one you ended up with in Question #1. New technology increases the amount of output a country can produce. This is shown in the graph by an upward shift of the production function. This causes immediate growth in output—called "catching-up" growth since it results from new technology. But a shift in the production function also shifts the investment curve. Make sure you shift both curves as shown in the graph below.

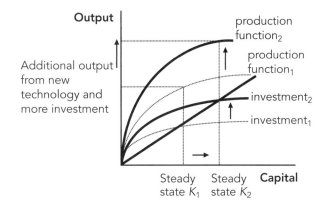

The shift in the investment curve causes a new steady state at a higher steady-state capital stock. As the economy moves from the old to the new steady state, capital accumulation and "catching-up" growth occurs. So the new technology ultimately causes both "cutting-edge" and "catching-up" growth to occur.

Topic: Better Ideas Drive Long-Run Economic Growth

4. There is an advantage to new technology since it results in a higher level of output than the increase in savings. Thus, new technology will result in more growth. We know new technology will result in a higher output level because it results in a higher production function, whereas higher savings does not shift the production function at all.

Topic: Solow Mode and the Economics of Ideas in One Diagram

5. Begin with the same graph as in previous questions. It is important to recognize in this problem that no curves will shift. Since the war destroys capital, it will simply move the economy to a lower capital stock. To illustrate, assume that the economy is initially at the steady state shown in the graph below. The war will knock the economy away from this steady state to a lower capital stock (and level of output), as shown. Then, over time, the economy will gradually move back toward its steady state—as capital accumulation occurs to replace the destroyed capital. As the economy moves back to its steady state, growth will occur. Since this growth results from capital accumulation, it is "catching-up" growth.

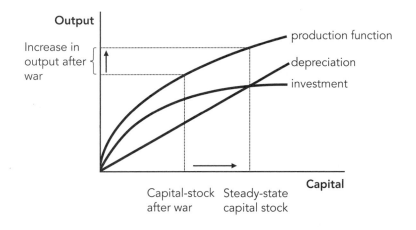

Topic: The Solow Model and Catch-Up Growth

6. Patents grant exclusive rights to all proceeds from the invention of an idea to the creator of the idea for a period of time. There are positive and negative effects of patents in terms of their effect on the creation of ideas. On the positive side, since patents guarantee that any proceeds from an idea will go to the inventor, it increases the incentive to create new ideas. This higher incentive causes more creative activity and more new ideas. On the negative side, since the patent essentially gives the inventor a monopoly on the use of the idea, it limits the widespread use of (or at least raises the price of using) the idea by the rest of society. This limited use (or higher price) of ideas limits the benefits—or spillovers—to society that result from the use of an idea. Limiting spillovers means that too few new ideas will be created.

Topic: Growth on the Cutting Edge: The Economics of Ideas

7. This is a mathematical problem that requires first solving for the steady-state capital stock and then using that solution to solve for the steady-state output level. In solving these types of problems, remember the following helpful math hints:

It is helpful to write all of the K terms in exponent form.
In doing so, remember that $\sqrt{K} = K^{1/2}$ and $K = K^1$. Also, remember that

$$\frac{1}{\sqrt{K}} = K^{-1/2}.$$

When working with exponents, multiplying two terms with the same base requires adding their exponents, for example, $K^1 \times K^2 = K^{(1+2)} = K^3$.

To solve for the steady-state capital stock, remember that the steady state occurs where *investment equals depreciation*. So, to solve for K, we have:

$$\text{Investment} = \text{Depreciation}$$
$$0.3\sqrt{K} = 0.03K$$
$$0.3K^{1/2} = 0.03K^1$$

To get all the K terms together on one side, divide both sides by $K^{1/2}$:

$$0.3 = 0.03K^1K^{-1/2}$$
$$0.3 = 0.03K^{1/2}$$
$$0.3 / 0.03 = K^{1/2}$$
$$10 = K^{1/2}$$

To solve for K, square both sides to get $K = 100$. So, the steady-state capital stock for this economy is $K = 100$.

Now, use $K = 100$ in the production function to solve for the steady-state output level:

$$Y = \sqrt{K}$$
$$Y = \sqrt{100}$$
$$Y = 10$$

So, the steady-state output level is $Y = 10$.

Topic: Why Capital Alone Cannot Be the Key to Economic Growth

8. Solving for K just as in the previous question:

$$\text{Investment} = \text{Depreciation}$$
$$0.4\sqrt{K} = 0.02K$$
$$0.4K^{1/2} = 0.02K^{1}$$

To get all the K terms together on one side, divide both sides by $K^{1/2}$:

$$0.4K^{1/2} = 0.02K^{1}K^{1/2}$$
$$0.4K = 0.02K^{1/2}$$
$$0.4 \,/\, 0.02K = K^{1/2}$$
$$20 = K^{1/2}$$

To solve for K, square both sides to get $K = 400$. So, the steady-state capital stock for this economy is $K = 400$.

Now, use $K = 400$ in the production function to solve for the steady-state output level:

$$Y = 5\sqrt{K}$$
$$Y = 5\sqrt{400}$$
$$Y = 5 \times 20 = 100$$

So, the steady-state output level is $Y = 100$.

Topic: Why Capital Alone Cannot Be the Key to Economic Growth

Answers to Multiple-Choice Questions

1. b, Topic: The Solow Model and Catch-Up Growth

2. a, Topic: The Solow Model and Catch-Up Growth

3. b, Topic: The Solow Model and Catch-Up Growth

4. c, Topic: The Solow Model and Catch-Up Growth

5. a, Topic: The Solow Model and Catch-Up Growth

6. a, Topic: The Solow Model and Catch-Up Growth

7. b, Topic: The Solow Model and Catch-Up Growth

8. b, Topic: The Solow Model and an Increase in the Investment Rate

9. a, Topic: The Solow Model and an Increase in the Investment Rate

10. d, Topic: The Solow Model—Details and Further Lessons

11. d, Topic: Solow and the Economics of Ideas in One Diagram

12. b, Topic: Better Ideas Drive Long-Run Economic Growth

13. d, Topic: The Solow Model and Conditional Convergence

14. d, Topic: Solow and the Economics of Ideas in One Diagram

15. d, Topic: The Solow Model and an Increase in the Investment Rate

16. c, Topic: Growing on the Cutting Edge: The Economics of Ideas

17. a, Topic: The Solow Model and Conditional Convergence

18. e, Topic: Growing on the Cutting Edge: The Economics of Ideas

19. c, Topic: Spillovers, and Why There Aren't Enough Good Ideas

20. a, Topic: The Solow Model and Catch-Up Growth

9 (27)

Saving, Investment, and the Financial System

Learning Objectives

In this chapter, you will learn:

> The roles of savers and investors in the economy

> How the financial system in an economy provides a "bridge" between savers and investors

> How to use supply and demand to analyze financial markets

> What causes failure of the financial system—and the consequences of such failures

> What circumstances led to the 2007–2008 financial system collapse

Summary

In general terms, this chapter is about savers and investors and the institutions—collectively called the financial system—that bridge the gap between the two. Before jumping into the details of this chapter, it is important to understand exactly what is meant by saving and investment and who are the savers and investors in the economy. **Saving** refers to income that is not spent on consumption. Saving is generated in the economy by households, firms, and others who do not spend all of their current income. **Investment** refers to the purchase of new capital goods, as we first learned in Chapter 6. Investment is generated by firms (businesses), entrepreneurs who want to start new businesses, and households who want new homes. Investment is important for growth in the economy (see Chapters 7 and 8 for more on this) and saving is important as a source of funds for that investment.

How Are Saving and Investment Related?

The relationship between saving and investment in an economy can be shown with a few simple steps. Beginning with the national spending identity from Chapter 6, we can write $Y = C + I + G + NX$. Recall that Y is GDP, C is consumption, I is investment, G is government purchases, and NX is net exports. For simplicity, if we assume a *closed* economy (one that does not engage in international trade) then $NX = 0$ and we can write $Y = C + I + G$. Some rearranging of terms provides $Y - C - G = I$. The expression on the left-hand side, $Y - C - G$, is what economists call *national saving*. If we use S to denote national saving, then we have $S = I$. This result says national saving and investment in a closed economy *must* be equal. (The relationship between saving and investment in an *open* economy will be explored in Chapter 20.)

Bridging the Gap between Savers and Investors

In thinking about the $S = I$ result, it is useful to think of S as being the *source* of funds and I as being the *use* of those funds. But since saving and investment are generated by different groups within the economy, there must be a way to get the funds from those who save to those who invest. The institutions of an economy that move funds from savers to investors are collectively referred to as the *financial system*. In the financial system, savers *lend* the funds they save and investors *borrow* those funds for investment. However, savers and investors rarely deal directly with one another. The role of the financial system in "bridging the gap" between savers and investors is demonstrated in Figure 9.1 (27.1) in the text. (In this figure, note that investors are referred to as "borrowers.")

Among the individual institutions that make up the financial system are banks, bond markets, and stock exchanges. These institutions are sometimes referred to as **financial intermediaries** because of the "middleman" role they play in moving funds from those who save to those who invest. Let's briefly describe the role of banks, bond markets, and stock exchanges in the financial system.

Banks serve the middleman role by taking deposits from savers/lenders and making loans to investors/borrowers. Note that the term "bank" is used broadly here, as there are many different names for institutions that operate on the basis of taking deposits and making loans. Some examples are savings and loans (S&Ls), savings banks, credit unions, investment banks, and venture capital firms. Regardless of name, all of these firms reduce risk for lenders by pooling funds together and evaluating the creditworthiness of potential borrowers. Banks also provide other financial services such as check-clearing and maintaining networks for funds transfers and cash withdrawals.

Bond markets are well-organized markets in which bonds are traded between buyers and sellers. A *bond* can most simply be thought of as a loan, where the borrower (investor) issues the bond and the lender (saver) buys the bond. Businesses that are large enough and reputable enough to borrow directly from individual lenders often borrow in this way. Governments also issue bonds for their borrowing needs. A bond promises to repay a fixed amount (called the *face value*) on a specified date (called the *maturity date*), sometimes with additional periodic payments that occur before the maturity date (called *coupon payments*). The amount of money initially paid (loaned) to obtain the bond is the *price* of the bond. Since paying a lower price initially implies a higher return when the face value is repaid at maturity, it is often said that bond prices and interest rates move in opposite directions. Note that the formula for calculating the rate of return (interest rate) on a zero-coupon bond is provided in the text as [(FV − Price)/Price] × 100, where FV is the face value of the bond.

The *stock market* is a market in which shares of stock are bought and sold. Corporations issue *stock* to raise funds for investment. However, instead of raising these funds by borrowing (as is the case with bonds), the companies issue shares of ownership in the company itself in exchange for these funds. Shareholders have a claim on the profits of the corporation, which may be paid out in the form of payments called *dividends*. Additionally, if the corporation is successful and its stock value increases, stockholders gain from the appreciation in the value of their stock.

While the details may differ, banks, bond markets, and stock exchanges all have in common their role as financial intermediaries—as institutions that facilitate the movement of funds from savers to investors.

The Market for Loanable Funds

We now know that savers provide the *source* of funds and investors provide the *use* of those funds. In other words, we could describe savers as *supplying* funds and investors as *demanding* funds. In this context, it is easy to model the exchange of funds between savers and investors using a supply and demand graph. This supply and demand model of the financial system is referred to as the **market for loanable funds**. This market is useful for demonstrating the determination of interest rates along with the quantity of funds traded between savers and investors.

In graphing the market for loanable funds, remember that the horizontal axis measures the quantity of funds traded and the vertical axis measures the price of those funds (called the interest rate). The supply and demand curves for this market are shown in Figures 9.3 (27.3) and 9.5 (27.5) in the text. It is important to remember that the *demand for borrowing* comes from investors who want to borrow funds for investment. The demand curve slopes downward, as usual, because a lower quantity of funds is demanded at higher interest rates. The *supply of saving* comes from savers who loan their savings. The supply curve slopes upward, as usual, because a higher interest rate attracts more savings. In other words, the demand and supply curves simply represent the two sides of the $S = I$ equation. Equilibrium in the market for loanable funds is a natural way to achieve the required balance between saving and investment in the financial system.

In using supply and demand analysis, it is always important to understand what factors can cause a shift in the supply and demand curves.

Factors that shift the *supply of saving* discussed in the text are:

> the desire to smooth consumption (which implies saving/borrowing at various stages in life)

> impatience (the desire to consume sooner rather than later)

> marketing or psychological factors (societal norms for saving)

> tax incentives for saving (such as tax-exempt savings accounts)

> economic conditions (such as recession) that cause uncertainty about the future

Factors that shift the *demand for borrowing* discussed in the text are:

> the desire to smooth consumption (implies saving/borrowing at various stages in life)

> the need to finance large investments (start-up capital for new ventures)

> tax incentives for investment (such as an investment tax credit)

> business cycle (recession/expansion) influences on the profit outlook for a firm

> changes in the government's demand for borrowing to finance deficits

So, for example, an increase in the government's demand for borrowing to finance large budget deficits will cause an increase (rightward shift) in the demand for borrowing (this example is shown in Figure 9.10 [27.10] in the text). Note that the interest rate is not listed as a factor that will shift supply or demand. This is because changes in the interest rate cause a *movement along* the supply or demand curve, not a shift in the curve.

Equilibrium in the market for loanable funds occurs where the supply and demand curves intersect. The equilibrium provides the equilibrium quantity of saving/borrowing and the equilibrium interest rate, as shown in Figure 9.6 (27.6) in the text. Several useful examples of shifts in supply and demand in the loanable funds market are shown in the text. Figure 9.7 (27.7) shows an increase in the supply of saving; Figure 9.8 (27.8) shows a decrease in the demand for borrowing; and Figure 9.9 (27.9) shows an increase in the demand for borrowing. You should familiarize yourself with these examples and work other examples for yourself. When it comes to successfully using supply and demand graphs, practice makes perfect!

Failure of the Financial System

Failure of the financial system occurs when circumstances prevent the efficient flow of funds from savers to investors. Visually, this amounts to "breaking the bridge" between savers and investors, as shown in Figure 9.11 (27.11) in the text. The text discusses four specific examples of problems that might lead to such failure of the financial system:

1. insecure property rights
2. interest rate controls
3. politicized lending and government-owned banks
4. bank failures and panics

Insecure property rights can mean that a person's savings are not immune from confiscation, freezes, or other restrictions imposed by government. For example, the text discusses the freezing of bank accounts for one year in Argentina during the 2001 recession. Naturally, such insecure property rights with respect to bank accounts does not encourage saving behavior. As a result, the supply of savings dries up and the economy is deprived of funds necessary for investment. Other examples of insecure property rights are also discussed in the text.

Interest rate controls refer to legal limits on how high an interest rate can be charged on a loan. Such interest rate controls (sometimes called ursury laws) are an example of what economists call *price ceilings*. As you may recall from your study of microeconomics, price ceilings cause shortages to occur in markets by holding prices artificially low. Figure 9.12 (27.12) demonstrates this effect in the market for loanable funds. The interest rate control causes the supply of savings to be too low and the demand for borrowing to be too high, thus causing a shortage in the market. This shortage results in too little investment in the economy.

Politicized lending refers to lending to politically favored parties rather than to the most efficient potential borrowers. This, of course, deprives funds for investment by efficient businesses and causes lower returns on investment. *Government-owned banks* naturally pay favors to political allies and so are obvious sources of politicized lending.

Bank failure refers to a situation in which a bank becomes insolvent and goes out of business. A *banking panic* occurs when fear of bank failure spreads throughout the banking system. Bank failures—or fears of a failure—cause depositors to lose or withdraw their savings from banks. This leads to a decrease in the supply of savings and a reduction in the intermediation services provided by banks. Bank failures were a key source of the economic collapse during the Great Depression when about half the banks in the United States failed.

The 2007–08 Financial Crisis

The last section of this chapter discusses the causes of the financial crisis of 2007-08. Specifically, three aspects of the crisis are discussed:

1. leverage
2. securitization
3. shadow banking

A **leverage ratio** is the ratio of debt to equity (D/E) for an asset. **Owner's equity** is the value of an asset minus the debt on the asset ($E = V - D$). Owner's equity provides a cushion against which the value of an asset may fall without becoming less than the loan used to secure the asset. As the amount of debt associated with an asset or a firm rises, its leverage ratio rises and we might say the owner of the asset or the firm is highly leveraged. Highly leveraged individuals and firms are a key part of the story of the financial crisis of 2007–08.

First, many homeowners became highly leveraged in their homes following the relaxation of government requirements for minimum down payments on home loans (also called mortgages). A lower down payment reduces the owner's equity in the home. Then, when home values started to fall around 2006, highly leveraged individuals simply abandoned or faced foreclosure on their mortgages when the value of the home fell below the loan amount. Banks that had made these loans were left with bad loans on their books. This circumstance caused a number of banks to fail and took many others to the brink of **insolvency**. Insolvency occurs when a firm's liabilities or debts become larger than the value of its assets. These bank failures and the risk of more failures going forward started the breakdown of the financial system in 2007 and into 2008.

Separately, many of these mortgages had been bundled together and sold around the world. This bundling and selling—or *securitization*—of mortgage-backed assets exposed individuals and firms around the world to losses as loan failures began to rise. Many of these assets were purchased by other types of banking institutions in the economy. Investment banks like Lehman Brothers bought many of these securities and even worse, they bought them with borrowed funds. So not only were homeowners highly leveraged, but so were the investment banks who bought the mortgage-backed securities. So, as home loan failures began to rise, the investment banks that held the mortgage-backed securities were at risk of becoming insolvent.

Investment banks like Lehman Brothers are part of what is called the "shadow banking system." This name derives from the fact that these types of institutions operated in the shadows of the commercial banking industry. By the mid-2000s, a large amount of the financial intermediation in the financial system was being performed by these institutions. Thus, insolvency and failure in the shadow banking system resulted in a significant decline of financial intermediation services in the economy.

In summary, the domino effect of defaults by homeowners, failures in the commercial banking system, and insolvency in the shadow banking system resulted in a collapse of the financial system in the U.S. economy and to some extent around the world. This financial collapse made the recession that was already underway following the housing market decline even worse.

Key Terms

saving income that is not spent on consumption goods

investment the purchase of new capital goods

time preference the desire to have goods and services sooner rather than later (all else being equal)

financial intermediary institutions such as banks, bond markets, and stock markets that reduce the costs of moving funds from savers to borrowers and investors

market for loanable funds the market in which suppliers of loanable funds (savers) trade with demanders of loanable funds (borrowers).

bond a sophisticated IOU that documents who owes how much and when payment must be made.

collateral something of value that by agreement becomes the property of the lender if the borrower defaults

crowding out the decrease in private consumption and investment that occurs when government borrows more

arbitrage the buying and selling of equally risky assets, which ensures that equally risky assets earn equal returns

stock a certificate of ownership in a corporation

initial public offering (IPO) the first time a corporation sells stock to the public in order to raise capital

owner's equity the value of an asset minus the debt associated with the asset ($E = V - D$)

leverage ratio the ratio of debt to equity (D/E)

insolvent term used to describe a firm whose liabilities exceed its assets

Traps, Hints, and Reminders

Remember that the word "investment" is used in this chapter in its true macroeconomic context—to describe the purchase of new capital by firms. This word was first defined in Chapter 6. The discussion of venture capitalists in the FedEx story (see "The Demand for Borrowing" section in the text) highlights the ease with which the word "investment" can be used out of the context intended in this chapter. There it is stated that venture capitalists were "*investors* willing to accept risk in return for a stake in future profits" of FedEx. In reality, venture capitalists are *savers* who supplied funds to be used for investment by FedEx. Be careful!

In Chapters 7 and 8, the word "institutions" was used to refer to the laws, rules, and regulations that structure incentives in an economy. In this chapter, "institutions" refer to the organizations that collectively make up the financial system in an economy.

Throughout this chapter, remember that *savers* are *lenders* who make up the *supply* side in the loanable funds market. Likewise, *investors* are *borrowers* who make up the *demand* side of the loanable funds market.

In working with the market for loanable funds, you should familiarize yourself with the basic concepts of supply and demand graphs. You can review these concepts in Chapter 3.

When using the market for loanable funds, always draw a supply and demand graph to work out problems. Do not try to imagine the graph in your mind. The graph can only help you if you *draw* it.

When working with the loanable funds market, it is important to remember that anything that affects *savings* will shift the *supply curve,* while anything that affects *investment* will shift the *demand curve.*

The federal government's budget position is an important factor in determining the overall demand for borrowing in the loanable funds market. Remember, a budget *deficit* requires the government to *borrow,* and the larger the deficit the more borrowing that will be required by the government. Thus, increases and decreases in the government's deficit will affect the red curve in Figure 9.10 (27.10), with increases shifting if farther to the right and decreases shifting if back to the left. The amount of government borrowing shown in Figure 9.10 (27.10) determines the amount of reduced consumption and reduced investment that results from the government's presence in the market. This reduced consumption and investment is sometimes referred to as **crowding out**.

Remember that a "bond" simply represents a loan from the buyer of the bond to the issuer of the bond.

Students are often confused by the idea of a bond's *price.* Remember that the price of a bond is simply the amount of money initially given to obtain the bond. This is different from the rate of return or *interest rate* on the bond. The interest rate is the difference between the bond's price and its *face value* (the amount repaid when the bond matures), expressed in percentage terms. Since the face value of a bond is fixed, the lower the price paid for a bond the higher the implied interest rate will be (and vice versa). This is why it is often said that bond prices and interest rates move in opposite directions.

A "zero-coupon" bond, often mentioned in this chapter, is a bond that has no coupon payments. This means the only payment involved is the payment of the bond's face value to the bondholder at the bonds' maturity date.

Self-Practice Questions

1. The study of financial institutions such as banks, stock markets, and bond markets is usually included in finance courses. Why are these finance topics covered in a macroeconomics course?

2. Imagine that you want to buy a zero-coupon bond that will pay $1,000 in one year. If the current interest rate is 5 percent on comparable bonds, what price should you expect to pay for the bond?

3. Suppose you own a $10,000 zero-coupon bond that you purchased for $9,100. What is the rate of return on this bond?

4. Imagine that life expectancy in the United States increases by 20 years, but the retirement age remains the same. How would you expect this to affect the loanable funds market?

5. Imagine that the government allows banks to offer a new type of savings account in which new deposits are tax deductible each year. How will this affect the market for loanable funds?

6. Imagine that the federal government comes up with a credible plan to reduce its budget deficit by several hundred billion dollars in the years ahead. What would happen to the ability of private businesses to borrow? What would happen to the real interest rate?

7. The Federal Deposit Insurance Corporation (FDIC) was established after the banking panics of the 1930s. The FDIC insures customers' deposits in the commercial banking system. How does deposit insurance help protect the integrity of the commercial banking system? How does this benefit the economy?

8. Jimmy and Joey both average $50,000 of income per year. Jimmy has a very stable income and always makes $50,000. Joey has a very unstable income. Sometimes he makes much more than $50,000 and sometimes much less. Which one needs functioning financial markets more?

Multiple-Choice Questions

1. Which of the following is a list of financial intermediaries?

a. banks, stock markets, bond markets

b. Congress, the President, the Supreme Court

c. the Fed, the Treasury, the Bureau of Printing and Engraving

d. property rights, judicial system, the Constitution

2. On the basis of their role in the financial system, venture capitalists are:

a. borrowers.

b. savers.

c. financial intermediaries.

d. investors.

3. In macroeconomics, investment includes:

a. buying stock.

b. buying bonds.

c. buying new equipment for your business.

d. depositing money in a savings account.

4. The life-cycle theory says that:

   a. all savings will eventually end up as investment.

   b. people try to save when they are making lots of money so they can borrow and continue to consume when they are making less money.

   c. all banks will eventually be purchased by one large bank.

   d. venture capitalists buy small companies, those companies prosper, and the venture capitalists eventually sell them and buy new companies.

5. Large investments such as Fred Smith's FedEx often require the firm to:

   a. borrow.

   b. save.

   c. lend.

   d. intermediate.

6. If the interest rate increases (all else remaining the same), what is likely to happen to the quantity of borrowing demanded?

   a. It will stay the same.

   b. It will increase.

   c. It will decrease.

   d. It will shift.

7. If the interest rate decreases (all else remaining the same), what is likely to happen to the quantity of saving supplied?

   a. It will stay the same.

   b. It will increase.

   c. It will decrease.

   d. It will shift.

8. If the government suddenly stopped funding public university education, the supply of loanable funds would likely:

   a. shift to the right.

   b. shift to the left.

   c. increase in quantity along the supply curve.

   d. decrease in quantity along the supply curve.

9. If the government gets rid of an investment tax credit, then what would happen in the market for loanable funds?

   a. Demand would shift to the right.

   b. Supply would shift to the right.

   c. Demand would shift to the left.

   d. Supply would shift to the left.

10. Coupon bonds are bonds that give:

    a. buyers a discount whenever they buy a bond.

    b. sellers a discount whenever they sell a bond.

    c. the owner coupons, which can be redeemed for interest payments before the maturity of the bond.

    d. the owner coupons, which can be redeemed for discounts on future bond purchases.

11. Two bonds with the same risk and same maturity should sell at the same price because of:

    a. the permanent-income hypothesis.

    b. arbitrage.

    c. the life-cycle theory.

    d. initial public offerings.

12. Who of the following would NOT be owners of a company?

    a. bondholders

    b. stockholders

    c. people who buy in an IPO

    d. venture capitalists

13. When the government freezes bank accounts, this is an example of:

    a. price controls.

    b. insecure property rights.

    c. inflation.

    d. bank panics.

14. Which of the following does NOT break the bridge between bank borrowers and savers?

    a. politicized lending

    b. interest rate controls

    c. bank failures

    d. consumption smoothing

15. Usury laws are a type of:

    a. price ceiling.

    b. price floor.

    c. credit shortage prevention rule.

    d. IPO

16. Forcing banks to lend to politically well-connected groups and individuals is an example of:

    a. price ceilings.

    b. interest rate controls.

    c. politicized lending.

    d. a bank panic.

17. A $1,000 zero-coupon bond that sells for $900 has a rate of return of:

    a. 1 percent

    b. 9 percent

    c. 10 percent

    d. None of the answers is correct.

18. Jim just passed away at the age of 90. While he was alive he had student loans to pay for college. He paid the loans off and saved for retirement during his working years. During retirement he lived off of his savings. He died with no assets and no debt. Based on this information, Jim was very successful at:

    a. smoothing his consumption.

    b. acting as a venture capitalist.

    c. delaying gratification.

    d. understanding time preference.

19. If the economy falls into a recession, what is likely to happen in the market for loanable funds?

    a. Supply will shift to the right.

    b. Supply will shift to the left.

    c. Demand will shift to the left.

    d. Demand will shift to the right.

20. When the government increases its borrowing, there are less funds available for other borrowers. This is known as:

    a. collateral.

    b. crowding out.

    c. insolvency.

    d. leverage.

21. If the interest rate increases, then the price of bonds will:

    a. go up.

    b. go down.

    c. not change.

    d. change in an unpredictable way.

Homework Quiz

1. Investment banks are an example of a:

   a. saver.

   b. investor.

   c. financial intermediary.

   d. venture capitalist.

2. Which of the following provides financial intermediation services for the economy?

   a. the Federal Reserve

   b. the Treasury

   c. the Securities and Exchange Commission (SEC)

   d. the commercial banking industry

3. Which of the following represents loaning money to a firm?

   a. buying a bond

   b. selling a bond

   c. buying stock

   d. selling stock

4. Which of the following will *shift* the demand for borrowing?

   a. a change in interest rates

   b. a change in the incentive to save

   c. a change in the size of government budget deficits

   d. All of the answers are correct.

5. If individuals become more patient with respect to their desire to consume, then:

   a. the demand to borrow will shift to the right.

   b. the demand to borrow will shift to the left.

   c. the supply of savings will shift to the right.

   d. the supply of savings will shift to the left.

6. If the government allows firms to take an investment tax credit on the purchase of new capital, then:

   a. the demand for borrowing will increase.

   b. interest rates will increase.

   c. the amount of investment will increase.

   d. All of the answers are correct.

7. A recession that reduces investment by firms will:

a. shift the supply of savings to the right.

b. shift the supply of savings to the left.

c. decrease the quantity of savings.

d. increase interest rates.

8. Record government budget deficits in the years ahead will:

a. increase interest rates.

b. decrease private investment.

c. increase savings.

d. All of the answers are correct.

9. For a $1,000 zero-coupon bond to provide a 3.5 percent rate of return, its price must be:

a. $966.18.

b. $650.45.

c. $285.71

d. None of the answers is correct.

10. The 2007–08 financial crisis is best described as:

a. a stock market crash.

b. a breakdown of financial intermediation in the commercial and shadow banking systems.

c. extremely high levels of default in the bond market.

d. All of the answers are correct.

Answer Key

Answers to Self-Practice Questions

1. These topics are included in a macroeconomics course because the financial system is an important part of an economy. An efficient financial system is essential for moving funds from savers to investors to ensure that the economy will have sufficient capital to sustain economic growth.

   Topic: Introduction

2. Rate of Return for a zero-coupon bond $= \dfrac{FV - \text{Price}}{\text{Price}} \times 100$.
   $5\% = [(1,000 - \text{Price})/\text{Price}] \times 100$.
   Make sure you don't put .05 on the left-hand side. Multiplying by 100 on the right-hand side of the equation takes care of this conversion. Now, solving for Price, we have:
   $.05 = (1,000 - \text{Price})/\text{Price}$
   $.05 \times \text{Price} = (1,000 - \text{Price})$
   $.05 \times \text{Price} + \text{Price} = 1,000$
   $\text{Price}(.05 + 1) = 1,000$
   $\text{Price} = 1,000/1.05$
   $\text{Price} = \$952.38$

   Topic: The Bond Market

3. Rate of return $= [(FV - \text{Price})/\text{Price}] \times 100 = [(10,000 - 9,100)/9,100] \times 100 = [900/9,100] \times 100 = 0.0989 \times 100 = 9.89\%$.

   Topic: The Bond Market

4. The logical effect on the loanable fund market if life expectancy, but NOT the retirement age, increases by 20 years is that people would save more to prepare for a longer retirement. This increase in savings will cause the supply of loanable funds to increase. The result will be a lower interest rate and an increase in the equilibrium level of savings/borrowing in the market. The graph will look like Figure 9.7 (27.7) in the text.

   Topic: Shifts in Supply and Demand

5. The new savings account provides a tax incentive for saving. This causes individuals across the economy to save more. The increase in savings will shift the supply of loanable funds to the right, causing lower interest rates and an increase in the equilibrium level of savings/investment. Again, the graph would look like Figure 9.7 (27.7) in the text.

   Topic: Shifts in Supply and Demand

6. If the federal government borrows several hundred billion fewer dollars in the years ahead, that would shift the demand for loanable funds to the left. Specifically, this could be shown by shifting the red curve in Figure 9.10 (27.10) to the left. This would decrease the real interest rate and make it easier for private businesses to borrow (in other words, it would reduce the crowding out of private investment).

   Topic: Shifts in Supply and Demand; The Bond Market

7. Deposit insurance is important because (1) it makes savers more willing to deposit their savings in commercial banks and (2) prevents depositors from suddenly withdrawing their funds when signs (or even rumors) of problems in the commercial banking system develop. This ensures a larger and more stable supply of funds in the commercial banking system and prevents sudden disruptions of financial intermediation services in the economy by preventing failures and panics in the banking system.

Topic: What Happens When Intermediation Fails?

8. Joey needs functioning financial markets more than Jimmy because Joey needs to be able to borrow when his income is low and lend when his income is high. This allows Joey to enjoy smooth consumption from year to year even though his income varies from year to year.

Topics: The Supply of Savings *and* The Demand to Borrow

Answers to Multiple-Choice Questions

1. a, Topic: Introduction

2. b, Topic: Figure 9.1

3. c, Topic: Introduction

4. b, Topic: The Demand to Borrow

5. a, Topic: The Demand to Borrow

6. c, Topic: The Demand to Borrow

7. c, Topic: The Supply of Savings

8. a, Topic: The Supply of Savings

9. c, Topic: The Demand to Borrow

10. c, Topic: Banks, Bonds, and Stock Markets

11. b, Topic: Banks, Bonds, and Stock Markets

12. a, Topic: Banks, Bonds, and Stock Markets

13. b, Topic: Insecure Property Rights

14. d, Topic: What Happens When Intermediation Fails?

15. a, Topic: What Happens When Intermediation Fails?

16. c, Topic: What Happens When Intermediation Fails?

17. d, Topic: The Bond Market

18. a, Topic: The Supply of Savings and The Demand to Borrow

19. c, Topic: Equilibrium in the Market for Loanable Funds

20. b, Topic: Banks, Bonds, and Stock Markets

21. b, Topic: Banks, Bonds, and Stock Markets

10

Stock Markets and Personal Finance

Learning Objectives

In this chapter you will learn about stock markets and personal investing. The topics covered include:

> Passive vs. Active Investing
> How to Really Pick Stocks, Seriously
> Other Benefits and Costs of Stock Markets

Summary

A mutual fund buys assets with money pooled from many customers. With **passive investing,** a saver buys a mutual fund that mimics a broad stock market index such as the Standard and Poor's 500 (S&P 500). With **active investing,** a saver buys a mutual fund that is run by managers who try to pick stocks to beat broad market indexes. Active investing has not been shown to give the saver a higher return than passive investing, however.

The **efficient markets hypothesis** says that the prices of traded assets reflect all publicly available information. This implies that it will be difficult for mutual fund managers to actually beat the broad market indexes. Only if you have information not in the market can you beat the market. Additionally, once you start buying or selling, based on that information, the market price will soon reflect your information.

The textbook authors offer four pieces of advice for savers who want to put their savings at risk. The first piece of advice is to diversify: that is, buy a variety of different assets so you do not have all your eggs in one basket.

The second piece of advice is that since the efficient markets hypothesis says that you cannot beat the market by stock picking, your best strategy is to **buy and hold** your diversified assets.

The third piece of advice is to avoid high brokerage fees. In other words, since the efficient markets hypothesis says that you cannot beat the market, do not pay high fees for stock-picking advice.

The fourth and final piece of advice is related to the buy and hold strategy, which is holding your diversified portfolio over a long period to take advantage of the power of compound returns to build wealth. The rule of 70 shows that a small difference in growth rates can lead to a large difference in wealth over decades. This rule states that an annual growth rate divided into 70 tells you the number of years it takes the growing asset to double in value. The textbook thus advises you to not try to beat the market, but to avoid high brokerage fees when buying, and holding, a well-diversified portfolio of assets for a long period advantage of the compounding of returns, which is what builds wealth.

Risk and return are related. The **risk-return trade-off** means higher returns come at the price of higher risk. For example, U.S. government T-bills are safe but have low return; corporate bonds earn a higher return than T-bills but are riskier. By riskier, the textbook means that corporate bond values fluctuate more than T-bill values. The S&P 500 has a higher return than corporate bonds, but the S&P is riskier than corporate bonds. Shares of stock in small companies have returns that are even higher than the S&P 500, but, they are riskier than the S&P 500. Risk implies that the value of an asset can go either up or down and also could, in the extreme, go to zero.

Stock markets are important since companies can use them to raise funds for start-up or expansion. Stock markets use stock prices to signal how well a company is being run. Finally, stock markets are a way of transferring control of a company from less competent people to more competent people.

Bubbles occur when asset prices are bid up higher than the underlying value of the asset. Eventually, however, a bubble must burst and then prices must fall to reflect the true value of the underlying asset. The bursting of price bubbles has sometimes been associated with recession.

Key Terms

efficient markets hypothesis the prices of traded assets reflect all publicly available information

buy and hold buying stocks and then holding them for the long run, regardless of what prices do in the short run

risk-return trade-off higher returns come at the price of higher risk

Traps, Hints, and Reminders

Sometimes students get confused about the trade-off between risk and return. They do not understand why the relationship exists. Imagine that there were two bonds you could buy. One is more risky than the other. Which would you pay more for? The less risky one, of course. But paying more for the less risky bond means that bond has a lower return.

The efficient markets hypothesis is similar to the idea that there is no such thing as a free lunch. If you could easily gather special information on stocks and make money, everyone would do that. That would get rid of your advantage.

Bubbles misallocate resources. For example, if there is a real estate bubble, then resources that would have gone to produce something else are drawn into real estate. This does not mean that investing in housing is bad; it means that consumers valued something else more, and that investors were confused.

The authors do suggest ways to get rich slow. For example, by using the power of compounding, the longer your money is invested, the bigger it will be at the end. Small amounts of money saved over a long period of time can be much bigger than large amounts of money invested for a short period of time. Another way to get rich slow is by diversifying your portfolio to protect yourself against the risk from single stocks. It also helps build your wealth when you can avoid high fees when choosing stocks.

Homework Quiz

1. You are actively investing when you
   a. buy and hold.
   b. try to beat the market.
   c. buy mutual funds that try to mimic broad market indexes.
   d. All of these answers are correct.

2. If you buy and hold a diversified portfolio of assets, you are engaging in
   a. active investment.
   b. passive investment.
   c. foolish investment.
   d. beating the market.

3. The Standard & Poor's 500 is
   a. a NASCAR event.
   b. a narrow index of U.S. bond prices.
   c. a broad index of U.S. stock prices.
   d. an international index of stock prices.

4. The efficient markets hypothesis says that
   a. because big firms are more efficient, they make all the money in stock markets.
   b. the prices of trade assets reflect all publicly available information.
   c. big firms are more efficient at picking stocks than individual investors.
   d. individuals are better at picking stocks than big firms.

5. Your stockbroker tells you that today's news means that Google will make much more money next year than anyone had predicted. He recommends a buy. Why might this be poor advice?

    a. He is just trying to unload his own stock.

    b. If it was in today's news, the price has already increased.

    c. Newspapers usually try to manipulate the stock market for their own gain.

    d. None of the answers is correct.

6. After the nuclear power plant in Chernobyl melted down and contaminated the Ukraine with radiation, American potato prices increased because

    a. people wanted to eat more potatoes.

    b. people were afraid to buy stocks.

    c. people were afraid to buy bonds.

    d. traders quickly realized that since Ukrainian potatoes were contaminated, American potato prices would rise.

7. The authors' advice for picking stock includes

    a. focus on one asset.

    b. buy and hold assets for long periods of time.

    c. pay what it takes to get advice from the best stock pickers.

    d. frequently dump some assets and buy others.

8. The authors' advice for picking stock includes

    a. diversify or hold many different assets.

    b. change the assets in your portfolio frequently.

    c. pay what it takes to get advice from the best stock pickers.

    d. only hold your portfolio for a short period of time.

9. The authors' advice for picking stock includes

    a. diversify or hold many different assets.

    b. avoid paying high brokerage fees.

    c. take advantage of compounding returns to build wealth.

    d. All of the answers is correct.

10. The rule of 70 implies that if an asset's annual growth rate is 2 percent, then the asset will double in value in

    a. 2 years.

    b. 35 years.

    c. 140 years.

    d. It will never double in value.

11. According to diversification, if you work in the auto industry you should
    a. invest heavily in auto stocks.
    b. split your portfolio equally between auto stocks and nonauto stocks.
    c. have relatively few auto stocks.
    d. buy companies that supply auto companies.

12. Rank the following asset categories from lowest risk to highest risk.
    a. U.S. T-bills, small stocks, S&P 500, corporate bonds
    b. corporate bonds, small stocks, S&P 500, T-bills
    c. U.S. T-bills, corporate bonds, S&P 500, small stocks
    d. U.S. T-bills, small stocks, corporate bonds, S&P 500

13. The relationship between risk and return of an asset is
    a. that as returns rise, so does risk.
    b. an inverse relationship.
    c. a negative relationship.
    d. that as return rise, risk falls.

14. When economists talk about bubbles they mean that
    a. you never know what will happen to the economy.
    b. sometimes markets bid up prices well above the value of the underlying asset.
    c. sometimes market participants spend too much time focusing on core competencies.
    d. sometimes stock prices float back and forth like soap bubbles.

15. Bubble bursts are hard on economies because
    a. the bubble led people to put resources in the wrong areas.
    b. people do not like to let asset prices get too high or too low.
    c. bubbles are not actually painful, since paper profits may go up and then down, but only on paper.
    d. the bubbles caused people to not buy assets before they burst.

Self-Practice Questions

1. Passive investing is when you
    a. buy and hold stocks.
    b. try to beat the market.
    c. buy mutual funds run by stock pickers who have a solid record of beating the market.
    d. All of the answers are correct.

2. If you pick stocks to try to beat the market, you are engaging in
   a. active investment.
   b. passive investment.
   c. conservative investment.
   d. illegal investment.

3. The idea that the prices of traded assets reflect all publicly available information is known as
   a. a speculative bubble.
   b. beating the market.
   c. diversification.
   d. the efficient markets hypothesis.

4. Your friend calls you with news from the morning paper that should make a certain stock more valuable. You should
   a. buy the stock and reap the reward.
   b. sell the stock because the paper is wrong.
   c. not buy or sell the stock because the information would already be reflected in the price of the stock soon after the paper was printed.
   d. not buy or sell the stock because this would be insider trading.

5. When financial economists talk about a stock's risk, they mean
   a. how much the stock's price moves up and down.
   b. how much the stock's price moves up or down compared to its previous movement.
   c. how the stock's price moves up or down along with the rest of the market.
   d. how high the price of the stock is.

6. The fall of a stock market price means that
   a. the stock is undervalued and its price will rise.
   b. the stock's price will continue to fall.
   c. most buyers and sellers negatively reevaluated their opinion of the stock.
   d. the stock's price will suddenly have more variance.

7. The text authors' advice for picking assets is to
   a. trade frequently.
   b. buy and hold assets for only short periods of time.
   c. avoid paying high brokerage fees.
   d. buy only one type of asset.

8. One piece of advice for picking assets that the text authors give is to
   a. buy and hold a well-diversified portfolio of assets.
   b. avoid paying high brokerage fees.
   c. take advantage of compounding returns to build wealth.
   d. All of the answers are correct.

9. Diversification means that if, for example, you work in the banking industry, you should

    a. invest heavily in bank stocks.

    b. split your portfolio equally between bank stocks and nonbank stocks.

    c. have relatively few bank stocks.

    d. buy stock only in financial companies.

10. Corporate bond returns are higher than the returns on

    a. T-bills.

    b. the S&P 500.

    c. shares of stock in small companies.

    d. All of the answers are correct.

11. If the return on corporate bonds rises, then you would expect the risk of corporate bonds to

    a. fall.

    b. rise.

    c. be unaffected.

    d. be unpredictable.

12. A bubble in a market is when the market price

    a. rises rapidly.

    b. falls rapidly.

    c. rises above the value of the underlying asset.

    d. is undervalued.

13. The rule of 70 implies that if an asset's annual growth rate is 5%, then the asset will double its value in

    a. 14 years.

    b. 70 years.

    c. 350 years.

    d. no specified amount of time.

14. If S&P 500 risk falls, then you would expect the return from the S&P 500 to

    a. fall.

    b. rise.

    c. be unaffected.

    d. be unpredictable.

15. Stock markets

    a. are where companies raise funds for start up or expansion.

    b. signal when companies are poorly managed.

    c. facilitate transfer of company control from less competent to more competent people.

    d. All of the answers are correct.

Answers to Self-Practice Questions

1. a, Topic: Passive vs. Active Investing

2. a, Topic: Passive vs. Active Investing

3. d, Topic: Passive vs. Active Investing

4. c, Topic: Passive vs. Active Investing

5. a, Topic: Passive vs. Active Investing

6. c, Topic: Passive vs. Active Investing

7. c, Topic: How to Really Pick Stocks, Seriously

8. d, Topic: How to Really Pick Stocks, Seriously

9. c, Topic: How to Really Pick Stocks, Seriously

10. a, Topic: How to Really Pick Stocks, Seriously

11. b, Topic: How to Really Pick Stocks, Seriously

12. c, Topic: How to Really Pick Stocks, Seriously

13. a, Topic: How to Really Pick Stocks, Seriously

14. a, Topic: How to Really Pick Stocks, Seriously

15. d, Topic: Other Benefits and Costs of Stock Markets

11 (28)

Unemployment and Labor Force Participation

Learning Objectives

In this chapter, you will learn:

> How unemployment is measured.

> About three different types of unemployment.

> What the "natural" rate of unemployment measures.

> Some of the basic determinants of labor force participation.

Summary

Measuring Unemployment

The first objective of this chapter is to explain how unemployment is measured. The official unemployment rate for the U.S. economy is measured monthly by the U.S. Department of Labor's Bureau of Labor Statistics (BLS). (You can check out their Web site and see the latest unemployment rate at www.bls.gov.)

To understand how unemployment is measured by the BLS, a few basic definitions are needed. The **labor force** is defined as the number of employed and unemployed people. In other words, the labor force includes everyone who is working or who *wants* to work. Anyone who does not want a job is not counted in the labor force. Examples of people *not* in the labor force include children, prisoners, retired persons, disabled persons, full-time students who don't want a job, or someone who, say, wins the lottery and decides not to work anymore.

An **unemployed** worker is someone who does not have a job but who is looking for work. Based on this definition, the official **unemployment rate** measured by BLS is the percentage of the labor force without a job. That is:

$$\text{Unemployment rate} = (\text{Unemployed}/\text{Labor Force}) \times 100.$$

Note that to be counted as unemployed by the BLS, you must be *looking* for work. A worker who quits looking for work but would still like to have a job is called a **discouraged worker**. Discouraged workers are not included in the official unemployment rate reported by the government, although BLS does have some broader measures of unemployment that include discouraged workers. The **underemployment rate** discussed in the text is one such measure. The underemployment rate includes discouraged workers and part-time workers who would like a full-time position.

Three Types of Unemployment

In addition to knowing how unemployment is measured, it is helpful to have some sense of what constitutes a "normal" amount of unemployment in the economy. For example, the unemployment rate in August, 2010 was 9.7 percent. Was this a good or bad number for the U.S. economy? To answer this question, we need to know something about the three different types of unemployment that occur. The three types of unemployment are:

> Frictional unemployment

> Structural unemployment

> Cyclical unemployment

Frictional unemployment is short-term unemployment caused by the ordinary difficulties of matching employee to employer. For example, a new high school or college graduate that has not yet found a job would be frictionally unemployed.

Structural unemployment is persistent, long-term unemployment caused by long-lasting shocks or permanent features of an economy that make it more difficult for some workers to find jobs. Long-lasting shocks that require restructuring in the economy will generally lead to unemployment in affected industries or sectors. Examples of such shocks discussed in the text are oil shocks, the shift from manufacturing to services, globalization and global competition, and new technology such as computers and the Internet.

Labor regulations such as unemployment benefits, minimum wages, powerful unions, and employment protection laws can also increase structural unemployment. The text discusses at some length how more extensive labor regulations in many European countries contribute to more structural unemployment than in the United States. Also discussed are **active labor market policies** that reduce structural unemployment by focusing on getting unemployed workers back to work. Such policies include job retraining, job-search assistance, work tests, and early employment bonuses.

Cyclical unemployment is unemployment associated with the business cycle. (Recall that the business cycle, first discussed in Chapter 6, refers to the periodic ups and downs in the economy.) For example, cyclical unemployment occurs when the economy goes into recession and firms lay off workers as GDP declines.

The Natural Unemployment Rate

Although unemployment is rarely considered a good thing, some amount of unemployment is inevitable in a dynamic economy. To get a sense of how much unemployment is normally expected, we can ask which of the three types of unemployment are "normal" types of unemployment. Alternatively, we can ask which type(s) of unemployment are associated with "bad" times or weakness in the economy. By definition, cyclical unemployment is unemployment associated with recession while frictional and structural unemployment are the result of more normal features of the economy such as job search, restructuring, or labor regulations. On this basis, we define the **natural unemployment rate** as frictional plus structural unemployment. As such, we can think of the natural rate of unemployment as the amount of unemployment that occurs in normal times.

Suppose the natural unemployment rate is 5 percent, a number in line with most current estimates of the natural rate. This suggests that the 9.7 percent unemployment rate in August, 2010 represents a higher-than-normal amount of unemployment in the economy. More specifically, it suggests that cyclical unemployment in the economy is roughly 4.7 percent of the labor force (9.7% − 5% = 4.7%). Cyclical unemployment indicates underlying weakness in the economy due to the business cycle. In other words, it implies that the unemployment rate has not yet returned to a normal level following the recent recession. (Such delays in the unemployment rate's decline following the end of a recession is sometimes referred to as a "jobless recovery." See Figure 11.7 [28.7] in the text for more on the jobless recovery.)

In this way, we can use the natural unemployment rate as a benchmark against which we can compare the official unemployment rate reported by the government. So, an unemployment rate higher than the natural rate suggests underlying business cycle weakness (or recession). On the other hand, an unemployment rate below the natural rate suggests a stronger-than-normal economy, probably near the peak of the business cycle (this is sometimes referred to as a "boom" or an "overheated" economy). When the unemployment rate is roughly equal to the natural rate, it is often said that the economy is at "full employment." Thus, full employment suggests that the only unemployment in the economy is that which we would normally expect to see—namely, frictional and structural unemployment.

In general, the unemployment rate is a good indicator of changes in economic activity over the course of the business cycle. Figure 11.8 (28.8) in the text shows how the official unemployment rate has fluctuated above and below the natural rate of unemployment since 1948. Note that spikes in unemployment correspond closely to periods of recession in the U.S. economy (as shown in Figure 11.5 [28.5]). The natural unemployment rate, on the other hand, changes very gradually over time and its movement is not related to the business cycle.

Labor Force Participation

The last section of the chapter discusses labor force participation, which refers to individuals' decisions about entering the labor force. Labor force participation is measured by the **labor force participation rate**, which is the percentage of the population that enters the labor force:

Labor Force Participation Rate = (Labor Force/Population) × 100.

The labor force participation rate in the United States is currently about 65%. This reminds us that there are a number of individuals in the population who do not want to work—that is, they do not participate in the labor force.

The chapter closes with a discussion of two factors that determine the labor force participation rate:

1. life-cycle effects and demographics
2. incentives

Life-cycle or demographic effects generally refer to the age profile of the population. The larger the percentage of working-age people in the population, the higher the labor force participation rate will be. As the population ages and a larger share of the population enters retirement age, labor force participation rates decline. This trend is expected in coming years in the United States as **baby boomers**—people born during the high-birth rate years of 1946–1964—enter retirement.

Incentives also affect labor force participation. Remember that incentives are rewards or penalties that motivate human behavior. There are a number of rewards and penalties that affect labor force participation. For example, some countries penalize workers who continue to work past normal retirement age. This penalty may come in the form of reduced government retirement benefits or higher payroll taxes. Such penalties are common in many European countries. Figure 11.9 (28.9) in the text shows that labor force participation is much lower in these European countries than in the United States because of these penalties.

One dramatic trend in the United States has been the increase in female labor force participation. Since the end of World War II, female labor force participation has doubled, from 35 percent in 1948 to 75 percent in 2008 (see Figure 11.11 [28.11] in the text). Cultural factors certainly played a role in this increase, but so did incentives. The text discusses one surprising incentive—the birth-control pill. The pill gave women a low-cost, reliable, and convenient method of controlling fertility. This lowered the cost of earning a professional degree by giving women more certainty about the consequences of sex. With the risk of pregnancy removed, women invested more in long-term education and their careers. This explains much of the dramatic rise in labor force participation among women in the United States.

Key Terms

labor force all workers, employed plus unemployed

unemployed adults who do not have a job but who are looking for work

unemployment rate the percentage of the labor force without a job

discouraged workers workers who have given up looking for work but who would still like a job

underemployment rate a Bureau of Labor Statistics measure that includes part-time workers who would rather have a full-time position and people who would like to work but have given up looking for a job

frictional unemployment short-term unemployment caused by the ordinary difficulties of matching employee to employer

structural unemployment persistent, long-term unemployment caused by long-lasting shocks or permanent features of an economy that make it more difficult for some workers to find jobs

median wage the wage such that one-half of all workers earn wages below the median and one-half of all workers earn wages above the median

union an association of workers that bargains collectively with employers over wages, benefits, and working conditions

employment at-will doctrine the most basic U.S. employment law, which says an employee may quit and an employer may fire an employee at any time and for any reason.

active labor market policies programs like work tests, job search assistance, and job retraining that focus on getting unemployed workers back to work

cyclical unemployment unemployment correlated with the business cycle

natural unemployment rate the rate of structural plus frictional unemployment

labor force participation rate the percentage of adults in the labor force

baby boomers the people born during the high-birth-rate years, 1946–1964

Traps, Hints, and Reminders

Remember that the unemployment rate measures the percentage of the *labor force* (not the entire population) that is unemployed.

Remember that someone is considered to be unemployed only if they are *actively looking for a job*. Someone who is not looking is not considered to be in the labor force and therefore would not be included in the official unemployment rate.

Discouraged workers (people who would like a job but have quit looking for work) are not counted in the official unemployment rate. They are included in some broader measures of unemployment such as the *underemployment rate.*

The number of discouraged workers is likely to grow larger during economic downturns (recessions), causing the underemployment rate to rise faster than the official unemployment rate.

The words "employment" and "unemployment" look similar on quizzes and exams. Read carefully!

Figure 11.3 (28.3) in the text shows how minimum wage laws and high union wages lead to unemployment in a supply and demand context. In either case, the wage is higher than the equilibrium or "market" wage and this results in a surplus of labor (in other words, unemployment).

There are two reasons why high unemployment and economic downturns (recessions) tend to go together: (1) Firms tend to lay off workers as output (GDP) falls during a downturn; (2) unemployed workers do not produce anything and this contributes further to the decline in output (GDP) during the recession.

Self-Practice Questions

1. Indicate what type of unemployment is illustrated by each of the following cases.

   a. Jim lost his job as a stockbroker when the recession hit.

   b. Omar left his job as a corporate lawyer to look for a less stressful position.

   c. Nancy lost her job in a furniture plant when it was outsourced to China.

   d. John lost his job at the local hamburger joint when the city passed a minimum wage law.

   e. Mary lost her job as a bank teller because of increased ATM usage for routine banking transactions.

   f. Sally lost her job at a restaurant during a recession and decided to go back to school full-time (without looking for a job) to become a teacher.

2. If the adult population is 200 million, and 100 million are working and 10 million are actively looking for a job, but not working, what is the unemployment rate?

3. If the adult population is 200 million, and 100 million are working and 10 million are actively looking for a job, but not working, what is the labor force participation rate?

4. Why is long-term unemployment so high in so many European countries?

5. What would you expect to happen to the unemployment rate during a recession? How about the natural rate of unemployment?

6. What factors affect structural unemployment?

7. Some unemployment exists even during economic boom periods. Explain.

8. What is a "jobless" recovery? How can unemployment rates be used to determine when a jobless recovery finally ends?

9. Suppose the government increases the official retirement age for people to become eligible to receive Social Security benefits to age 80. How would you expect this change to affect labor force participation rates?

Multiple-Choice Questions

1. If there are 200 million adults with 170 million in the labor force and 8 million actively looking for a job but not currently working, then what is the *unemployment* rate?

   a. 4.0 percent

   b. 4.7 percent

   c. 4.9 percent

   d. 85 percent

2. If there are 200 million adults with 170 million in the labor force and 8 million actively looking for a job but not currently working, then what is the labor force participation rate?

   a. 4.0 percent

   b. 4.7 percent

   c. 89 percent

   d. 85 percent

3. Esther is currently working for income but also looking for a job on monster.com. Esther is:

    a. employed.

    b. not in the labor force.

    c. unemployed.

    d. discouraged.

4. Raquel was working at the local mill, but soon after it closed she got discouraged and quit looking for a job. In calculating the official unemployment rate, Raquel will be considered:

    a. employed.

    b. not in the labor force.

    c. unemployed.

    d. naturally employed

5. Which of the following is a shortcoming of the official unemployment rate as a measure of national economic performance?

    a. It does not count "discouraged" workers.

    b. It does not differentiate between part-time and full-time employment.

    c. It does not account for people who accept lower-quality jobs than they are qualified for.

    d. All of the answers are correct.

6. If a country enacts new unemployment insurance that provides the unemployed with more money for a longer period, we would expect:

    a. unemployed people to find jobs more quickly.

    b. fewer people to lose their jobs.

    c. the unemployment rate to go down.

    d. the unemployment rate to go up.

7. Labor market regulations generally affect which type of unemployment?

    a. frictional unemployment

    b. structural unemployment

    c. cyclical unemployment

    d. All of the answers are correct.

8. Which of the following are examples of active labor market policies?

    a. paying a bonus to people who find a job

    b. forcing people who get unemployment insurance to prove that they are actively looking for a job

    c. providing job training and job search assistance

    d. All of the answers are correct.

9. Which of the following policies would be likely to increase the duration of unemployment?

   a. providing higher unemployment benefits

   b. providing unemployment benefits for a longer period of time

   c. providing housing assistance to unemployed people

   d. All of the answers are correct.

10. Employment "at will" means that you can be fired:

    a. for good reasons only.

    b. for any reason at any time.

    c. only if you agree.

    d. only under certain circumstances, such as when employers and union organizers agree.

11. The United States has employment "at will" but some restrictions do exist. Which one of the following is a U.S. restriction?

    a. You may not fire someone simply because the economy is bad.

    b. You may not fire someone simply because of his or her race or religion.

    c. You may not fire someone simply because that person doesn't show up for work on time.

    d. You may not fire someone without first issuing a warning.

12. Keith just graduated from high school and is in the process of looking for a job. Keith is:

    a. structurally unemployed.

    b. cyclically unemployed.

    c. frictionally unemployed.

    d. not yet in the labor force.

13. Grace works as a framer for a construction company. During the recent downturn, she got laid off. If she is actively looking for employment, she is:

    a. structurally unemployed.

    b. cyclically unemployed.

    c. a discouraged worker.

    d. frictionally unemployed.

14. Byron lost his job as a travel agent when people switched to purchasing their own airline tickets on the Internet. Even though Byron is still looking for a job, Byron is:

    a. structurally unemployed.

    b. cyclically unemployed.

    c. a discouraged worker.

    d. frictionally unemployed.

15. Which of the following would be a cause of structural unemployment?

    a. Jobs are lost when an economy shifts away from agriculture and becomes more industrial.

    b. Jobs are lost due to outsourcing to China.

    c. Jobs are lost when a typewriter factory shuts down due to increased use of computers for word processing.

    d. All of the answers are correct.

16. Which of the following best describes the unemployment rate during an economic boom?

    a. The unemployment rate rises above the natural rate.

    b. The unemployment rate falls, but remains above the natural rate.

    c. The unemployment rate falls below the natural rate.

    d. The unemployment rate will be equal to the natural rate.

17. Labor force participation differs depending on people's ages. Which group has the lowest labor force participation rate?

    a. 16–19

    b. 25–54

    c. 65+

    d. None of the answers is correct.

18. Higher income tax rates do what to labor force participation?

    a. They increase it because people have to work more just to survive.

    b. They increase it because people know that their hard work is going to benefit society.

    c. They decrease it because higher taxes reduce the benefit of work.

    d. None of the answers is correct.

19. Which of the following is credited with encouraging the participation of women in the U.S. labor force?

    a. the shift from a manufacturing to a service economy

    b. the invention of the birth control pill

    c. social and cultural changes

    d. All of the answers are correct.

20. Which of the following explains why labor force participation rates of older workers are lower in many European countries?

    a. Fewer people live to old age in these countries.

    b. There was no "baby boom" in these countries.

    c. These countries penalize workers who continue to work past the normal retirement age.

    d. All of the answers are correct.

Homework Quiz

1. Which of the following is NOT included in the natural unemployment rate?
   a. cyclical unemployment
   b. frictional unemployment
   c. structural unemployment
   d. None of the answers is correct

2. When the unemployment rate equals the natural rate, we would expect:
   a. cyclical unemployment to be high.
   b. structural unemployment to be low.
   c. frictional unemployment to be low.
   d. cyclical unemployment to be zero.

3. Which of the following policies is likely to reduce the duration of unemployment in an economy?
   a. increasing unemployment benefits
   b. reducing the length of time unemployment benefits are provided
   c. providing food stamps to unemployed people
   d. All of the answers are correct.

4. Which of the following remains fairly stable over the course of the business cycle?
   a. frictional unemployment
   b. structural unemployment
   c. the natural unemployment rate
   d. All of the answers are correct.

5. In an adult population of 234.1 million, 145.5 million are employed and 9.4 million are unemployed but actively looking for work. What is the unemployment rate in this economy?
   a. 6.1 percent
   b. 6.5 percent
   c. 4.0 percent
   d. None of the answers is correct.

6. In an adult population of 234.1 million, 145.5 million are employed and 9.4 million are unemployed but actively looking for work. What is the labor force participation rate in this economy?

   a. 6.5 percent

   b. 62.2 percent

   c. 66.2 percent

   d. None of the answers is correct.

7. An increase in the unemployment rate over a period of time likely indicates that the economy is:

   a. overheated.

   b. booming.

   c. in recession.

   d. at full employment.

8. According to the official unemployment rate reported by the government, a "discouraged" worker is considered to be:

   a. employed.

   b. unemployed.

   c. not in the labor force.

   d. None of the answers is correct.

9. A textile worker who loses his or her job due to outsourcing to India (but who is still actively looking for work) is said to be:

   a. frictionally unemployed.

   b. structurally unemployed.

   c. cyclically unemployed.

   d. underemployed.

10. The official unemployment rate reported by the government includes:

   a. frictional unemployment.

   b. structural unemployment.

   c. cyclical unemployment.

   d. All of the answers are correct.

Answer Key

Answers to Self-Practice Questions

1. a. cyclical unemployment

    b. frictional unemployment

    c. structural unemployment

    d. structural unemployment

    e. structural unemployment

    f. Sally is not unemployed since she left the labor force to go back to school (and is not currently looking for a job).

    Topic: Frictional Unemployment; Structural Unemployment; Cyclical Unemployment

2. The unemployment rate is (10 million looking)/(100 million working + 10 million looking) = 10/110 = 0.0909 × 100 = 9.1%.

    Topic: Defining Unemployment

3. The labor force participation rate is (100 million working + 10 million looking) divided by the 200 million adult population = 110 million/200 million = 110/200 = 0.55 × 100 = 55%.

    Topic: Labor Force Participation

4. Labor regulations in these countries generally contribute to higher levels of structural unemployment. Higher unemployment benefits, longer-term unemployment benefits, and other benefits to the unemployed (such as housing assistance) reduce the cost of being unemployed and cause higher levels of unemployment. Minimum wage laws and stronger unions that raise wages also reduce the demand for workers, thus contributing to higher unemployment.

    Topic: Labor Regulations and Structural Unemployment

5. The unemployment rate will increase during recessions, driven by the increase in cyclical unemployment. The natural rate of unemployment, on the other hand, does not change during recessions. This is because it measures unemployment that normally occurs and so is not related to business cycle downturns.

    Topic: Cyclical Unemployment; The Natural Unemployment Rate

6. Structural unemployment is affected by oil shocks, shifts that require restructuring of the economy such as the shift from services to manufacturing, globalization and global competition, and fundamental technology shocks like computers and the Internet. Labor market regulations can also contribute to structural unemployment.

    Topic: Structural Unemployment

7. Even during times when the economy is unusually strong there will be some unemployment. This is because there will always be people searching for new jobs or better jobs (frictional unemployment) and reallocations of jobs resulting from shocks and new technology in the economy (structural unemployment). These normally occurring types of unemployment determine the natural unemployment rate.

    Topic: Frictional Unemployment; Structural Unemployment; The Natural Unemployment Rate

8. A "jobless" recovery refers to a period of time during which unemployment remains high (above the natural unemployment rate) following the end of a recession. The jobless recovery will be over when the unemployment rate falls to a level near the natural unemployment rate.

Topic: Cyclical Unemployment

9. A delay in the age required to receive Social Security benefits increases the cost of retiring (or reduces the benefit of retiring). As more people delay retirement, more individuals will remain in the labor force. This would increase the number of "working-age" people in the population, thus increasing the labor force participation rate.

Topic: Life-Cycle Effects and Demographics; Incentives

Answers to Multiple-Choice Questions

1. b, Topic: Defining Unemployment

2. d, Topic: Labor Force Participation

3. a, Topic: Defining Unemployment

4. b, Topic: Defining Unemployment

5. d, Topic: How Good of an Indicator Is the Employment Rate?

6. d, Topic: Labor Regulations and Structural Unemployment

7. b, Topic: Labor Regulations and Structural Unemployment

8. d, Topic: Labor Regulations and Structural Unemployment

9. d, Topic: Labor Regulations and Structural Unemployment

10. b, Topic: Structural Unemployment

11. b, Topic: Structural Unemployment

12. c, Topic: Frictional Unemployment

13. b, Topic: Cyclical Unemployment

14. a, Topic: Structural Unemployment

15. d, Topic: Structural Unemployment

16. c, Topic: Cyclical Unemployment; The Natural Unemployment Rate

17. c, Topic: Life-Cycle Effects and Demographics

18. c, Topic: Life-Cycle Effects and Demographics; Incentives

19. d, Topic: Incentives

20. c, Topic: Incentives

12 (29)

Inflation and the Quantity Theory of Money

Learning Objectives

In this chapter, you will learn:

> What economists mean by "inflation"

> How to measure inflation

> How to "deflate" nominal to real values

> What causes inflation

> Why inflation and deflation are bad for the economy

Summary

What Is Inflation?

Inflation refers to an increase in the average level of prices—or price level—over time in an economy. Since inflation refers to the *average* level of prices, it is important to remember that it does not mean *all* prices are rising. Indeed, the prices of some goods could actually fall as inflation occurs. This point is illustrated by Figure 12.1 (29.1) in the text, which shows that inflation is like an elevator. The inflation elevator lifts the *average* level of prices from an average of 100 in Year 1 to an average of 200 in Year 10. But within the elevator, some individual prices may be falling even as inflation occurs.

Inflation can also be thought of as a *decline in the value of money* over time. When the value—or purchasing power—of money declines, it takes more money to purchase goods and services. That is, prices rise. In this respect, rising prices are actually a symptom of the underlying problem with inflation, namely a decline in the value of money.

How Is Inflation Measured?

In order to measure inflation, we need a measure of the price level. To measure the price level, economists use a *price index*. A price index is a number that measures the average level of prices in a given period relative to the average level of prices in some "base" period. Some examples of price indexes are the Consumer Price Index (CPI), the GDP Deflator, and the Producer Price Indexes (PPI). These prices indexes are briefly described in the text. The key difference between them is the set of goods used to calculate the index. The CPI uses a set of typical consumer goods while the PPI includes intermediate goods used by businesses to produce final goods. The GDP deflator is calculated using nominal and real GDP data, so it covers all final goods and services produced in the economy (see Chapter 6 for more on the GDP Deflator).

Regardless of which price index is used, the interpretation is the same. Specifically, all price indexes are set up so that the index number for a given period provides a comparison of prices in that period against prices in some "base" period. To illustrate, consider the GDP Deflator:

$$\text{GDP Deflator}_t = \frac{\text{Nominal GDP}_t}{\text{Real GDP}_t} \times 100$$

For example, nominal GDP in 2010 was \$14,526.5 billion and real GDP in 2010 was \$13,088.0 billion (in 2005 prices). The GDP Deflator for 2010 would be calculated as:

$$\text{GDP Deflator}_{2010} = \frac{\$14,526.5 \text{ billion}}{\$13,088.0 \text{ billion}} \times 100 = 111$$

A price index of 111 means that prices in 2010 are 1.11 times higher than they were in the base year of 2005. Note that the base year for the GDP Deflator is the year whose prices are used in the calculation of real GDP. Note also that if the GDP Deflator is calculated for the base year of 2005, the result will be 100 since nominal and real GDP are always equal in the base year. All price indexes are set up to equal 100 in the base year, which makes sense given the interpretation of a price index (in other words, prices in year t are 1.00 times what they were in the base year if year t is the base year).

As an additional example, nominal GDP in 2000 was \$9,951.5 billion while real GDP was \$11,216.4 billion (in 2005 prices). This implies a GDP Deflator of 88.7 in 2000 (check the math for yourself). A price index of 88.7 means that prices in 2000 were 0.887 times what they were in the base year of 2005.

With a price index in hand, it is easy to measure inflation. Inflation is measured by calculating the **inflation rate**, as follows:

$$\text{Inflation rate} = \frac{P_2 - P_1}{P_1}$$

where P_2 is the price index in year 2 and P_1 is the price index in year 1. Although it is not shown in the formula, inflation rates are usually multiplied by 100 to express the result in percentage form. For example, if the Consumer Price Index is 217.158 in 2009 and 220.186 in 2010, the inflation rate would be:

$$\frac{220.186 - 217.158}{217.158} = 0.0139$$

or 1.39 percent after multiplying by 100. This means that prices increased 1.39 percent on average between 2009 and 2010. Note that if prices are *falling* over time, the inflation rate will be a *negative* number. In this case, we would say that **deflation** has occurred.

Deflating Nominal to Real Values

Another important use of price indexes is to adjust dollar values from different years for the affects of inflation. For example, suppose a new Ford sedan cost $4,200 in 1972 and $30,000 in 2010. Can we simply conclude that the price of new Ford sedans increased by roughly seven times between 1972 and 2010? The answer is no. Dollar values from different years cannot be compared in this way because inflation has eroded the value of the dollar over time. In order to make the values comparable, we must adjust for inflation. This technique is discussed in the Appendix to this chapter in the text.

To make dollar values from different years comparable, the figures must be adjusted so that all figures are expressed in the *same year's dollars*. This can be done by either converting the 1972 figure to a 2010 dollar value or by converting the 2010 figure to a 1972 dollar value. Alternatively, both figures could be converted to base-year dollars. Converting dollar values from one year into dollar values of another year is often called *deflating* nominal into real (inflation-adjusted) values.

In general, the formula for deflating a nominal value expressed in year-x dollars to a (real) value expressed in year-y dollars is as follows:

$$(\text{nominal}) \text{ value in year-}x \text{ dollars} \times \frac{P_y}{P_x} = (\text{real}) \text{ value in year-}y \text{ dollars}$$

To illustrate, let's consider the increase in the prices of new Ford sedans noted above. The prices given previously are nominal values (expressed in current-year dollars). The Consumer Price Index can be used to adjust for inflation. The CPI was 42.5 in 1972 and 220.186 in 2010, with the base year being the 1982–1984 period. Using the formula above, we can adjust the 1972 (nominal) price of the car to *real* 2010 dollars as follows:

$$\$4,200 \times (220.186/42.5) = \$4,200 \times 5.18 = \$21,756.$$

Since this figure is expressed in 2010 dollars, it is directly comparable to the $30,000 price from 2010. Thus, we can conclude that the real price of new Ford sedans increased from $21,756 to $30,000 between 1972 and 2010.

To deflate the 2010 value to 1972 dollars, the calculation would be:

$$\$30,000 \times (42.5/220.186) = \$30,000 \times 0.193 = \$5,791.$$

This figure can be compared to the 1972 price of $4,200. Again, we conclude that the real price of new Ford sedans increased between 1972 and 2010.

An alternative method of deflating involves adjusting both nominal prices to base-period dollars. Noting that the price index will always have a value of 100 in the base period, the formula for deflating can be written as follows:

$$\text{(real) value in base-period dollars} = \frac{100}{P_x} \times \text{(nominal) value in year-}x\text{ dollars}$$
$$= \frac{\text{(nominal) value in year-}x\text{ dollars}}{\left(\dfrac{P_x}{100}\right)}$$

Adjusting both nominal car prices to base-period (1982–1984) dollars, we have:

$$\frac{\$4,200}{\left(\dfrac{42.5}{100}\right)} = \$9,882 \text{ (in 1982–84 dollars)}$$

$$\frac{\$30,00}{\left(\dfrac{220.186}{100}\right)} = \$13,625 \text{ (in 1982–84 dollars)}$$

With both figures in base-year dollars, we again see that the real price of new Ford sedans increased between 1972 and 2010.

Note that the same answer is obtained in this example—namely, that the real price of new Ford sedans increases—regardless of which year's dollars we convert the nominal figures to. Another useful example that involves adjusting house prices for inflation is shown in the Appendix to this chapter in the text.

What Causes Inflation?

Recall that inflation involves a *decline in the value of money*. So, if we ask "what causes inflation?" we are really asking "what causes the value of money to fall?" The simple answer to this question is "the quantity of money available." The idea that the quantity of money determines its value is known as the **Quantity Theory of Money**. In a nutshell, the Quantity Theory of Money describes the relationship between the quantity of money in an economy and the price level in that economy.

To understand the Quantity Theory of Money, begin with the following example. Suppose nominal spending (GDP) in an economy in a given year is $14 trillion while the money supply is only $2 trillion. How is it possible that $2 trillion of money can support $14 trillion of spending? It is only possible if each dollar of money supply is spent seven times, on average, during the year. The average number of times a dollar is spent is called the **velocity of money**. If we denote the velocity of money by v, the money supply by M, and nominal GDP by $P \times Y_R$, where P is the price level and Y_R is real GDP, then we can define the velocity of money as:

$$v = (P \times Y_R)/M.$$

In our numerical example above, we calculate velocity as $v = (P \times Y_R)/M = \$14$ trillion/$\$2$ trillion $= 7$. Upon rearranging terms in the previous equation, we can write:

$$M \times v = P \times Y_R.$$

This equation is actually an identity, which means this relationship *must* always hold true by definition. This identity is useful for understanding the relationship between the quantity of money (M) and the price level (P) in an economy. The identity is often written in terms of *growth rates* instead of levels:

$$\vec{M} + \vec{v} = \vec{P} + \vec{Y_R}.$$

The arrows over the letters denote "growth rates," and note that the multiplication signs have become plus signs. From left to right, the variables in the identity are now the growth rate of money, the growth rate of velocity, the growth rate of prices or *inflation*, and the growth rate of real GDP.

Now let's look at each variable in the identity. It turns out that velocity is relatively stable over long periods of time in an economy, so its growth rate is likely to be zero or a very low number. Similarly, the growth rate of real GDP is likely to be a very low number, usually between 2 percent and 10 percent for most economies, since growth in real output in an economy is limited by real factors of production such as capital, labor, and technology. Since both $\vec{v}$ and $\vec{Y_R}$ are likely to be zero or very low numbers, we end up with the result that $\vec{M}$ and $\vec{P}$ will be approximately equal. In other words, growth in money roughly determines growth in prices, or inflation, in an economy. This relationship between money and prices is known as the Quantity Theory of Money.

In practice, the Quantity Theory says that if the government keeps growth in the money supply low and stable, inflation will be low and stable over time. On the other hand, if the money supply grows at extraordinarily high rates, inflation will be extraordinarily high. This explains episodes of *hyperinflation* in which inflation rates are extremely high such as in Zimbabwe, discussed in the opening of this chapter in the text.

One other key prediction of the Quantity Theory is worth noting. Since velocity is thought to be stable over long periods of time and an economy's long-run real growth rate does not depend on money (recall from Chapter 7 that an economy's real growth rate is determined by real factors of production in the long run), the *only* long-run effect of increases in the rate of money growth is inflation. In other words, an increase in money growth does not have any effect on the economy's real growth rate in the long run and only causes inflation. This result is often described by saying that "*money is neutral in the long run.*"

Why Inflation (and Deflation) Are Bad for an Economy

Since many people think of inflation simply as rising prices, many people believe that the only problem with inflation is that they can afford to buy fewer goods and services with their money. Actually, this is not generally the problem with inflation. Recall that inflation refers to a decline in the value of money. This means that, not only are prices rising as the value of money falls, but so are all other things measured in dollar terms—such as workers' wages and salaries. Note that if wages and salaries are rising along with prices, there is no change in the *real* value or "purchasing power" of workers' incomes. So, what many people believe is bad about inflation is actually not the real problem with inflation. So what, then, is the problem with inflation?

Inflation causes a number of problems in an economy. Some of these problems are discussed at the end of this chapter in the text. These problems include:

> Price confusion and money illusion
> Inflation redistributes wealth
> Hyperinflation and the breakdown of financial intermediation
> Inflation interacts with other taxes
> Inflation is painful to stop

Price confusion refers to the fact that inflation makes price "signals" difficult to interpret. Without inflation, prices send signals that direct economic behavior. In a world of rapidly and unpredictably changing prices, these signals become difficult to read. In particular, it becomes difficult to determine whether price changes are nominal or real. Individuals normally respond to real price changes. The confusion caused by inflation, however, often causes people to mistakenly respond to nominal price changes—an affliction referred to as **money illusion**. The loss of informational content in prices causes inefficiency and misallocation of resources in the economy.

Inflation redistributes wealth from lenders to borrowers because it deflates the real value of fixed loan payments. The result is that borrowers end up paying lenders back dollars that are worth less than those initially loaned. So, inflation redistributes wealth from lenders to borrowers. (Note that this is only true of *unexpected* inflation, since expected inflation will be accounted for by the lender charging a higher nominal interest rate. The **Fisher effect** says that the nominal interest rate (i) will equal the real interest rate (r) plus expected inflation ($E\pi$): $i = r + E\pi$). Governments with large amounts of debt are able to take advantage of the redistributive effects of inflation by printing money. Printing more money increases inflation (recall the discussion of the Quantity Theory above) and allows the government to redistribute wealth back to itself. Printing money to reduce the real value of government debt is called **monetizing the debt**.

Hyperinflation causes a breakdown of financial intermediation because the redistributive properties of inflation become so severe that borrowers and lenders will refuse to enter into long-term loans. The breakdown of borrowing and lending causes real problems for the economy (recall the discussion of collapses in financial intermediation in Chapter 9).

Inflation interacts with other taxes by pushing taxpayers into higher income tax brackets—a process described as "bracket creep"—unless tax brackets are adjusted for inflation. This is another way inflation can result in a transfer of resources from the private sector to the government.

Once it begins, *inflation is painful to stop*. Since inflation is generally caused by excessive money growth (recall the discussion of the Quantity Theory above), reducing inflation can only be accomplished by reducing money growth. Reducing money growth, however, will generally have a negative impact on the economy in terms of slowing economic growth in the short run—that is, pushing the economy toward recession.

In closing, note that most of these problems would also occur in cases of *deflation*. This is especially true of problems caused by price confusion. And unexpected deflation would redistribute wealth from borrowers to lenders, again causing a potential breakdown of financial intermediation. This implies that avoiding these problems requires an environment without inflation or deflation—often referred to as *price stability*.

Key Terms

inflation an increase in the average level of prices

inflation rate the percentage change in the average level of prices (as measured by a price index) over a period of time

real price a price that has been corrected for inflation

Quantity Theory of Money the idea that when v and Y are fixed, increases in M must cause increases in P

velocity of money *(v)* the average number of times a dollar is spent on final goods and services in a year

deflation a decrease in the average level of prices

disinflation a reduction in the inflation rate

money illusion when people mistake changes in nominal prices for changes in real prices

Nominal rate of return the rate of return that does not account for inflation

Real rate of return the nominal rate of return minus the inflation rate

Fisher effect the tendency of nominal interest rates to rise with expected inflation rates.

monetizing the debt when the government pays off its debts by printing money

Traps, Hints, and Reminders

Although inflation is usually defined as a period of rising prices, remember that it is also useful to think of inflation as a decline in the value or "purchasing power" of money. Likewise, deflation can be thought of as an increase in the value of money.

In using price indexes to calculate inflation rates, remember that there are several price indexes to choose from. The price indexes discussed in the text are the Consumer Price Index, GDP Deflator, and Producer Price Indexes. Regardless of which price index you choose, they are interpreted the same way and used the same way to calculate inflation rates.

Remember that a positive inflation rate means that prices are *rising* over time (or that inflation has occurred). A negative inflation rate means that prices are *falling* over time and that deflation has occurred.

Do not confuse *deflation* with another term defined in the text: **disinflation**. Deflation refers to falling *prices* over a period of time, while disinflation refers to a period of falling *inflation rates*. Note that if the inflation rate falls from, say, 5 percent to 2 percent, inflation is still occurring and prices are still rising, albeit at a slower rate. In this case, disinflation has occurred, not deflation. Deflation only occurs when the inflation rate becomes *negative*.

Remember that a little arrow over a variable means the "growth rate" of that variable. In particular, $\vec{P}$ is the growth rate of prices, or the *inflation rate*.

In working with the $\overrightarrow{M} + \vec{v} = \overrightarrow{P} + \overrightarrow{Y_R}$ identity, remember that the $\vec{v}$ term is usually considered to be zero (since velocity is usually stable over time). The $\overrightarrow{Y_R}$ term is usually considered to be fixed at some low rate like 3 percent (as determined by the economy's real factors of production). This leaves nearly all of the variation across the two sides of the identity with the $\overrightarrow{M}$ and $\overrightarrow{P}$ variables, so that changes in money growth determine the inflation rate.

Remember that deflation entails many of the same costs in the economy as inflation. For example, while inflation redistributes wealth from lenders to borrowers (making fixed loan payments easier for borrowers to make as nominal incomes rise), deflation redistributes wealth from borrowers to lenders (making fixed loan payments more difficult to make as nominal incomes fall).

Self-Practice Questions

1. If the price level is 134 in 2008 and 149 in 2009, what is the inflation rate over this period?

2. If the nominal rate of interest was 7 percent last year and the inflation rate was 6 percent, what was the real rate of interest?

3. Why does volatility in the inflation rate make it harder for businesses to get loans?

4. Why do economists think that increases in the money supply cause prices to rise instead of changes to other variables such as velocity or real growth?

5. Suppose the Consumer Price Index in 1987 is 428 with a base year of 1967. What does this tell us about prices in 1987?

6. Provide three historical examples of incredible hyperinflation. What do all episodes of hyperinflation have in common?

7. If your older brother paid $27,000 for college tuition in 1999, what is the real price of his college tuition in 2009 dollars? The consumer price Index was 164.7 in 1999 and 212.174 in 2009.

8. The price of pocket calculators has fallen from $375 in 1972 to just a few dollars in 2009. Why doesn't that prove that the United States has had deflation instead of inflation?

9. If velocity is constant and the economy's real growth rate is 3 percent, what rate of money growth will achieve price stability?

10. A decline in the inflation rate from 10 percent to 3 percent implies that deflation has occurred. True or false? Explain.

Multiple-Choice Questions

1. Which of the following is TRUE about inflation?

   a. The prices of some goods may fall as inflation occurs.

   b. Inflation implies a decline in the value of the dollar.

   c. Inflation is an increase in the average level of prices.

   d. All of the answers are correct.

2. If the Consumer Price Index (CPI) rises from 328.4 in 1986 to 340.7 in 1987, the rate of inflation over this period would be:

   a. 3.7 percent.

   b. −3.7 percent.

   c. −3.6 percent.

   d. 103.7 percent.

3. If, on average, what cost $1.00 in 1982 costs $2.00 in 2010, you would expect the Consumer Price Index in 2010 (with a base year of 1982) to be:

   a. 0.5.

   b. 50.

   c. 200.

   d. 2.

4. Which of the following price indices measures the prices of not only final goods but also intermediate goods?

   a. CPI

   b. GDP deflator

   c. PPI

   d. Government Services Index

5. What is the difference between real and nominal interest rates?

   a. Real interest rates are on loans for which the borrower has put up real estate as collateral. Nominal interest rates are on loans with no collateral.

   b. Real interest rates adjust for changes in GDP. Nominal interest rates don't.

   c. Real interest rates are adjusted for inflation. Nominal interest rates aren't.

   d. Real interest rates are for loans between the Fed and banks. Nominal interest rates are between individuals and banks.

6. If you borrowed money at a 12 percent *nominal* interest rate and the inflation rate is 7 percent, what is your *real* interest rate?

   a. 12 percent

   b. 1.7 percent

   c. 19 percent

   d. 5 percent

7. Which of the following countries had very high inflation rates between 2002 and 2007?

   a. Japan

   b. Zimbabwe

   c. United States

   d. China

8. The Quantity Theory of Money says that inflation is primarily caused by:

   a. excessive growth in the money supply.

   b. increases in the rate of nominal spending in the economy.

   c. increases in the velocity of money.

   d. increases in real GDP.

9. The price of gasoline increased from $2.50 per gallon in 2006 to $3.50 per gallon in 2010. If the CPI was 203.1 in 2006 and 220.186 in 2010, then we can conclude that:

   a. the real price of gasoline declined from 2006 to 2010.

   b. the real price of gasoline increased from 2006 to 2010.

   c. the real price of gasoline stayed the same from 2006 to 2010.

   d. the real price of gasoline cannot be determined without knowing the base year.

10. If the inflation rate falls from 4 percent in 2005 to 2 percent in 2006, then:

    a. disinflation has occurred.

    b. deflation has occurred.

    c. the value of money has increased.

    d. the price level has declined.

11. If people are worried about inflation and begin spending their money faster before prices rise, then:

    a. the velocity of money will remain unchanged.

    b. the effect on the velocity of money cannot be predicted.

    c. the velocity of money will increase.

    d. the velocity of money will decrease.

12. The idea that "money is neutral" in the long run means:

    a. money can't make people happy in the long run.

    b. changes in money supply don't affect real GDP in the long run.

    c. changes in the inflation rate do not affect the interest rate in the long run.

    d. changes in the money supply don't affect prices in the long run.

13. "Money illusion" refers to the idea that:
    a. money can buy happiness.
    b. people become confused when trying to spend money from other countries.
    c. people mistake nominal changes for real changes.
    d. people can never really know the real interest rate.

14. If velocity is constant and real growth is 3 percent in a country, a 10 percent money growth rate will result in:
    a. 13 percent inflation.
    b. 10 percent inflation.
    c. 7 percent inflation.
    d. 3 percent deflation.

15. When a country uses inflation to reduce the real value of its debt, this is known as:
    a. deflating the debt.
    b. monetizing the debt.
    c. rolling over the debt.
    d. distributing the debt.

16. Unexpected inflation redistributes wealth:
    a. from the rich to the poor.
    b. from the poor to the rich.
    c. from borrowers to lenders.
    d. from lenders to borrowers.

17. A key problem with inflation in an economy is that:
    a. people come to enjoy their inflated salaries, but the salaries can't go up forever.
    b. higher prices reduce the purchasing power of workers' salaries.
    c. financial intermediation can break down if the inflation becomes severe enough.
    d. All the answers are correct.

18. Which of the following is a problem with deflation?
    a. It causes redistributions of wealth that can cause a breakdown of financial intermediation.
    b. Stopping it will cause a recession.
    c. It causes people to pay more taxes.
    d. There is no problem with deflation; falling prices are good for the economy.

19. Episodes of hyperinflation are caused by:
    a. severe recessions.
    b. extreme economic booms.
    c. extremely high money growth rates.
    d. All of the answers can cause hyperinflation.

20. Inflation is difficult to stop because:

    a. people like it and won't vote for politicians who want to stop it.

    b. the government doesn't know how to stop it.

    c. stopping it usually causes a recession.

    d. no one knows what causes it.

Homework Quiz

1. Which of the following price indexes includes prices of *all* final goods and services produced in the U.S. economy?

    a. Consumer Price Index

    b. Producer Price Index

    c. GDP Deflator

    d. All of the answers are correct.

2. If the GDP Deflator is 200 in 2004 and 205.7 in 2005, what is the inflation rate?

    a. 103 percent

    b. 5.7 percent

    c. 2.9 percent

    d. 2.7 percent

3. Suppose you decide to loan a friend some money. If you want to earn a *real* return of 5 percent on the loan and you expect inflation to be 2 percent over the period of the loan, what *nominal* interest rate should you charge your friend?

    a. 7 percent

    b. 5 percent

    c. 3 percent

    d. 2.5 percent

4. A price index of 300 means that:

    a. prices on average are 3 percent higher than in the base year.

    b. prices on average are 300 times higher than in the base year.

    c. prices on average are 300 percent higher than in the base year.

    d. prices have tripled since the base year.

5. Suppose your mother earned a wage of $2.25 per hour in 1975, when the CPI was 52.3. If the CPI is 220.2 today, what is the value of your mother's 1975 wage in current dollars?

    a. $9.47

    b. $4.95

    c. $4.30

    d. $0.53

6. If the velocity of money remains stable at 4 and real growth in the economy is 4 percent over a period of time, what rate of money growth will provide price stability (zero inflation) during this period?

   a. 0 percent

   b. 4 percent

   c. 8 percent

   d. Not enough information to determine the answer.

7. If the inflation rate falls from 10 percent to 3 percent, then:

   a. prices on average have declined by 7 percent.

   b. deflation has occurred.

   c. the value of the dollar has increased.

   d. None of the answers is correct.

8. The key insight of the Quantity Theory of Money is that:

   a. the velocity of money cannot change.

   b. inflation is caused by excessive real GDP growth.

   c. increases in the money supply cause higher prices.

   d. inflation causes higher interest rates.

9. Hyperinflation is caused by:

   a. losing a major war.

   b. extremely high rates of money growth.

   c. severe recessions.

   d. All of the answers are correct.

10. A major problem caused by inflation is:

    a. price confusion and money illusion.

    b. redistributions of wealth.

    c. a potential breakdown of financial intermediation.

    d. All of the answers are correct.

Answer Key

Answers to Self-Practice Questions

1. $(149 - 134)/134 = 0.11194 \times 100 = 11.194$ percent.

   Topic: Defining and Measuring Inflation

2. Real rate of interest $= 7\% - 6\% = 1\%$.

   Topic: Inflation Redistributes Wealth

3. Volatility in the inflation rate makes it difficult for businesses to get loans because it makes it difficult to predict the rate of inflation in the future. The expected rate of inflation in the future is important for determining the nominal interest rate to charge on loans (as a result of the Fisher effect). Both borrowers and lenders want to make sure that they don't get hurt by unexpected changes in the inflation rate, but making the prediction is difficult when the inflation rate is highly volatile.

   Topic: Inflation Redistributes Wealth

4. Velocity tends to be stable over time and real growth rates in an economy depend on the real factors of production, not the money supply. This leaves only the level of prices to rise when the money supply increases, as can be seen in the $M \times v = P \times Y_R$ relationship when v and Y_R are fixed.

   Topic: The Cause of Inflation

5. It tells us that prices in 1987 are 4.28 times higher than they were in the base year of 1967. In other words, what cost \$1.00 on average, in 1967 would cost \$4.28 in 1987.

   Topic: Price Indexes

6. Zimbabwe, Hungary, and Germany have all experienced serious hyperinflation (see Table 12.2 [29.2] in the text). All episodes of hyperinflation have in common extraordinarily high rates of inflation caused by extraordinarily high rates of money growth.

   Topic: Inflation in the United States and Around the World; The Quantity Theory of Money

7. $(212.174/164.70) \times \$27{,}000 = \$34{,}782.62$.

   Topic: Defining and Measuring Inflation

8. The fall in the price of pocket calculators doesn't mean that the United States has experienced deflation. Pocket calculators are just one item. Inflation and deflation refer to changes in *lots* of prices, not just one price.

   Topic: Defining and Measuring Inflation

9. If velocity is constant, the Quantity of Money Theory implies that Inflation money growth $=$ inflation $+ 3\%$. Price stability requires an inflation rate of zero and inflation will be zero only if money growth $= 3\%$.

   Topic: The Quantity Theory of Money

10. This statement is false. The decline in the inflation rate is referred to as *disinflation*, not deflation. Since the inflation rate is still positive at 3 percent, prices are still rising, albeit at a much slower rate than before.

    Topic: The Cause of Inflation

Answers to Multiple-Choice Questions

1. d, Topic: Defining and Measuring Inflation

2. a, Topic: Defining and Measuring Inflation

3. c, Topic: Price Indexes

4. c, Topic: Price Indexes

5. c, Topic: Inflation Redistributes Wealth

6. d, Topic: Inflation Redistributes Wealth

7. b, Topic: Inflation in the United States and Around the World

8. a, Topic: The Cause of Inflation

9. b, Topic: Appendix: Get Real! An Excellent Adventure

10. a, Topic: The Cause of Inflation

11. c, Topic: The Quantity Theory of Money

12. b, Topic: The Quantity Theory of Money

13. c, Topic: Price Confusion and Money Illusion

14. c, Topic: The Quantity Theory of Money

15. b, Topic: Inflation Redistributes Wealth

16. d, Topic: Inflation Redistributes Wealth

17. c, Topic: Inflation Redistributes Wealth

18. a, Topic: Inflation Redistributes Wealth

19. c, Topic: The Cause of Inflation

20. c, Topic: Inflation Is Painful to Stop

13 (30)

Business Fluctuations: Aggregate Demand and Supply

Learning Objectives

In this chapter, you will learn:

> How to use the AD-AS model.

> How real shocks and demand shocks cause business cycle fluctuations.

Summary

The primary purpose of this chapter is to introduce the *aggregate demand–aggregate supply* (or AD-AS) model. The model is used to explain how business cycle fluctuations occur in the economy. In the end, the model will show that there are two causes of business fluctuations: real shocks and demand shocks. It is important that you learn how to use the AD-AS model because it is used extensively in the remainder of the book.

The AD-AS model consists of three curves: the aggregate demand (AD) curve, the Solow growth curve, and the short-run aggregate supply (SRAS) curve. We will introduce each curve individually and put them together to build the model. Along the way we will see how business fluctuations occur and learn how to analyze the effects of various types of shocks on the economy.

The Aggregate Demand (AD) Curve

Let's begin with the **aggregate demand curve**, which *shows combinations of real growth and inflation for a specified rate of nominal spending growth in the economy.* Take time to read this definition again; it explains exactly what the AD curve shows. First, note that it shows combinations of *real growth* and *inflation*. So, we begin with a graph that measures real GDP growth on the horizontal axis and the inflation rate on the vertical axis. This will be the graph that is used throughout our discussion of the AD-AS model. Second, the AD curve is drawn for a *specified* rate of nominal spending growth. Let's now put these ideas together to graph the AD curve.

Recall the quantity theory of money from Chapter 12, which gives the equation:

$$\vec{M} + \vec{v} = \vec{P} + \vec{Y}_R.$$

Remember that both sides of this equation represent nominal spending growth. Note also that the right-hand side of this equation includes the inflation rate $(\vec{P})$ and real growth $(\vec{Y}_R)$. This is just what we need to draw the AD curve. So, let's specify a rate of nominal spending growth, say 5 percent. Substituting this nominal spending growth rate on the left-hand side of the equation gives:

$$5\% = \vec{P} + \vec{Y}_R.$$

Now, just think about what combinations of $\vec{P}$ and $\vec{Y}_R$ will give this 5 percent spending growth rate. In other words, think $5 + 0$, $1 + 4$, $2 + 3$, etc. When these combinations are graphed, it provides the AD curve for a spending growth rate of 5 percent. This AD curve is shown in Figure 13.3 in the text. Note that when the AD curve is drawn, it is important to indicate the rate of spending growth that was specified.

Now that we know what the AD curve looks like, let's think about what will cause it to shift in the graph. Actually, it's quite easy to see. Since the AD curve is drawn assuming a *specified* rate of spending growth, the curve will shift if that rate of spending growth changes. For example, an increase in spending growth from 5 percent to 7 percent would shift the AD curve to the right, as shown in Figure 13.4 in the text. But let's think about what would cause this to happen. Looking at the previous equation shown, it is clear that a change in either $\vec{M}$ or $\vec{v}$ could cause a change in the spending growth rate. This tells us that either a change in money growth or a change in velocity growth could cause a shift in the AD curve.

Changes in money growth, $\vec{M}$, are straightforward; they are the result of central bank policy. But what causes a change in velocity growth, $\vec{v}$? Remember that the velocity of money measures how quickly money is spent in the economy. So any change in the rate of spending will affect velocity. But how would this occur? We know that there are four categories of spending in the economy: consumption (C), investment (I), government purchases (G), and net exports (NX). Therefore, anything that affects any of these categories of spending will affect velocity and, thus, shift the AD curve. This could include changes in consumer confidence, the business outlook, taxes, consumer wealth, government spending, or changes in exports and imports. Table 13.2 in the text provides a list of factors that will shift AD, and it is important that you are familiar with these factors. Remember that anything that *increases* one of the spending components will shift AD to the *right*. Likewise, *decreases* in spending shift AD to the *left*.

Shifts in the AD curve are called **aggregate demand shocks**. A rightward shift of the AD curve is called a *positive* demand shock, while a leftward shift of the AD curve is a *negative* demand shock.

The Solow Growth Curve

The next curve in our model is called the *Solow growth curve*. This curve shows the economy's *potential* growth rate, also called the **Solow growth rate**. Recall from Chapter 7 that this potential growth rate depends on the existing factors of production (capital, labor, and technology) in the economy. The name "Solow" comes from the economist, Robert Solow, who first proposed the importance of these factors in determining an economy's potential growth rate.

To graph the Solow growth curve in our graph with real growth on the horizontal axis and inflation on the vertical axis, we must think about the relationship between the economy's Solow growth rate and the inflation rate. That turns out to be simple. Since the economy's potential (Solow) growth rate depends on existing factors of production and not on the inflation rate, there is no relationship. Graphically speaking, "no relationship" translates to a *vertical* Solow growth curve. In other words, the Solow growth rate will be the same regardless of the rate of inflation. The Solow growth curve is drawn in Figure 13.5 in the text (assuming a 3 percent Solow growth rate).

Next, let's think about shifts in the Solow growth curve. Again, this turns out to be simple. Any factor that affects the economy's ability to produce goods and services will cause the Solow growth curve to shift. This means any change in the existing factors of production (capital, labor, or technology) will shift the curve. In addition, changes in the supplies of other important resources—such as oil—will shift the curve. Finally, anything that affects the productivity of these resources or the efficiency with which they are used will shift the curve. This might include weather, wars, or government regulations, among other things. Anything that *increases* the economy's productive capability shifts the curve to the *right*; *decreases* in the economy's ability to produce cause a shift to the *left*. Table 13.1 in the text provides a list of factors that shift the Solow growth curve. Again, it is important that you are familiar with these factors.

Shifts in the Solow growth curve are called **real shocks** (or productivity shocks). A rightward shift of the Solow growth curve is called a *positive* real shock, while a leftward shift is a *negative* real shock.

Real Shocks in the AD-AS Model

Now that we have two of the curves in our AD-AS model, let's take a look at how real shocks affect the economy. In particular, we want to consider whether real shocks can cause business cycle fluctuations.

Remember that **business fluctuations** are movements in the economy's real growth rate above and below its trend (long-run average) growth rate. Figure 13.1 in the text shows that there is considerable movement of growth rates around the long-run average of 3.3 percent in the U.S. economy. Can real shocks in our AD-AS model explain this movement?

To answer this question, let's put the AD curve and Solow growth curve together, as shown in Figure 13.6 in the text. It is useful to think of the point at which the two curves intersect as a *long-run equilibrium* in the economy. As with most "equilibrium" situations in economics, this equilibrium is where the economy will end up *once prices have fully adjusted*. The term "long run" is used to describe this equilibrium to remind you that *full price adjustment* has occurred and the economy will remain at this equilibrium until something happens to change it (such as a shift in one of the curves).

The equilibrium determines the economy's real growth rate (on the horizontal axis) and inflation rate (on the vertical axis). Since the Solow growth curve is vertical, the economy's equilibrium growth rate will be the Solow growth rate of 3 percent. Given the Solow growth rate at 3 percent and spending growth at 10 percent, the inflation rate at the equilibrium *must be* 7 percent. (This is because all points on the AD curve must add to 10 percent. So, if growth is 3 percent at the equilibrium, inflation must be 7 percent since 3% + 7% = 10%.)

Now, let's think about how business cycle fluctuations can occur in this graph. Since the Solow growth curve is vertical, the equilibrium growth rate will always be the Solow growth rate, regardless of where the AD curve intersects the Solow growth curve. In other words, demand shocks will not affect the economy's growth rate. The only way for the economy's growth rate to change (that is, for business fluctuations to occur) is for the Solow growth curve itself to shift. That is, a *real* shock must occur. This is shown in Figure 13.7 in the text, where positive and negative real shocks cause the growth rate to fluctuate from −1 percent to 7 percent as the Solow growth curve shifts right and left. Note that a growth rate of −1 percent implies that real GDP is declining and that a **recession** has occurred.

So, we have demonstrated the first source of business fluctuations in the economy: real shocks. The text provides some good examples of how real shocks drive business fluctuations. For example, real shocks caused by droughts in India and oil shocks in the United States are linked to business cycle fluctuations in these countries.

The Short-Run Aggregate Supply (SRAS) Curve

A key implication of the two-curve version of the AD-AS model discussed above is that demand shocks cannot cause business fluctuations; only real shocks matter. This is the reason for introducing the third, and final, curve in our model. But first, a bit of historical context will help to set the stage.

During the Great Depression in the 1930s, the British economist John Maynard Keynes argued that insufficient demand was driving the economy's woes. More specifically, Keynes argued that insufficient demand could cause the economy to become stuck at a rate of growth well below the economy's potential (or Solow) growth rate and remain there for relatively long periods of time. The reason for the economy's sluggishness, Keynes argued, was "sticky wages and prices." Sticky wages and prices mean that wages and prices are *slow to adjust* to their equilibrium following a shock. Note that Keynes never denied the existence of a long-run equilibrium (implying full price adjustment); he simply argued that the price adjustment process might be sufficiently slow to keep the economy away from its long-run equilibrium for long periods of time. Thus, Keynes's famous quote: "In the long run, we're all dead!"

Note that a subtle aspect of the *long-run* equilibrium discussed above is that *full price adjustment* has occurred once the economy reaches this long-run equilibrium. But what if price adjustment is very slow (that is, prices are sticky)? This means the economy will not quickly move to the long-run equilibrium on the Solow growth curve shown in Figure 13.6. Instead, the economy could remain somewhere away from the Solow growth rate for long periods of time. Periods of time during which prices have *not* fully adjusted are called the *short run*.

To understand the performance of the economy in the short run, we need to add the final curve to our AD-AS model. The **short-run aggregate supply (SRAS) curve** *shows the relationship between inflation and real growth when prices are sticky* (in other words, in the short run). It is important to note that the relationship between inflation and real growth in the short run will be a *positive* relationship. That is, increases in inflation will imply an increase in the economy's real growth rate, and vice versa. This positive relationship between inflation and real growth in the short run suggests an *upward-sloping* SRAS curve. Note that this is different from the relationship between inflation and real growth in the long run implied by the Solow growth curve. Recall that the vertical nature of the Solow growth curve implies *no relationship* between inflation and real growth in the long run.

Intuitively, the positive relationship between inflation and real growth in the short run is a result of the economic decisions individuals and businesses make in response to changes in inflation. All such decisions are based on some expectation of inflation. When actual inflation (π) differs from expected inflation (E[π]), individuals and firms respond by changing how hard they work and how much they produce. One possible reason for this behavior is **nominal wage confusion**, which is workers' tendency to respond to nominal wage changes rather than real wage changes when inflation occurs.

To illustrate, suppose expected inflation is E(π) = 3%. If actual inflation is less than 3 percent (that is, π < E[π]), workers will work less and firms will produce less in response to lower than expected wages and prices. As a result, real growth in the economy will be below the Solow rate. This scenario is shown by point A in the following graph. Similarly, when π > E(π) real growth in the economy will exceed the Solow rate, as shown by point C in the graph. Note that such discrepancies between actual and expected inflation can only persist in the short run. In the long run, all unexpected inflation becomes expected (that is, π = E[π]) and real growth will equal the Solow rate (point B in the graph). Together, points A, B, and C provide an upward-sloping relationship between inflation and real growth in the short run. This is the short-run aggregate supply curve.

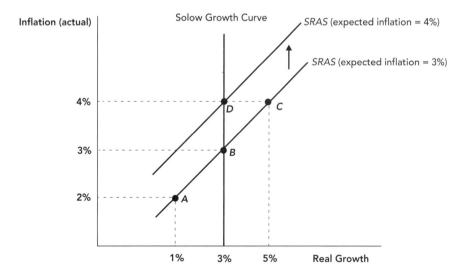

Note that the position of the SRAS curve is "anchored" by the expected rate of inflation (shown as point B in the graph). The anchor point is the point at which SRAS intersects the Solow growth curve, and this point is determined by expected inflation. Thus, the label for the curve indicates the expected rate of inflation. This also makes it easy to see what causes the SRAS curve to shift. When the expected rate of inflation changes, the SRAS curve shifts accordingly. For example, if expected inflation rises from 3 percent to 4 percent, the SRAS curve will shift up and to the left (as the anchor point moves from point B to point D in the graph). It is important to note that changes in *actual* inflation cause *movements along* the SRAS curve in the short run, while changes in *expected* inflation cause *shifts* in the SRAS in the long run.

Finally, notice that the SRAS curves shown in the previous graph are drawn as straight lines. This allowed us to emphasize the upward-slope of the curves. The SRAS curves in the text are drawn with an initially flat slope at low growth rates and an increasingly steep slope at higher growth rates. See Figure 13.11 in the text, for example. This shape makes sense because the SRAS curve should eventually become vertical as the economy approaches its physical growth limit determined by resource and technology growth.

Demand Shocks in the AD-AS Model

Now, with the SRAS curve in hand, we can examine Keynes's notion of short-run equilibrium in response to a demand shock. Begin by combining all three of the curves derived in this chapter in a single graph. Figure 13.11 in the text shows all three curves together. The point at which all three curves intersect is a long-run equilibrium. As before, the long-run equilibrium implies the economy is operating at its potential (or Solow) growth rate following full-price adjustment.

Let's now consider what happens when a demand shock hits the economy. Recall from earlier that there are two sources of demand shocks:

1. changes in money growth ($\vec{M}$) caused by the Fed

2. changes in velocity growth ($\vec{v}$) caused by changes in consumption, investment, government, or net export spending growth

We will look at each of these sources of demand shocks separately since they have a different effect on the economy in the long run. Let's begin with a positive demand shock caused by an increase in money growth. As shown in Figure 13.12 in the text, the increase in money growth shifts the AD curve outward. This causes the economy to move from its initial long-run equilibrium at point a to a *short-run equilibrium* at point b. At the short-run equilibrium, the economy's growth rate has increased to 6 percent. In business cycle terms, the economy is in a "boom" period. Also at point b, the inflation rate has increased to 4 percent. The fact that inflation at 4 percent now exceeds expected inflation at 2 percent is why output growth exceeds the Solow rate in the short run (that is, the economy has moved up along the SRAS curve). To summarize, this short-run equilibrium indicates that positive demand shocks can cause business fluctuations during periods when prices are sticky—just as Keynes suggested.

A short-run equilibrium, however, cannot last forever. Figure 13.13 in the text shows the economy's long-run response to the increase in money growth. Specifically, in the long run, prices will adjust, and unexpected inflation becomes expected. This means the SRAS curve shifts up and to the left until a long-run equilibrium is achieved at point c. This adjustment involves the real growth rate in the economy returning to the Solow growth rate in the long run. The increase in the money supply has one lasting effect, however, since the inflation rate will be higher at the new long-run equilibrium. Thus, money remains "neutral" in the long run, even though it was not neutral in the short run (recall the discussion of monetary "neutrality" from Chapter 12).

The possibility of this type of short-run equilibrium implies that a decrease in money growth would have the opposite effect on the economy, possibly pushing it into a lengthy recession. This possibility is illustrated in Figure 13.14 in the text. Again, it is clear that demand shocks can cause business fluctuations when prices are sticky.

Next, let's look at a negative demand shock caused by a decline in consumer spending (or, equivalently, one of the other spending components). Remember, this type of demand shock shifts the AD curve through a change in velocity growth, $\vec{v}$. The effect is shown in Figure 13.15 in the text. In the short run, the effect is identical to the demand shock caused by a decline in money growth: a recession occurs at point b. The difference with this demand shock, however, is in the economy's long-run response. Instead of the SRAS curve shifting to restore long-run equilibrium, this time the AD curve will eventually shift back to the right to restore long-run equilibrium. The reason for this return shift of the AD curve is that changes in the spending components are likely to be temporary, since growth rates in the components of AD cannot permanently change without affecting the economy's long-run growth rate (which must be the Solow rate). A key implication of this scenario is that inflation rates will return to their original level at point a. This confirms the result obtained in Chapter 12 that sustained increases in inflation require an increase in the rate of money growth (which has not happened here).

Concluding Remarks

The AD-AS model has shown us that there are two sources of business fluctuations: real shocks and demand shocks. In addition, the AD-AS model provides a framework that is useful for demonstrating the effects of various shocks on the economy's growth rate and inflation rate—in both the short run and the long run. As an application to close the chapter, the AD-AS model is used to illustrate the Great Depression. Here, we summarize the major shocks that contributed to the Great Depression and their causes.

Demand Shocks Contributing to the Great Depression
1. A decrease in consumption growth brought about by a stock market crash (which itself may have been brought on by a monetary contraction to burst a stock market bubble) causing the AD curve to shift to the left.

2. A decrease in money growth (actually a decrease in the money supply by more than one-third) brought about by a massive banking panic across the nation.

3. A decrease in investment growth brought about by the uncertain business environment as unemployment rose and consumer confidence fell.

4. A decrease in net export growth brought about by a reduction in world trade resulting from retaliation over the Smoot-Hawley Tariffs.

The effects of these negative demand shocks are shown in Figure 13.16 in the text.

Real Shocks Contributing to the Great Depression (not shown in Figure 13.16)
1. Reduced financial intermediation resulting from bank failures reduced the efficiency of the financial system.

2. Reduced specialization resulting from decreases in world trade reduced the efficiency of resource use.

3. Severe drought associated with the "Dust Bowl" caused a negative productivity shock.

Key Terms

aggregate demand curve a curve that shows all the combinations of inflation and real growth that are consistent with a specified rate of spending growth

aggregate demand shock a rapid and unexpected shift in the AD curve

Solow growth rate the rate of economic growth given the existing real factors of capital, labor, and ideas

real shock (or productivity shock) an increase or decrease in the economy's fundamental ability to produce goods and services and, thus, the Solow growth rate

business fluctuations fluctuations in the growth rate of real GDP around its trend growth rate

recession a significant, widespread decline in real income and employment

short-run aggregate supply (SRAS) curve a curve that shows the positive relationship between inflation and real growth during the period when prices are sticky

nominal wage confusion what occurs when workers respond to their nominal wage instead of their real wage

menu costs the costs of changing prices

Traps, Hints, and Reminders

> The AD-AS model requires the use of graphs and it is crucial that you learn how to use them. The material may seem complex at first, but practice makes perfect. Always draw the AD-AS graph and use it to help you answer questions. Never try to imagine the graph or figure out the answer in your head. The more you use the graph, the easier it will be. The key is to learn how to shift the curves and then read the graph to see the effects of those shifts—or shocks—on the economy.

> Remember that you must be familiar with the factors that will shift the curves in the AD-AS model in order to use it successfully. Take the time to learn these factors along with the direction of the shifts. Causes of real shocks are listed in Table 13.1. Causes of demand shocks are listed in Table 13.2.

> Remember that the terms "long run" and "short run" used in this chapter have very specific meanings. Both relate to the adjustment of prices. The long run is a period of time long enough that prices have *fully* adjusted. The short run is a period of time short enough that prices have *not* fully adjusted (that is, prices are "sticky" in the short run). The length of the short run and long run involves the speed with which price adjustment occurs. If prices are very slow to adjust, the short run could be a *long* time. This is exactly what Keynes argued in the 1930s.

> It follows from the previous point that a *short-run* equilibrium is where the economy will be *before* prices have fully adjusted and a *long-run* equilibrium is where the economy will be *after* prices have fully adjusted. The notion of a

short-run equilibrium follows directly from Keynes's assertion that prices may be sticky, giving rise to an economy that may become stuck (in a short-run equilibrium) far away from its long-run equilibrium for a considerable period of time. In other words, according to Keynes, the short run could be a *long* time.

> There is another useful way to think about the economy's Solow growth rate. It is the growth rate that prevails in the economy *in the long run*—that is, after enough time has passed for prices to *fully adjust*. This means the Solow growth curve is where the economy will end up once prices have fully adjusted—that is, in the long run. Note that if prices adjust quickly, the long run will be a *short* time.

> Remember a concept discussed in Chapter 12: *money is neutral in the long run*. This concept implies that a change in money growth has no effect on the economy's growth rate in the long run. This idea is supported by the AD-AS model since a change in money growth that shifts AD will not affect the economy's growth rate in the long run (once prices have fully adjusted and the economy returns to its Solow growth rate). However, if prices and wages are sticky, changes in money growth will affect the economy's growth rate in the short run. This implies that money will *not* be neutral in the short run.

> Remember that changes in $\vec{M}$ can be permanent while changes in $\vec{v}$ are generally temporary. This means that demand shocks caused by changes in $\vec{M}$ are generally followed by a shift in SRAS to restore long-run equilibrium, while demand shocks caused by changes in $\vec{v}$ are usually followed by a return shift in AD to restore long-run equilibrium. The short-run (business cycle) effects of the two types of shocks are identical.

> In the text, real shocks are shown early in the chapter with only the Solow growth curve and AD curve in the graph. When all three curves are present, a real shock will shift the Solow growth curve, as usual, but the SRAS curve will also shift. Ultimately, the SRAS curve must shift to restore long-run equilibrium on the new Solow growth curve. As always, the shift in SRAS results from the adjustment in expected inflation (as unexpected inflation becomes expected in the long run).

> Sometimes the term "unexpected" inflation is used to describe cases in which π and $E(\pi)$ are different. For example, suppose expected inflation is $E(\pi) = 3\%$. If the Fed unexpectedly increases money growth to shift AD to the right, the actual inflation rate will rise in the short run, say, to $\pi = 4\%$. This increase in actual inflation above expected inflation can be described as "unexpected" inflation; in other words, $\pi > E(\pi)$. The unexpected inflation causes a movement along the SRAS curve in the short run (this is the movement to the short-run equilibrium when AD shifts) and a shift in the SRAS curve in the long run as the unexpected inflation becomes expected (as $E[\pi]$ adjusts to shift SRAS to the left to restore long-run equilibrium). Note that this is exactly the same story shown in Figures 13.12 and 13.13, except that we are now using the term "unexpected" to describe the events in the story. Note that unexpected inflation—that is, π and $E(\pi)$ being different—is a requirement for all short-run equilibrium positions in the AD-AS model. This is why the change in money growth by the Fed must be *unexpected* to have any effect on real growth.

Self-Practice Questions

1. Draw the basic AD-AS diagram for an economy that is in long-run equilibrium. Assume the economy's Solow growth rate is 3 percent and the rate of spending growth is 5 percent. What will the actual (equilibrium) and expected rate of inflation be? Make sure you correctly label the axes and curves in your graph.

2. What are "real" shocks in the context of the AD-AS model? What are some real world events that could cause a real shock to occur?

3. Explain what each of the following variables means: $\vec{M}, \vec{v}, \vec{P}$, and $\vec{Y}_R$.

4. What are "demand" shocks in the context of the AD-AS model? What real world events could cause a demand shock to occur?

5. Why is the Solow growth curve vertical in the AD-AS graph?

6. If the Solow growth rate for an economy is 4 percent and the rate of spending growth is 10 percent, what will the actual (equilibrium) and expected rate of inflation be at long-run equilibrium? Illustrate graphically using an AD-AS graph.

7. Draw two separate AD-AS (side by side) graphs showing long-run equilibrium for an economy. Show how a recession caused by a negative *real* shock would differ from one caused by a negative *demand* shock. Explain your answer.

8. Is it possible for the economy to experience faster growth with lower inflation at the same time? Is this possible even in the long run? Illustrate your answer graphically.

9. The term *stagflation* was used to describe the occurrence of a recession along with high inflation in the mid-1970s. What kind of shock is required to cause stagflation?

10. Use the AD-AS model to show the effect of an unexpected increase in the growth rate of the money supply by the Fed. Explain your answer. Are there any negative effects of this policy?

11. How would your answer to question 10 be different if the increase in money growth had been expected rather than unexpected?

12. Draw a graph that shows the economy in recession as a result of a negative demand shock. How would your graph differ if the demand shock is caused by a change in money growth as opposed to a change in spending growth?

Multiple-Choice Questions

1. The AD-AS model is most useful for explaining what causes
   a. the economy's long-run growth rate.
   b. inflation.
   c. stock market fluctuations.
   d. movements in GDP growth above and below its trend rate.

2. In the AD-AS model, business fluctuations are caused by
   a. aggregate demand shocks.
   b. real shocks.
   c. both demand shocks and real shocks.
   d. neither demand shocks nor real shocks.

3. When drawing the AD-AS graph, what is measured on the vertical axis?
   a. prices
   b. GDP
   c. employment
   d. inflation rate

4. When drawing the AD-AS graph, what is measured on the horizontal axis?
   a. inflation
   b. expected inflation
   c. GDP
   d. GDP growth rate

5. Which of the following would shift the Solow growth curve?
   a. a severe earthquake
   b. expectations
   c. changes in the money supply
   d. animal spirits

6. Which of the following would shift the aggregate demand curve?
   a. a severe hurricane season
   b. new technology
   c. increase in oil supplies
   d. an increase in government purchases

7. The Solow growth curve is vertical because
   a. the Solow growth rate does not depend on inflation.
   b. prices and wages are flexible in the long run.
   c. money is "neutral" in the long run.
   d. All of the answers are correct.

8. The SRAS curve is upward sloping because

   a. labor markets quickly adjust to equilibrium.

   b. wages and prices are fully flexible in the short run.

   c. prices and wages are sticky in the short run.

   d. None of the answers is correct; the SRAS curve is vertical.

9. If nominal spending growth is 5 percent, and the economy is in recession at a −1 percent real growth rate, what is the inflation rate?

   a. 6 percent

   b. 5 percent

   c. 4 percent

   d. There is not enough information to determine the answer.

10. Sticky wages and prices are incorporated in the AD-AS model by the

    a. Solow growth curve.

    b. short-run aggregate supply curve.

    c. aggregate demand curve.

    d. All of the answers are correct.

11. Which of the following scenarios could result in a recession?

    a. Aggregate demand decreases and wages are flexible.

    b. Aggregate demand decreases and wages are sticky.

    c. Aggregate demand increases and wages are flexible.

    d. Aggregate demand increases and wages are sticky.

12. The AD-AS model predicts that unexpected changes in money growth will have an effect on the economy's real growth rate

    a. only in the short run.

    b. only in the long run.

    c. in both the short run and the long run.

    d. in neither the short run nor the long run; money is always neutral.

13. A change in expected inflation causes

    a. a shift of the Solow growth curve.

    b. a movement along the SRAS curve.

    c. a shift of the SRAS curve.

    d. a shift of both the Solow growth curve and the SRAS curve.

14. If the economy is in a recession that has decreased real growth and increased inflation, such a situation would be caused by

    a. an inward shift of the Solow growth curve.

    b. an outward shift of the Solow growth curve.

    c. an inward shift of the aggregate demand curve.

    d. an outward shift of the aggregate demand curve.

15. New technology has an immediate effect on which of these curves?

a. short-run aggregate supply curve

b. aggregate demand curve

c. Solow growth curve

d. None of the answers is correct.

16. The economy's *long-run* response to an unexpected increase in money growth by the Fed involves

a. a shift in the AD curve.

b. a shift in the Solow growth curve.

c. a shift in the SRAS curve.

d. a movement along the SRAS curve.

17. If nominal spending growth equals 6 percent, and the real growth rate equals 4 percent, what is the inflation rate?

a. 4 percent

b. 10 percent

c. 2 percent

d. 2/3 percent

18. If there is a positive demand shock, which of the following scenarios would occur in the *short run*?

a. The inflation rate would increase and real growth would decrease.

b. The inflation rate would increase and real growth would increase.

c. The inflation rate would decrease and real growth would decrease.

d. The inflation rate would decrease and real growth would increase.

19. If fear causes individuals to spend less, and firms to invest less, it would have which of the following effects?

a. AD would shift in.

b. AD would shift out.

c. SRAS would shift in.

d. Solow growth curve would shift in.

20. The Great Depression was the result of

a. neither AD shocks nor real shocks.

b. mostly AD shocks but also some real shocks.

c. AD shocks but not real shocks.

d. real shocks but not AD shocks.

Homework Quiz

1. Business fluctuations refer to

   a. stock market fluctuations.

   b. changes in the inflation rate.

   c. movement of the economy's growth rate around its trend.

   d. All of the answers are correct.

2. Which of the following is an example of a *positive* real shock?

   a. a decrease in oil supplies

   b. a severe drought

   c. an advance in technology

   d. All of the answers are correct.

3. Which of the following is an example of a *negative* demand shock?

   a. a decrease in consumer confidence

   b. a decrease in money growth

   c. a decrease in business investment

   d. All of the answers are correct.

4. The "long run" is a period of time

   a. long enough that prices and wages are "sticky."

   b. long enough that prices and wages are fully flexible.

   c. longer than one year.

   d. longer than three years.

5. If the economy is in long–run equilibrium at a Solow growth rate of 4 percent and a nominal spending growth rate of 5 percent, the expected rate of inflation must be

   a. −1 percent.

   b. 1 percent.

   c. 9 percent.

   d. There is not enough information to determine the answer.

6. The economy's *long-run* response to a decrease in the rate of consumer spending involves

   a. a shift in the AD curve.

   b. a shift in the Solow growth curve.

   c. a shift in the SRAS curve.

   d. None of the answers is correct.

7. What type of shock could be responsible for an increase in growth and a decrease in the inflation rate?

    a. a positive real shock

    b. a positive demand shock

    c. a negative real shock

    d. a negative demand shock

8. An increase in expected inflation from 4 percent to 8 percent causes

    a. the AD curve to shift left.

    b. the AD curve to shift right.

    c. the SRAS curve to shift left.

    d. the SRAS curve to shift right.

9. If there is a negative demand shock, which of the following scenarios would occur in the short run?

    a. a decrease in real growth and an increase in inflation

    b. a decrease in real growth and a decrease in inflation

    c. an increase in real growth and an increase in inflation

    d. an increase in real growth and a decrease in inflation

10. The economy's long-run response to an unexpected increase in money growth involves

    a. an increase in the inflation rate.

    b. an increase in expected inflation.

    c. a return to the Solow growth rate.

    d. All of the answers are correct.

Answer Key

Answers to Self-Practice Questions

1. Your graph should look like Figure 13.11 in the text. The ability to draw the AD-AS graph from memory is important. The equilibrium and expected rate of inflation will be 2 percent. Make sure you indicate the expected rate of inflation in the label for your SRAS curve. Also, make sure you indicate the rate of spending growth in the label for your AD curve.

   Topic: Aggregate Demand Shocks and the Short-Run Aggregate Supply Curve

2. Real shocks are shown in the AD-AS model by a shift of the Solow growth curve. Recall that when the Solow growth curve shifts, in the full model, however, so does SRAS. Ultimately, SRAS must shift to establish a new long-run equilibrium on the new Solow growth curve (as shown in the following graph). Anything that affects the economy's ability to produce goods and services will cause a real shock. Some examples would be changes in technology, education, population, or other important resources (such as oil supplies). Also, drought (or other large-scale weather events), earthquakes (or other major natural disasters), or war could cause real shocks.

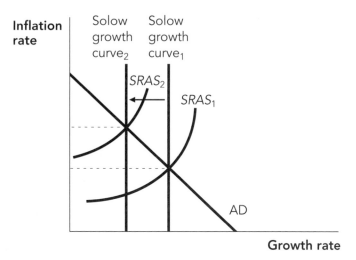

   Topic: The Solow Growth Curve

3. $\overrightarrow{M}$ is the rate of money growth; $\vec{v}$ is the rate of velocity growth; $\overrightarrow{P}$ is the rate of price growth or inflation; and $\overrightarrow{Y_R}$ is the rate of real GDP growth.

   Topic: The Dynamic Aggregate Demand Curve

4. Demand shocks are shown in the AD-AS model by a shift of the AD curve. Events that could cause a demand shock are changes in money growth by the Fed or changes in velocity growth. Changes in velocity growth result from changes in the rates of spending by consumers, businesses, and government, or net exports. Thus, any factor that affects these categories of spending (such as confidence, wealth, uncertainty, taxes, etc.) could cause a demand shock.

   Topic: The Dynamic Aggregate Demand Curve

5. The vertical nature of the Solow growth curve shows that there is no relationship between inflation and real growth in the economy in the long run. In other words, money (which ultimately drives inflation) is "neutral" in the long run. This means that money does not help produce goods and services in the economy. Instead, the economy's potential or "Solow" growth rate is determined by the existing resouces such as labor, capital, and technology.

Topic: The Solow Growth Curve

6. With a Solow growth rate of 4 percent and spending growth at 10 percent, the actual (equilibrium) and expected rate of inflation will be 6 percent at long-run equilibrium.

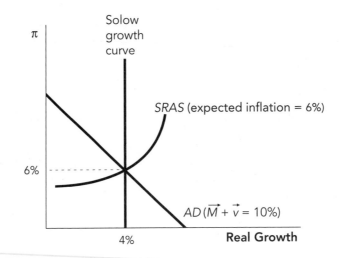

Topic: Aggregate Demand Shocks and the Short–Run Aggregate Supply Curve

7. See the following graphs. New curves are in bold. Notice that when the Solow growth curve shifts inward the inflation rate increases, but when the aggregate demand curve shifts inward the inflation rate decreases.

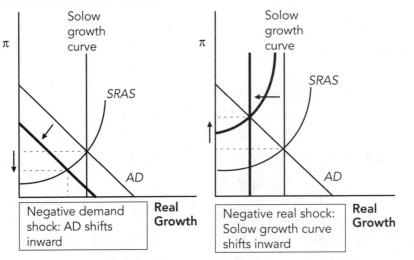

Topic: Real Shocks; Aggregate Demands Shocks and the Short–Run Aggregate Supply Curve

8.

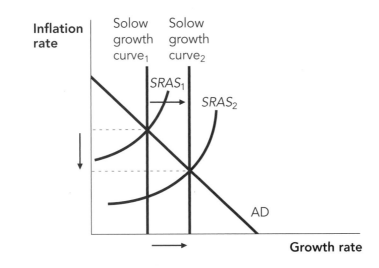

Yes, faster growth and lower inflation would be the result of a positive real shock. This effect is shown in the graph provided. Since a new long-run equilibrium occurs on the new Solow growth curve, this effect can last even in the long run if the new Solow growth curve remains in its new position.

Topic: Real Shocks

9. Only a negative real shock can cause a recession accompanied by higher inflation. See the following graph. Recall that a recession caused by a negative demand shock will result in lower inflation. See question 7.

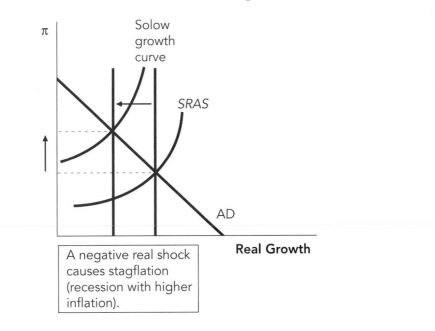

A negative real shock causes stagflation (recession with higher inflation).

Topic: Real Shocks

10. The unexpected increase in money growth will shift AD to the right. This causes a "boom" in the economy in the short run (point *b*). While a boom may seem like a good thing, it also causes higher inflation. In the long run, SRAS shifts and the economy returns to its Solow growth rate (point *c*). But inflation is even higher at the new long-run equilibrium. Thus, a negative effect of the policy is the higher inflation it causes in the economy.

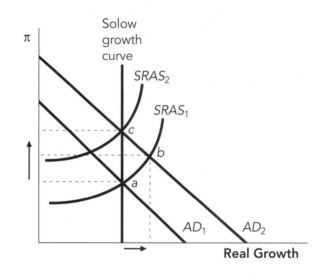

Topic: Real Growth

11. The same graph from question 10 can be used here. If the change in money growth is expected, the economy immediately moves from its initial long-run equilibrium (point *a*) directly to the new long-run equilibrium (point *c*). This is because an expected increase in money growth causes expected inflation to rise *immediately*, so SRAS shifts along with AD when the increase in money growth occurs. There will be no short-run equilibrium (point *b*). This means there is no boom in the short run, but the economy will still experience higher inflation as a result of this policy.

Topic: Aggregate Demand Shocks and Real Shocks

12. The negative demand shock will push the economy into recession at point *b*, regardless of whether the shock is caused by a change in money growth or velocity (spending) growth. But in the long run, there will be different effects depending on the cause of the shock. If the shock is the result of a change in money growth, SRAS will shift right to restore Solow growth at point *c* (and a lower inflation rate). If the shock is a result of a change in velocity growth, the AD curve will shift back to the right to restore long-run equilibrium at point *a* (and the initial inflation rate).

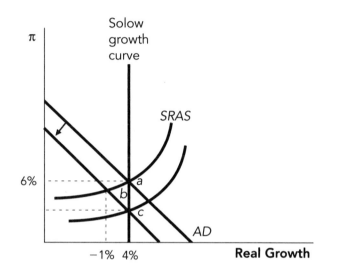

Topic: Aggregate Demand Shocks and the Short-Run Aggregate Supply Curve

Answers to Multiple-Choice Questions

1. d, Topic: Introduction

2. c, Topic: Introduction

3. d, Topic: The Dynamic Aggregate Demand Curve

4. d, Topic: The Dynamic Aggregate Demand Curve

5. a, Topic: The Solow Growth Curve

6. d, Topic: Shocks to the Components of Aggregate Demand

7. d, Topic: The Solow Growth Curve

8. c, Topic: Aggregate Demand Shocks and the Short-Run Aggregate Supply Curve

9. a, Topic: The Dynamic Aggregate Demand Curve

10. b, Topic: Aggregate Demand Shocks and the Short-Run Aggregate Supply Curve

11. b, Topic: Aggregate Demand Shocks and the Short-Run Aggregate Supply Curve

12. a, Topic: Aggregate Demand Shocks and the Short-Run Aggregate Supply Curve

13. c, Topic: Aggregate Demand Shocks and the Short-Run Aggregate Supply Curve

14. a, Topic: Shifts in the Solow Growth Curve

15. c, Topic: Shifts in the Solow Growth Curve

16. c, Topic: Aggregate Demand Shocks and the Short-Run Aggregate Supply Curve

17. c, Topic: The Dynamic Aggregate Demand Curve

18. b, Topic: Aggregate Demand Shocks and the Short-Run Aggregate Supply Curve

19. a, Topic: Shocks to the Components of Aggregate Demand

20. b, Topic: Understanding the Great Depression: Aggregate Demand Shocks and Real Shocks

14 (31)

Transmission and Amplification Mechanisms

Learning Objectives

In this chapter, you will learn:

> How transmission mechanisms can turn small, isolated shocks into larger, economy-wide business cycles

> How real shocks and demand shocks can interact with one another—that is, how one type of shock can lead to the other

Summary

The focus of this chapter is to explain how small shocks whose effects are seemingly limited to specific sectors of the economy can spread to produce larger events that affect the broader economy—therefore causing business cycle effects. The economic forces that amplify shocks and spread them across time and sectors of the economy are called *transmission mechanisms*. This chapter discusses five transmission mechanisms:

1. Intertemporal substitution

2. Uncertainty and irreversible investments

3. Labor adjustment costs

4. Time bunching

5. Collateral damage from shocks to net worth

In addition to amplifying and transmitting the initial shocks that hit the economy, transmission mechanisms can cause important interactions between real and demand shocks. That is, one type of shock can lead to the other. Let's now take a look at each of these transmission mechanisms in more detail.

Intertemporal substitution refers to individuals' decisions about how to allocate consumption, work, and leisure across time to maximize well-being. Generally, people choose to work when the reward for work is the greatest and, alternatively, choose to enjoy leisure time or engage in other non-work activities when the opportunity cost of that time (i.e., the reward for work) is the lowest. For example, during times of severe drought, farmers may choose to devote less time to work in the fields and more time to leisure, since the reward for working the fields is lower. This means output will not only be lower because of the drought's direct effect on the productivity of the land, but also because farmers spend less time working the land. Thus, the initial effects of the negative productivity shock are magnified by workers' subsequent decisions to work less. In terms of the AD-AS model introduced in the previous chapter, this effect causes larger shifts in the Solow growth curve, as shown in Figure 14.3 in the text.

Uncertainty and irreversible investments refer to the effects shocks—especially negative shocks—have on investment decisions. Uncertainty refers to people's tendency to rethink how the world works following shocks. This uncertainty causes businesses to hold off on investment spending. In addition, many investment projects are *irreversible*. This means that, once completed, the investment is only productive for its current use and it cannot be undone and re-invested for other uses in a productive manner. Because of this, investors tend to hold off on investment until they are certain the environment is such that the project will pay off. Note that investment—or business spending—affects the AD curve. Thus, this transmission mechanism provides a channel through which negative real shocks (by causing uncertainty) can be amplified through subsequent shifts in the AD curve (as investment spending declines as a result of the uncertainty).

Labor adjustment costs are the costs of shifting workers from declining sectors of the economy to growing sectors. Because of these costs and the difficulties in making rational decisions about relocating to new areas and new industries, people often hold off on making the move. Such delays can result in longer periods of high unemployment and low output in the economy, thus drawing out the negative effects of an initial shock over time.

Time bunching refers to the tendency for similar economic activities to be coordinated at common points in time. In other words, it is generally more efficient if a person chooses to invest, produce, or sell at the same time as other people are investing, producing, or selling. This phenomenon can spread the effects of shocks across other sectors of the economy. For example, if a negative shock reduces farm productivity and farmers spend less time in the fields (as a result of intertemporal substitution explained above), then it is also likely that tractor salesmen, seed vendors, and fertilizer suppliers will also work less at the same time.

Collateral damage refers to secondary economic problems that result from negative shocks to equity or net worth. (Recall from Chapter 9 that **equity** or net worth is the value of an asset minus the debt associated with that asset.) Because of collateral damage, a real shock that initially reduces asset values or wealth in one part of the economy can be spread to other parts of the economy through subsequent demand shocks. The initial decline in wealth lowers equity. Lower equity, in turn, increases economic risk and decreases the ability of individuals or businesses to adjust to changing circumstances. This causes reductions in consumer spending, bank lending and borrowing, and business investment—all of which amounts to a negative demand shock that exacerbates the effect of the initial shock. An example of collateral damage is the reluctance of banks to make loans to businesses in an uncertain economic environment (that is, during a recession). The restricted credit environment reduces investment (business spending) and makes the recession worse. Note that this effect also provides a channel through which an initial shock on the supply side (real shock) can be followed by a demand shock.

Key Terms

intertemporal substitution individuals' choices about how to allocate consumption of goods, work, and leisure across time to maximize well-being

irreversible investments investments that have high value only under specific conditions and cannot be easily moved, adjusted, or reversed if conditions change

labor adjustment costs the costs of shifting workers from declining sectors of the economy to growing sectors

time bunching the tendency for economic activities to be coordinated at common points in time

equity the value of an asset minus the debt associated with it, $E = V - D$

collateral damage secondary economic problems that result from negative shocks to equity or net worth

Traps, Hints, and Reminders

> Remember that this chapter builds on the previous chapter, where we learned that real shocks (shifts in the Solow growth curve) and demand shocks (shifts in the AD curve) were the key sources of business cycle activity in the economy. This chapter shows how small, isolated shocks that hit the economy can be amplified and transmitted across the economy to cause business cycle effects.

> Remember that there are three types of effects that transmission mechanisms can have on the initial shocks that hit the economy. They can (1) amplify the size of a shock (make small shocks have larger effects); (2) transmit the effect of a shock across space and time (move the effect of a shock to other parts of the economy and to other time periods); and (3) cause interactions between real and demand shocks (so that one type of shock causes the other).

> Intertemporal substitution and time bunching are closely related and can be easily confused. Remember that intertemporal substitution refers to *individual* decisions about when to engage in certain activities, where the decision is based on the reward for that activity. Time bunching refers to the tendency for large *groups* of people to coordinate their decisions about when to engage in certain activities, where the decision is based on coordinating the activity with others. The confusion between intertemporal substitution and time bunching occurs because the grouping that occurs with time bunching is based on higher rewards associated with grouping behavior. In other words, both mechanisms involve higher rewards for engaging in activities at certain times. Remember, if

the decision involves coordinating activities with other groups, it is generally interpreted to be time bunching. If it is an individual decision that does not involve others, it is intertemporal substitution.

> Collateral damage caused by a negative shock to equity is similar to the effects of uncertainty on irreversible investment. Recall that uncertainty causes postponement of investment projects because adjustment costs (the cost of un-doing the investment) are too large when the investment is irreversible. Thus, an initial real shock that causes uncertainty can cause a subsequent demand shock by affecting investment. An equity shock has a similar type of effect on the economy. This is because the equity shock initially causes uncertainty and increases adjustment costs which, in turn, cause negative demand effects through declines in consumer spending, bank lending or borrowing, and business investment. Thus, the effect of the initial (equity) shock is exacerbated through subsequent demand-side shocks.

Self-Practice Questions

1. What do economists mean by transmission mechanisms?

2. Do transmission mechanisms make business cycle fluctuations more or less severe? Explain.

3. What are the five transmission mechanisms?

4. College enrollments tend to increase during recessions. This is an example of which transmission mechanism? Explain.

5. Government policy often encourages home ownership in the United States, but owning a home can often make it more difficult to relocate to take a new job, especially during a recession. This is an example of which transmission mechanism? Explain.

6. It is well known that the Christmas holiday causes a seasonal economic fluctuation. This effect is an example of which transmission mechanism(s)? Explain.

7. Explain how irreversible investment can cause an initial real shock to result in a secondary demand shock.

8. If there is a negative shock to the economy that adversely affects some industries more than others, which transmission mechanism will be most likely to come into play?

9. Explain the role that banks play in transmitting economic fluctuations following a shock to asset prices or net worth.

10. How is the collateral damage caused by a negative shock to net worth similar to the effects of irreversible investments as a transmission mechanism?

Multiple-Choice Questions

1. Transmission mechanisms

    a. transfer shocks to other countries around the world.

    b. reduce the impact of shocks on the economy.

    c. make business cycle fluctuations more severe.

    d. All of the answers are correct.

2. Which of the following is a list of the transmission mechanisms?

    a. intertemporal substitution, collateral damage, production costs, irreversible investments

    b. labor adjustment costs, intertemporal substitution, collateral damage, irreversible investments, time bunching

    c. monetary shocks, intertemporal substitution, flexible wages and prices, production costs, and irreversible investment

    d. collateral damage, intertemporal investment, sticky prices and wages, time bunching, and labor adjustment costs

3. With transmission mechanisms present, the effect of a negative real shock on the economy will be

    a. stronger than without a transmission mechanism.

    b. weaker than without a transmission mechanism.

    c. the same with or without a transmission mechanism.

    d. weakened by some transmission mechanisms but strengthened by others.

4. Everyone working at the same time is an example of which mechanism?

    a. labor adjustment costs

    b. time bunching

    c. irreversible investments

    d. intertemporal substitution

5. Bartenders wanting to work the Friday and Saturday evening shifts is an example of which transmission mechanism?

    a. intertemporal substitution

    b. irreversible investments

    c. sticky wages and prices

    d. time bunching

6. After Hurricane Katrina hit New Orleans and the Gulf Coast, many homeowners waited to rebuild their houses until new building code rules had been enacted. This is an example of which mechanism?

    a. labor adjustment costs

    b. intertemporal substitution

    c. sticky wages and prices

    d. uncertain/irreversible investments

7. If in 2020, interstellar space travel becomes possible and the crab/fish population in Alaska dies out, workers will need to move from Alaska to Sioux Falls, SD (the headquarters of space travel). Which transmission mechanism is likely to have the largest effect on the Alaskan economy as a result of these developments?

a. labor market adjustment costs

b. intertemporal substitution

c. irreversible investments

d. time bunching

8. Now that you are in college, your mom is thinking of going from part-time work to full-time work outside the home. Which mechanism is at work when she considers whether there have been positive or negative shocks to the economy recently?

a. labor market adjustment costs

b. intertemporal substitution

c. irreversible investments

d. time bunching

9. In 2013, the L.A. Clippers (a basketball team) win back-to-back championships. You and your friends decide to have one giant blowout to celebrate all on one day instead of having a very tiny celebration every day for the rest of year. This would be an example of

a. labor market adjustment costs.

b. intertemporal substitution.

c. irreversible investments.

d. time bunching.

10. Transmission mechanisms affect the economy by

a. magnifying the impact of shocks.

b. transferring the impact of shocks across different sectors of the economy and across time.

c. causing interactions between real and demand shocks (so that one type of shock can cause the other).

d. All of the answers are correct.

11. What is the difference between time bunching and intertemporal substitution?

   a. Time bunching is your decision to invest or work at the same time as other people. Intertemporal substitution is your decision to work when the gains from working are highest.

   b. Intertemporal substitution is your decision to invest or work at the same time as other people. Time bunching is your decision to work when the gains from working are highest.

   c. Time bunching is when individuals don't move to better positions because it is costly to do so. Intertemporal substitution is when people change their behavior because investments are irreversible.

   d. Intertemporal substitution is when people are afraid to invest, while time bunching is when people want to work harder when the returns to working are highest.

12. Collateral damage refers to the negative effects from

   a. high asset prices.

   b. negative shocks to equity or net worth.

   c. everyone trying to do things at the same time.

   d. engaging in an irreversible investment.

13. Falling home prices caused a decline in bank lending during the recent recession. This is an example of

   a. time bunching.

   b. irreversible investment.

   c. collateral damage.

   d. intertemporal substitution.

14. The amount of equity an owner has in an asset will decrease if

   a. the debt on the asset falls.

   b. the price of the asset rises.

   c. the price of the asset falls.

   d. the interest rate falls.

15. Imagine that there is a negative shock to the economy that causes businesses to be especially uncertain about the future. Which curve is affected by this new uncertainty?

   a. short-run aggregate supply

   b. aggregate demand

   c. Solow growth curve

   d. All of the answers are correct.

Homework Quiz

1. Which of the following is NOT a transmission mechanism?

a. collateral damage from shocks to net worth

b. sticky prices and wages

c. intertemporal substitution

d. labor adjustment costs

2. Transmission mechanisms can cause

a. small shocks to have large effects on the economy.

b. large shocks to have small effects on the economy.

c. shocks to spread to other countries around the world.

d. All of the answers are correct.

3. John is a sales associate at a retail store. The store pays "time and a half" (or 1.5 times the regular hourly wage) to all associates who work on Sundays. John volunteers to work every Sunday. This is an example of

a. labor adjustment costs.

b. sticky wages.

c. intertemporal substitution.

d. time bunching.

4. Christmas tree farmers tend to work very long hours during the months of October through December. This is an example of

a. labor adjustment costs.

b. sticky wages.

c. intertemporal substitution.

d. time bunching.

5. Uncertainty has a large impact on investment because most investment is

a. irreversible.

b. sensitive to changes in interest rates.

c. based on long-term decisions.

d. None of the answers is correct.

6. Raju was laid off from his job as a skilled carpenter in Orlando. He's thinking about moving to Charlotte where he has a job offer from a construction company, but he's unsure if it will be worth the cost of the move. This is an example of

a. time bunching.

b. intertemporal substitution.

c. labor adjustment costs.

d. collateral damage.

7. Many farmers take their vacations in the winter. This is an example of
   a. time bunching.
   b. intertemporal substitution.
   c. labor adjustment costs.
   d. collateral damage.

8. Malik is planning to work more hours selling ice cream at the beach in August than in November. This is an example of
   a. time bunching.
   b. intertemporal substitution.
   c. labor adjustment costs.
   d. collateral damage.

9. The willingness of banks to lend is an important part of which transmission mechanism?
   a. time bunching
   b. intertemporal substitution
   c. labor adjustment costs
   d. collateral damage

10. Because of the nature of investment, a positive real shock that decreases business uncertainty about the future is likely to also cause
   a. a negative real shock.
   b. a negative demand shock.
   c. a positive demand shock.
   d. an even larger positive real shock.

Answer Key

Answers to Self-Practice Questions

1. Transmission mechanisms are forces that spread the effect of a shock throughout the economy and magnify the effect of the shock.

   Topic: Introduction

2. Transmission mechanisms make economic fluctuations more severe by making negative shocks worse and positive shocks better. They can also make fluctuations more severe by spreading the effects of shocks to parts of the economy not directly affected by an initial shock and by making the effects of shocks last longer through time.

   Topic: Introduction

3. The five transmission mechanisms are collateral damage from shocks to net worth, labor adjustment costs, intertemporal substitution, time bunching, and irreversible investment.

   Topic: Introduction

4. The increase in college enrollments during a recession is an example of intertemporal substitution. More people decide to go to college during recessions because jobs are hard to find and the opportunity cost of going to college (in terms of lost wages and income) is lower during times of recession.

   Topic: Intertemporal Substitution

5. It can be difficult to sell a home without incurring a large financial loss during a recession. This can make the decision to relocate very costly during a recession, thus preventing the unemployed from moving to accept new job opportunities. This is an example of labor adjustment costs.

   Topic: Labor Adjustment Costs

6. Seasonal fluctuations are similar to regular business cycle fluctuations. December is a boom and January is a bust. This seasonal effect is a result of both intertemporal substitution and time bunching. Individuals and businesses work harder leading up to the Christmas season because their goods and services are more likely to sell during Christmas than January. Spending more time working when it is more profitable is an example of intertemporal substitution. But people also are involved in time bunching by doing their shopping when the largest variety is available.

   Topic: Intertemporal Substitution; Time Bunching

7. Recognizing the effect of uncertainty is the key to understanding how irreversible investment affects business fluctuations. An initial real shock which slows the economy causes uncertainty about the profitability of investment projects. Because many investments are irreversible (cannot be undone or converted to other uses), businesses will postpone investment spending until the uncertainty is resolved and it is clear the investment will be profitable. This postponement of investment projects following the initial real shock causes a secondary demand shock through the reduction in investment spending. The secondary demand shock further weakens the economy.

   Topic: Uncertainty and Irreversible Investments

8. If there is a negative shock to the economy that adversely affects some industries more than others, labor adjustment costs are most likely to affect the economy because in this case workers need to move from the most affected industry to other industries.

   Topic: Labor Adjustment Costs

9. During booms, asset prices and net worth rises. This increases cash flows and makes banks more likely to give loans. Increased borrowing supports more consumer spending and business investment, therefore reinforcing the boom. During recessions, the process works in reverse and banks make fewer loans, thereby making the recession worse. This is an example of collateral damage caused by an initial shock to net worth.

   Topic: Collateral Damage

10. Collateral damage following a shock to net worth is similar to the effects of irreversible investment because both of these transmission mechanisms are driven largely by uncertainty. Negative shocks to net worth increase uncertainty about the ability of individuals and businesses to repay loans. Banks reduce their willingness to lend which reduces consumer and business spending, thus causing a negative demand shock that exacerbates the effect of the initial shock. Similarly, irreversible investments cause a secondary demand shock (via a reduction in investment) when uncertainty is present.

    Topic: Collateral Damage

Answers to Multiple-Choice Questions

1. c, Topic: Introduction

2. b, Topic: Introduction

3. a, Topic: Introduction

4. b, Topic: Time Bunching

5. d, Topic: Time Bunching

6. d, Topic: Uncertainty and Irreversible Investments

7. a, Topic: Labor Adjustment Costs

8. b, Topic: Intertemporal Substitution

9. d, Topic: Time Bunching

10. d, Topic: Introduction

11. a, Topic: Time Bunching; Intertemporal Substitution

12. b, Topic: Collateral Damage

13. c, Topic: Collateral Damage

14. c, Topic: Collateral Damage

15. b, Topic: Uncertainty and Irreversible Investments

political influence. Along with long terms for the Governors, this makes it difficult for elected politicians to control the Fed.

Let's now turn to the Fed's role in controlling the nation's money supply.

How Money Is Created in the Economy

The Fed plays a key role in creating money in the economy because of its unique ability to issue money. But even with this powerful ability, the Fed's control of the money supply is not complete. This is because there are others that play a role in determining the nation's money supply, namely commercial banks and the public. Let's see how the Fed, commercial banks, and the public unwittingly work together to create money in the economy.

The Fed's ability to create money is often described as "printing money," although in reality the Fed usually creates money electronically—without a printing press—by increasing the amount of money in the accounts it holds for its commercial bank customers. The funds commercial banks hold with the Fed are called *reserves* and the accounts in which they are held are called *reserve accounts*. Commercial banks are required by law to hold a certain amount of reserves. The Fed's infusion of funds directly into a bank's reserve account is just the first step in the money creation process. To understand the rest of the story, we must look at how banks use these funds.

The amount of reserves a bank holds is expressed as a share of its customers' *deposits* into the bank. This share of reserves to deposits is called the **reserve ratio**. In other words, the reserve ratio is RR = reserves/deposits. For example, if 10 cents of every dollar a customer deposits is held in reserves, the reserve ratio is 0.1. But it is the money *not* held in reserves that is important in understanding how money is created in the economy. This is because banks generally *loan out* the portion of customer deposits not held in reserves. That is, if 10 cents of every dollar in deposits is held as reserves, the other 90 cents is available for loans. This type of banking system, where banks hold a portion of customer deposits as reserves and loan out the rest, is called a **fractional reserve banking** system.

When a bank makes a loan, it is just as if that bank has created new money. This is because the money that is loaned will generally end up being redeposited in another bank (perhaps after being spent to buy a house, a car, to build a new business, etc.). Remember, bank deposits are "money" so the new deposit is like new money. Once re-deposited, the bank will keep 10 cents of every dollar in reserves and loan out the other 90 cents. And the process is repeated when this new loan is redeposited. With each new loan there is another new deposit, and then another new loan, and so on. The only thing that eventually stops the process is that each new loan is smaller than the one before (because 10 percent of every new deposit is held as reserves, thus making the next loan only 90 percent of the previous one). Eventually, the loan amount will reach zero and the process stops.

After round after round after round of loans and new deposits are made, how much new money (deposits) will have been created? The answer can be determined by the following equation:

$$\Delta MS = \Delta \text{Reserves} \times MM.$$

This equation says that the change in the money supply (amount of new deposits created) equals the initial change in reserves by the Fed multiplied by the **money multiplier**. The money multiplier is the amount of money created for each dollar increase in reserves. The money multiplier (MM) is related to the reserve ratio (RR) as follows:

$$MM = \frac{1}{RR}.$$

So, if the Fed electronically injects $1,000 of new reserves into the reserve account of a commercial bank and the reserve ratio is 0.1, the amount of new money created in the economy (after round after round of loans and new deposits) will be:

$$\$1,000 \times \frac{1}{0.1} = \$1,000 \times 10 = \$10,000.$$

A more detailed description of the money multiplier process is provided in the Appendix to this chapter in the text.

How the Fed Controls the Money Supply

Now that we have a general idea of how money is created in the economy, we can take a closer look at how the Fed controls the money supply. The Fed uses three tools to control the money supply:

1. Open market operations

2. Discount rate lending and the Term Auction Facility

3. Paying interest on reserves held by banks at the Fed

Open Market Operations

Earlier, we described how the Fed could electronically increase the amount of reserves held by a commercial bank in its reserve account at the Fed. This was the initial increase in reserves that started the whole process that resulted in multiple rounds of bank loans and new deposits in the banking system—the so-called money multiplier process—that ultimately increased the money supply by some multiple of the initial increase in reserves. But how does the Fed decide how to accomplish the initial increase in reserves to get this process started?

The initial increase in reserves is not a random act by the Fed. Instead, the Fed deliberately buys U.S. government bonds. To pay for its bond purchases, the Fed increases the reserves of the bank or bond dealer who sold the bonds. This bond purchase by the Fed is called an **open market operation**. More specifically, in this case, an open market *purchase* has occurred. Remember that open market purchases *increase* reserves in the banking system to get the money multiplier process started.

The Fed can also use open market operations to remove reserves from the banking system. To accomplish this, the Fed *sells* bonds from its huge portfolio of securities. This operation is called an open market *sale*. The bank or securities dealer who buys the bonds from the Fed must pay for them, so the Fed reduces their reserve account to facilitate the payment. So, the open market sale *decreases* the reserves in the banking system, causing the money multiplier process to work in reverse as banks reduce loans.

The Fed's use of open market operations allows it to control short-term interest rates. This can be seen, first, by recognizing that the Fed usually buys and sells short-term government bonds to carry out its open market operations. The buying and selling of short-term bonds directly affects short-term interest rates on these bonds (see Chapter 9 for more on the relationship between bond prices and interest rates). Further, the Fed is able to use its open market operations to control the **federal funds rate**, which is the interest rate at which commercial banks loan money to each other overnight. Since open market operations affect the amount of reserves in the banking system, they affect the supply and demand of reserves that banks use for these overnight loans to each other. If the Fed wants to control longer-term interest rates, it sometimes purchases or sells longer-term government securities, a process called **quantitative easing** (for purchases) or **quantitative tightening** (for sales).

Discount Rate Loans and the Term Auction Facility

The Fed can also increase reserves in the banking system by loaning money to commercial banks. These loans are called *discount loans* and the interest rate charged by the Fed is the **discount rate**. The Fed sets the discount rate and allows banks to borrow. These discount loans have the same effect of increasing reserves in the banking system as open market operations. However, discount rate borrowing is not used nearly as extensively by the Fed as open market operations. Banks are often reluctant to borrow from the Fed, fearing it may be a sign of weakness at the bank. For this reason, commercial banks usually borrow from one another at the federal funds rate in normal times.

The Fed's willingness to loan to commercial banks in times of need gives rise to another important role of the central bank—namely as a **lender of last resort**. In this role, the Fed is able guard against what is called **systemic risk**, which is the risk that the failure of one financial institution will bring down other institutions.

During the financial crisis of 2007-08, the Fed initiated a new loan program called the *Term Auction Facility*. It is similar to discount rate lending, except that the Fed announces the amount it wishes to loan and continues to lower the interest rate on those loans (in a sort of auction) until it reaches that amount of lending. With traditional discount rate lending, the Fed simply sets the discount rate and allows banks to decide how much to borrow (and often that amount is small as discussed above).

Paying Interest on Reserves

The Fed began paying interest on reserves commercial banks hold in their reserve accounts in 2008. Previously, reserves earned no interest and banks generally tried to lend out most of their reserves. This caused problems for the Fed at times when it wanted banks to have more reserves on hand (and make fewer loans). By paying interest on reserves and varying the rate of interest, the Fed can influence banks' holdings of reserves and, thus, the money supply in the economy.

Concluding Remarks

While much has been said about the Fed and its control of the money supply, it is important to remember the big picture. The Fed's ultimate goal in controlling the money supply is to influence the economy by shifting the aggregate demand (AD) curve. Changes in the money supply shift AD when increases in the money supply and lower interest rates cause an increase in borrowing for consumption and investment spending. But there is much uncertainty in this process. The Fed's control of the money supply (M1 and M2) is uncertain because it is unclear how much banks will loan and how much the public will want to borrow. It is also uncertain how much interest rates and spending will respond to changes in the money supply. And, it is unclear how long it will take for changes in the money supply to translate into a shift in AD. These issues of monetary policy will be discussed in more detail in the next chapter.

Key Terms

money a widely accepted means of payment

liquid asset an asset that can be used for payments or, quickly and without loss of value, be converted into an asset that can be used for payments

fractional reserve banking when banks hold only a fraction of deposits in reserve, lending the rest

reserve ratio, RR, the ratio of reserves to deposits

money multiplier, MM, the amount the money supply expands with each dollar increase in reserves. $MM = 1/RR$

Federal Funds rate the overnight lending rate from one major bank to another

quantitative easing when the Fed buys longer-term government bonds or other securities

quantitative tightening when the Fed sells longer-term government bonds or other securities

open market operations occur when the Fed buys and sells government bonds

discount rate the interest rate banks pay when they borrow directly from the Fed

lender of last resort the Fed's role in lending money to banks and other financial institutions when no one else will

solvency crisis the crisis that occurs when banks become insolvent

insolvent bank when a bank has liabilities that are greater than its assets

liquidity crisis the crisis that occurs when banks are illiquid

illiquid bank when a bank has short-term liabilities that are greater than its short-term assets but overall has assets that are greater than its liabilities

systemic risk the risk that the failure of one financial institution can bring down other institutions as well

moral hazard situation that occurs when banks and other financial institutions take on too much risk, hoping that the Fed and regulators will later bail them out

Traps, Hints, and Reminders

> There is a lot of new vocabulary in this chapter. Be sure you are familiar with the new terms.

> Note that the Fed has perfect control over the monetary base, but not the money supply. Recall that the monetary base is currency plus bank reserves. Since the Fed issues currency and can directly inject reserves into the banking system, their control over the monetary base is certain. However, their control over broader measures of the money supply, such as M1 and M2, is not perfect. Commercial banks (by making loans) and the public (by depositing money into banks and borrowing) play are large role in determining these measures of the money supply.

> Make sure you understand the money creation process from start to finish. It begins when the Fed increases reserves in the commercial banking system (this can be accomplished using open market operations or discount loans). Once the reserves appear in the banking system, the next part of the money creation process begins as banks begin loaning the new funds. With each loan, funds are redeposited elsewhere in the banking system, causing yet another loan to occur, and so on. In the end, the new deposits represent new money in the economy and the amount of new deposits will be multiple times the initial increase in reserves by the Fed. This is called the money multiplier process.

> Practice problems using the money supply equation: $\Delta MS = \Delta \text{Reserves} \times MM$. Remember that $MM = 1/RR$. This means, for example, that a reserve ratio (RR) of 0.2 implies a money multiplier (MM) of $1/0.2 = 5$. A money multiplier of 5 implies that an injection of \$1 million in new reserves by the Fed will increase the money supply by \$5 million in the end.

> When calculating the money multiplier (MM), remember to use the reserve ratio (RR) in decimal form. For example, if banks are holding 10 percent of deposits in reserves so that RR is 0.1, use 0.1 in the formula for the money multiplier to obtain $MM = 1/0.1 = 10$.

> Do not be misled by the name "federal funds" rate. Federal funds are funds loaned from one commercial bank to another in overnight loans. The funds do *not* come from the Fed. Loans from the Fed to commercial banks are called discount loans and the interest rate on them is called the discount rate.

> It may be helpful to draw a supply and demand diagram of the market for Federal funds. The federal funds rate is shown on the vertical axis. Equilibrium in this market determines the Federal funds rate (FFR$\star$ in the figure that follows).

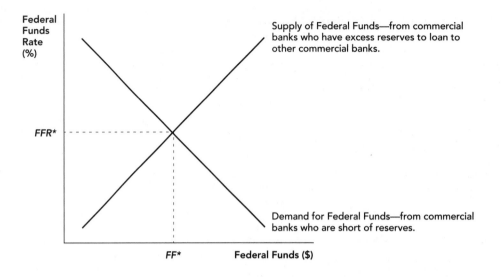

> The diagram of the federal funds market can be used to illustrate how the Fed is able to influence short-term interest rates (such as the federal funds rate) by using open market operations. For example, an open market purchase pushes the federal funds rate down, as shown in the following figure.

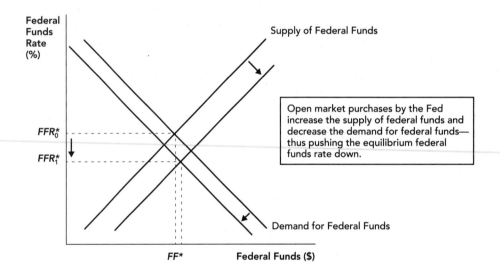

> Remember that there are two types of open market operations: purchases and sales. It may be useful to draw silly pictures such as the following to help you remember how open market operations affect the money supply in the economy. The key to understanding the effect on the money supply is to remember which way the money is flowing.

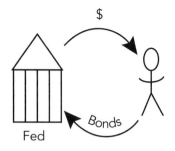

Open market purchases: The Fed buys bonds and issues new money to pay for them. This *increases* reserves in the banking system and ultimately the money supply.

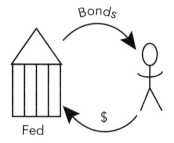

Open market sales: The Fed sells bonds and receives money as payment. This *decreases* reserves in the banking system and ultimately the money supply.

Self-Practice Questions

1. What is the central bank in the United States, what is its primary function, and how does it carry out this function?

2. What three measures of the money supply are discussed in this chapter?

3. How is money created *directly* by the Fed?

4. How is money created *indirectly* by fractional reserve banking?

5. We often think of the Fed as controlling the money supply. Explain how the Fed, in reality, controls only a small part of the money supply.

6. If the Federal Reserve credits your account with an extra $10,000 and banks have a reserve ratio of 0.05, how much will the money supply increase? Show your work.

7. Explain how an open market purchase by the Fed causes lower interest rates in the economy.

8. What is systemic risk and how does the Fed deal with it?

9. What does it mean that a central bank is independent? What makes the Fed independent?

10. Why doesn't the Fed know how much money will be created through the money multiplier process?

Multiple-Choice Questions

1. Which of the following can create money?
   a. the U.S. Congress
   b. the Federal Reserve System
   c. the U.S. Department of the Treasury
   d. All of the answers are correct.

2. Which of the following is a function of the Federal Reserve?
   a. taking deposits from the public
   b. making loans to the public
   c. taking deposits from commercial banks
   d. All of the answers are correct.

3. Of the following means of payment which is *most* liquid?
   a. currency
   b. checkable deposits
   c. savings deposits
   d. money market mutual funds

4. The M1 measure of the money supply includes
   a. currency only
   b. currency and savings deposits
   c. currency and checkable deposits
   d. currency and bank reserves

5. Which of the following is the largest or broadest measure of the money supply?
   a. monetary base
   b. M1
   c. M2
   d. None of the answers is correct.

6. Credit cards are counted in which definition of money?
   a. monetary base
   b. M1
   c. M2
   d. None of the answers is correct.

7. The Fed has the most control over which measure of the money supply?
   a. M1
   b. M2
   c. monetary base
   d. checking deposits

8. In a fractional reserve banking system, the reserve ratio will be
   a. equal to 1.
   b. greater than 1.
   c. less than 1.
   d. equal to 0.

9. The money multiplier process refers to changes in the money supply that come
   a. directly from the Fed.
   b. directly from the Treasury.
   c. directly from printing new currency.
   d. indirectly from commercial bank loans.

10. If banks are holding 100 percent of deposits in reserves, the money multiplier will be
    a. 0.
    b. 1.
    c. 10.
    d. 100.

11. If $1,000 of new reserves issued directly by the Fed results in a $5,000 increase in the money supply, the reserve ratio must be
    a. 0.05.
    b. 0.1.
    c. 0.2.
    d. 1.

12. If the Fed buys $100,000 worth of U.S. government bonds and the reserve ratio is 0.1, how much will the money supply increase?
    a. $10,000
    b. $90,000
    c. $1,000,000
    d. None of the answers is correct.

13. What is the Federal Funds rate?
    a. the interest rate the government pays to borrow money from the public
    b. the interest rate people pay to borrow money from the government
    c. the rate banks pay to borrow money from the Fed
    d. the rate banks pay to borrow money from each other overnight

14. How is the discount rate set?

    a. It is set by a majority vote among commercial banks.

    b. It is determined by the supply and demand of funds in the commercial banking system.

    c. It is simply announced by the Treasury.

    d. It is simply announced by the Fed.

15. If the Fed wishes to *decrease* the money supply, it could

    a. conduct open market purchases.

    b. decrease the discount rate.

    c. increase the interest rate it pays on reserves held by commercial banks.

    d. All of the answers are correct.

16. The Term Auction Facility was designed to

    a. encourage banks to borrow money from the Fed.

    b. bail out Chrysler and GM.

    c. discourage banks from borrowing from one another.

    d. discourage banks from borrowing money from the Fed.

17. Systemic risk is

    a. the risk that one financial institution's failure will lead to many other institutions failing.

    b. the risk that your bank will become illiquid just because of a rumor.

    c. the risk that your bank will make risky loans knowing that depositors will be repaid with FDIC money.

    d. the risk that aggregate demand will collapse.

18. Which of the following is likely to *increase* the Federal Funds rate?

    a. open market purchases

    b. open market sales

    c. a decrease in the discount rate

    d. a decrease in the interest rate the Fed pays on bank reserves

19. The Fed's control of the money multiplier process is incomplete because

    a. it does not know how many loans banks will want to make.

    b. it does not know how much currency the public will deposit into the banking system.

    c. it does not know how many loans the public will demand.

    d. All of the answers are correct.

20. The members of the Board of Governors of the Federal Reserve System hold terms that are

    a. four years long and renewable.

    b. four years long and nonrenewable.

    c. 14 years long and renewable.

    d. 14 years long and nonrenewable.

Homework Quiz

1. Which of the following is a function of the Federal Reserve System?

    a. loaning money to commercial banks

    b. maintaining deposit accounts for the U.S. Treasury

    c. maintaining reserve accounts for commercial banks

    d. All of the answers are correct.

2. Which of the following is included in the monetary base?

    a. currency only

    b. currency and total bank deposits

    c. currency and total bank reserves

    d. currency and checkable deposits

3. Which of the following is likely to be the *least* liquid asset?

    a. a famous Renoir painting stolen from an art museum

    b. checkable deposits

    c. currency

    d. gold

4. If the reserve ratio is 1, then

    a. banks loan out all of their deposits.

    b. banks loan out none of their deposits.

    c. banks hold no reserves.

    d. banks will make some loans and hold some reserves.

5. If banks are holding 50 percent of deposits in reserves, the money multiplier will be:

    a. 0.5.

    b. 2.

    c. 20.

    d. 50.

6. If the Fed wishes to increase the money supply by $1 million and the reserve ratio in the banking system is 0.2, they would need to conduct

   a. open market sales of $50,000.

   b. open market sales of $200,000.

   c. open market purchases of $50,000.

   d. open market purchases of $200,000.

7. The discount rate is

   a. the interest rate on loans from the Fed to commercial banks.

   b. the interest rate on overnight loans between commercial banks.

   c. the interest rate on loans from the Fed to the Treasury.

   d. the interest rate the Fed pays commercial banks for reserves.

8. If the Fed wishes to *increase* the money supply, it could

   a. conduct open market sales.

   b. decrease the discount rate.

   c. increase the interest rate it pays on reserves held by commercial banks.

   d. All of the answers are correct.

9. Which of the following moves by the Fed would *decrease* the Federal Funds rate?

   a. open market purchases

   b. a decrease in the discount rate

   c. a decrease in the interest rate paid on bank reserves

   d. All of the answers are correct.

10. An increase in the money supply by the Fed is intended to

   a. decrease interest rates.

   b. increase business and consumer spending.

   c. increase aggregate demand.

   d. All of the answers are correct.

Answer Key

Answers to Self-Practice Questions

1. The U.S. central bank is the Federal Reserve System. Its primary function is to control the money supply in the U.S. economy. It affects the money supply by carrying out open market operations, making discount rate loans, and paying interest on reserves it holds for commercial banks.

   Topic: What Is the Federal Reserve System?; How the Fed Controls the Money Supply

2. The three measures of the money supply are the monetary base, M1, and M2. The monetary base is currency plus total bank reserves held at the Fed. M1 is currency plus checkable deposits. M2 is M1 plus savings deposits, money market mutual funds, and small-time deposits.

   Topic: The U.S. Money Supplies

3. Money is created *directly* by the Fed when it increases reserves in the banking system. These new reserves are used to pay for government bonds purchased by the Fed in its open market purchases, thus injecting money directly into the economy.

   Topic: How the Fed Controls the Money Supply

4. Money is created *indirectly* through fractional reserve banking when banks make loans. Bank loans lead to spending (to buy new cars, houses, etc.) and the money is usually redeposited elsewhere in the banking system. This redeposit results in additional loans, spending, and redeposits, and so on. In this way, an initial infusion of reserves by the Fed can cause the money supply to increase by many times more than the amount of the initial infusion. This is known as the money multiplier process.

   Topic: Fractional Reserve Banking, the Reserve Ratio, and the Money Multiplier

5. The Fed directly controls the monetary base (currency plus bank reserves) only. Other components of the money supply, however, are controlled by commercial banks' willingness to make loans and the public's willingness to deposit funds into banks and borrow from banks.

   Topic: The U.S. Money Supplies

6. If the Fed increases your account by $10,000, you might spend every penny of it. But as long as the money eventually ends up as deposits in banks, they will lend most of it out. In particular, a reserve ratio of 5 percent implies that banks will hold 5 percent in reserves and loan out the rest. The money supply equation can be used to calculate how much money will ultimately be created through loans in the banking system:

   $$\$10,000 \times 1/RR = \$10,000 \times 1/.05 = \$10,000 \times 20 = \$200,000$$

   Topic: Fractional Reserve Banking, the Reserve Ratio, and the Money Multiplier

7. When the Fed buys bonds, it increases the demand for bonds, which pushes up the price of bonds, thus lowering the interest rate. (Remember from Chapter 9 that bond prices and interest rates are inversely related.) In addition, the open market purchase increases reserves in the banking system. This increases the supply of federal funds nd pushes the federal funds rate down. A lower federal funds rate allows banks to borrow reserves and make loans at lower interest rates. The graph of the federal funds market shown in the "Traps, Hints, and Reminders" section is useful for illustrating this effect.

   Topic: Open Market Operations and Interest Rates

8. Systemic risk is the risk that failure of one financial institution will cause other financial institutions to fail, causing a domino effect of failures in the financial system. The Fed is able to guard against systemic risk by acting as a lender of last resort—by lending to troubled institutions when no one else will. For example, banks can borrow from the Fed through discount loans or from the Term Auction Facility.

   Topic: The Federal Reserve and Systemic Risk

9. Economists think of the Fed as independent because it is not closely controlled by politicians. Being independent means, for example, that the Fed can't easily be pressured inot increasing the money supply just before an election. This independence is achieved in several ways. Members of the Board of Governors have long terms that outlast those of the President. In addition, the Fed funds itself through profits it earns from its banking and other financial operations. This means the Fed is free from Congressional budgetary control and does not need to carry favor with Congress or the President in order to get funding for its operations.

   Topic: Who Controls the Fed?

10. The uncertainty arises because the Fed doesn't know how much money banks will hold in reserves (as opposed to loaning out money), how much money the public will continue to deposit in banks, and how many loans the public (consumers and businesses) will want to borrow from banks.

    Topic: Fractional Reserve Banking, the Reserve Ratio, and the Money Multiplier

Answers to Multiple-Choice Questions

1. b, Topic: What Is the Federal Reserve System?

2. c, Topic: What Is the Federal Reserve System?

3. a, Topic: The U.S. Money Supplies

4. c, Topic: The U.S. Money Supplies

5. c, Topic: The U.S. Money Supplies

6. d, Topic: The U.S. Money Supplies

7. c, Topic: How the Fed Controls the Money Supply

8. c, Topic: Fractional Reserve Banking, the Reserve Ratio, and the Money Multiplier

9. d, Topic: Fractional Reserve Banking, the Reserve Ratio, and the Money Multiplier

10. b, Topic: Fractional Reserve Banking, the Reserve Ratio, and the Money Multiplier

11. c, Topic: Fractional Reserve Banking, the Reserve Ratio, and the Money Multiplier

12. c, Topic: Fractional Reserve Banking, the Reserve Ratio, and the Money Multiplier

13. d, Topic: How the Fed Controls the Money Supply

14. d, Topic: How the Fed Controls the Money Supply

15. c, Topic: How the Fed Controls the Money Supply

16. a, Topic: How the Fed Controls the Money Supply

17. a, Topic: The Federal Reserve and Systemic Risk

18. b, Topic: How the Fed Controls the Money Supply

19. d, Topic: Revisiting Aggregate Demand and Monetary Policy

20. d, Topic: Who Controls the Fed?

16 (33)

Monetary Policy

Learning Objectives

In this chapter, you will learn:

> How monetary policy works in the "best-case" scenario
> About some problems that complicate the use of monetary policy—and their implications
> How a commitment to low inflation complicates monetary policy
> How a real shock puts the Fed in a difficult position

Summary

Monetary policy refers to changes in the money supply by the Federal Reserve in an attempt to stabilize business cycle fluctuations. This chapter explains how monetary policy works and identifies some problems that make it difficult to use in practice. The AD-AS model is used extensively in this discussion, so it is important that you are familiar with the material presented in Chapter 13. This chapter ignores the administrative issues related to how the Fed carries out monetary policy (these are discussed in Chapter 15).

Monetary Policy in the Best-Case Scenario

Monetary policy involves the appropriate adjustment of the money supply by the Fed in response to an AD shock. Consider the Fed's response to a negative demand shock, as shown in Figure 16.1 in the text. The initial demand shock shifts AD to the left, pushing the economy into recession at point *b*. If the Fed can respond with sufficient speed and precision, it can shift the AD curve back to the right to move the economy back to point *a*, thus ending the recession. Note that the appropriate policy in this case is an *increase* in the growth rate of the money supply. The use of policy in this direction—to shift AD to the *right*—is called *expansionary* monetary policy. (The use of policy in the opposite direction—to shift AD to the *left*—would be called *contractionary* monetary policy.)

Note two important points about this best-case use of monetary policy. First, the advantage of using policy is not the recovery itself, but the *speed* of the recovery. The economy will eventually recover from the recession even if the Fed does not use policy. Recall the discussion of the economy's long-run response to demand shocks in Chapter 13. Since AD shocks caused by a change in private spending are generally temporary, AD will recover and the economy will eventually return to point *a on its own* in the long run. Thus, the advantage of using policy is getting the economy out of recession *quicker* than by doing nothing.

The second important point regarding the best-case scenario is that the initial shock that causes the recession must occur from the demand side. Only shifts in AD set the stage for the best-case scenario because monetary policy works through shifts in the AD curve. This allows policy in response to AD shocks to "undo" the initial shock without causing other complicating factors. Later, we will see that the use of monetary policy in response to real shocks is considerably more complicated.

Timing and Precision Problems Plague the Use of Policy

The use of monetary policy as demonstrated in Figure 16.1 assumes the Fed is able to act quickly and precisely. There are a number of real-world problems, however, that make this outcome difficult to achieve. Two problems are listed in the text. Here, we break the second problem into three parts and discuss.

Problems that Make Monetary Policy Difficult to Carry Out Effectively

1. The Fed must operate in real time while much of the data about the current state of the economy are unknown.

2. The Fed's control of monetary policy is incomplete and subject to uncertain lags:
   a. The Fed's control of the money supply is incomplete.
   b. The impact of changes in money growth on AD is uncertain.
   c. It takes time for changes in money growth to shift AD.

Looking at Figure 16.1, it is clear what the Fed *needs* to do. With the economy in recession at point *b*, the Fed needs to increase AD to achieve a recovery at point *a*. But what if we did not know the exact position of the economy? Then it becomes much harder to carry out the perfect policy. It's like turning the lights out in the Fed's board room and asking them to make policy decisions in the dark. This is the reality the Fed faces due to delays in obtaining accurate data on the current state of the economy. For instance, GDP data are first released about a month after the end of each quarter. Then, that figure is revised—sometimes substantially—about a month after the first estimate and again about a month after that. It is conceivable that a recession could be underway with little conclusive evidence until three to six months after the fact. This delay is sometimes referred to as the *recognition lag*. The recognition lag means the Fed will have to make policy decisions "in the dark" or wait for more conclusive data to arrive. This, of course, makes it harder for the Fed to get the precision and timing of its policy just right.

The second problem with using monetary policy is that the Fed's control of the money supply is incomplete. Recall from Chapter 15 that the Fed only directly controls the monetary base. Measures of the money supply, such as M1 or M2, ultimately depend on how many loans commercial banks are willing to make and on the public's willingness to take on such loans (or even deposit currency in banks in the first place). This uncertainty makes it difficult for the Fed to get the precision of its policy just right.

Even if the Fed's control of the money supply were complete, uncertainty would remain regarding the impact of monetary policy on the economy. The chain of events through which changes in the money supply ultimately affect AD—called the *transmission mechanism* of monetary policy—includes at least the following steps: changes in money growth → changes in interest rates → changes in consumption and investment spending → shift in AD. Since the cause and effect relationships at each step of this process are uncertain, the impact of monetary policy changes on the economy is uncertain.

Finally, it takes time for changes in monetary policy to be transmitted to the economy. The lag between monetary policy changes at the Fed and their impact on the economy is estimated to be between 6 and 18 months, and this lag varies from one occurrence of policy to another, making the exact length of the lag impossible to predict. This delay in policy's effect is sometimes called the *effectiveness lag*. Again, this makes it difficult to get the timing of policy just right.

How Policy Problems Affect Policy Outcomes

To summarize, all of these problems make it difficult for the Fed to get the timing and/or precision of monetary policy just right. So what impact does this have on policy outcomes? Figure 16.2 in the text demonstrates how imprecise policy can result in too much or too little policy, causing policy to over- or undershoot the desired Solow growth rate at point *a*. Next, we will see how such overshooting could lead to higher inflation and put the Fed in a difficult position down the road.

To demonstrate the potential impact of timing problems with the use of policy, consider the graph below. The graph shows the movement of real GDP as the economy enters a recession, which begins at time t_0. Because of the recognition lag, the recession is not recognized until t_1. Then, even if policy is implemented quickly after t_1, it does not impact the economy until t_2 because of the effectiveness lag. When the policy actually hits the economy, the stimulus causes the economy (which has already recovered from the recession) to overheat more than would be the case without the policy. Thus, the use of policy increases business cycle volatility rather than decreases it.

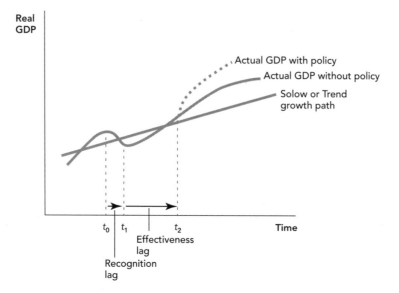

Of course, this does not prove that policy will always make business fluctuations more severe, but it shows that increased volatility is possible, especially in cases in which the recession is relatively mild and short-lived. Because of the potential for policy to increase business cycle volatility, many Fed critics argue that monetary policy should be carried out using "rules" rather than "discretion." In other words, critics agree the Fed should always follow a set rule—such as a constant 2 percent money growth rate—instead of actively manipulating monetary policy in response to business fluctuations.

Additional discussion of the type of damage that can occur when the Fed's timing and/or precision is off is discussed toward the end of this chapter in the text (see the section "When the Fed Does Too Much"). It explains how the Fed may have kept interest rates too low for too long following the 2001 recession, thus contributing to a housing bubble that set the stage for the 2007–2009 recession. Although there is still debate over the Fed's role in this instance, the mere possibility illustrates the potential for ill-timed or imprecise policy to make business fluctuations worse rather than better.

A Commitment to Low Inflation Complicates Monetary Policy

So far, we have focused on the Fed's goal of stabilizing business fluctuations (keeping the economy's growth rate as close to the Solow rate as possible). Sometimes, however, the Fed is concerned about another goal: keeping inflation low and stable. Price stability is often regarded as a central objective of monetary policy because inflation is ultimately caused by excessive money growth (as discussed in Chapter 12). This means the Fed is the government agency best suited to keep inflation under control. Unfortunately, a commitment to price stability in the long run is often in conflict with the Fed's desire to influence real growth in the short run. This conflict can put the Fed in the position of having to make some very difficult choices.

Consider the overshooting that resulted from the imprecise policy in Figure 16.2. This overshooting causes the economy to "overheat" with higher inflation at point *d*, as shown in the following graph. Even worse, if higher inflation expectations become set in, SRAS will shift left in the long run. The result is even higher inflation at point *e*. Since inflation carries its own problems for an economy (see the discussion in Chapter 12 for details), it is generally viewed as a problem to avoid. So, the Fed decides to pursue a policy to reduce inflation—often called a **disinflation** policy. The policy required to reduce inflation is a decrease in the growth rate of the money supply. Since this is a contractionary monetary policy, it will shift AD to the left. The economy moves to point *f* in the short run. While the policy is successful at reducing inflation, it also pushes the economy into recession. In other words, the desire to achieve lower inflation puts the Fed in the difficult position of having to choose between continuing with high inflation or risking a recession to reduce it.

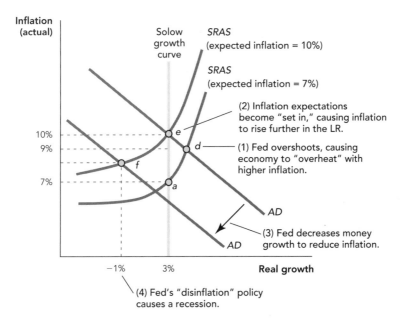

To avoid such policymaking dilemmas, the Fed often speaks forcefully about its commitment to low inflation, so as to keep inflation *expectations* from getting out of hand. The Fed's commitment to a given policy and its willingness to act in defense of that commitment is referred to as the Fed's **credibility**. Credibility can also be described as the Fed's willingness to "stick to its policy." Credibility is essential in keeping inflation expectations under control and avoiding policy dilemmas like the one described above. A real-world example of this type of policy dilemma is the disinflation of the early 1980s orchestrated by Paul Volcker as Fed chairman, as discussed in the text.

Real Shocks Complicate Monetary Policy

Another instance that highlights the conflict between achieving business cycle stability and price stability is the case of an adverse real shock. An example is a sharp decrease in oil supplies that shifts the Solow growth curve and SRAS curve to the left, as shown in Figures 16.3 and 16.4 in the text. The economy falls into recession at point *b* following the oil shock. Note that inflation is also higher at point *b*, causing the double problem of recession and inflation at the same time—a condition sometimes referred to as *stagflation*. The dilemma for the Fed is whether to focus on reducing inflation or fighting the recession.

In Figure 16.3, the Fed focuses on fighting inflation. This requires contractionary monetary policy, which shifts the AD curve to the left. This moves the economy to point *c*. While the policy is successful in reducing inflation, it makes the recession worse. In Figure 16.4, the Fed focuses on fighting the recession. This requires expansionary monetary policy, which shifts AD to the right. With a move to point *c*, the policy alleviates the recession somewhat, but results in a much higher inflation rate. Even worse, if higher inflation expectations become set in, SRAS will shift left, pushing inflation even higher. In summary, the Fed once again finds itself in a difficult position with no good policy options available.

Concluding Remarks

This chapter in the text concludes with a discussion of whether or not monetary policy could or should be used to deflate asset price bubbles—such as the housing price bubble that formed in the mid-2000s. There are two basic problems with using monetary policy in this way. First, it is hard to recognize when a bubble is forming. After all, if everyone knew it was a bubble, it would not continue to form or would deflate on its own. Therefore, it is hard to recognize *when* such a policy is needed until it's too late. Second, it is hard to use monetary policy to pinpoint specific markets like housing. Monetary policy impacts the broader economy. So, using contractionary policy to deflate a bubble in a specific market—even if successful—would come at the cost of slower growth across the entire economy.

Key Terms

disinflation a significant reduction in the rate of inflation

deflation a decrease in prices, that is, a negative inflation rate

credible refers to a monetary policy in which it is expected that a central bank will stick with its policy

market confidence acts as one of the Federal Reserve's most powerful tools in its influence over expectations, not its influence over the money supply

Traps, Hints, and Reminders

> The ideas in this chapter are not terribly difficult as long as you are comfortable working with the AD-AS model presented in Chapter 13. It may be useful to review this material. Remember that monetary policy works by shifting the AD curve. Expansionary policy (an increase in money growth) shifts AD to the *right* while contractionary policy (a decrease in money growth) shifts AD to the *left*.

> The discussion of inflation expectations becoming "set in" simply refers to the adjustments in expected inflation, $E(\pi)$, that shift SRAS to restore long-run equilibrium in the AD-AS model (as discussed in Chapter 13). This adjustment is important in this chapter because an increase in expected inflation causes higher (actual) inflation and, thus, presents a new problem for the Fed to deal

with. This is why the Fed is often viewed as trying to keep inflation *expectations* under control. This is where the Fed's *credibility* comes into play. If everyone *believes* the Fed will not allow inflation to get out of control, expected inflation will remain low. This, in turn, helps to keep actual inflation low.

> Do not confuse the terms "disinflation" and "deflation." They mean completely different things. Disinflation refers to a decrease in the inflation rate. Deflation, on the other hand, refers to a decrease in prices (which implies a negative inflation rate). In other words, deflation is the opposite of inflation (since it implies falling prices instead of rsising prices) while disinflation is a decrease in the rate of inflation. Even with disinflation, the economy will continue to experience inflation as long as the inflation rate is positive. Only when the inflation rate becomes negative will deflation occur.

Self-Practice Questions

1. Why is it hard for the Fed to get monetary policy "just right?"

2. Draw a graph that shows the economy operating above its Solow growth rate due to a positive demand shock. What type of policy should the Fed use to stabilize the economy? Illustrate this policy in your graph, assuming the Fed gets the policy just right.

3. If the economy as a whole is in a recession due to decreased demand, what type of policy should the Fed pursue to end the recession? Illustrate graphically. How might the Fed make a mistake in trying to fix things? Show the potential impact of these mistakes in your graph.

4. Explain the role of "expectations" and "credibility" in monetary policy.

5. Explain what happens if there is a negative real shock to the economy and the Fed tries to stimulate the economy. Illustrate graphically. Would the outcome be different if the Fed instead decided to try to keep inflation low?

6. How does the policy shown in question #2 impact the Fed's desire to keep inflation low?

7. In question #2, suppose the Fed had NOT used monetary policy. How would the decision NOT to use policy affect the Fed's desire to keep inflation low?

8. Why would it have been hard for Alan Greenspan to pop the real estate bubble that began to form in the mid-2000s?

9. What is a "disinflation" policy? What dilemma does it present for the Fed?

10. Draw an AD-AS graph that shows an economy operating at its Solow growth rate with 10 percent inflation. Explain the dilemma the Fed faces if it concentrates on trying to reduce inflation to one percent. Illustrate the use of this policy graphically.

Multiple-Choice Questions

1. Monetary policy affects the economy by shifting the

a. AD curve.

b. SRAS curve.

c. Solow growth curve.

d. None of the answers is correct.

2. Imagine that consumers borrow and spend less, thus shifting the AD curve inward. Which of the following is the best response by the Fed?

a. increase the discount rate

b. increase the rate of money growth

c. increase the interest rate

d. increase the federal funds rate

3. Why it is difficult for the Fed to shift the aggregate demand curve by just the right amount following a demand shock?

a. The Fed's control of the money supply is incomplete.

b. The Fed's control of the AD curve is uncertain.

c. The Fed's control of bank lending and borrowing is incomplete.

d. All of the answers are correct.

4. Why is it difficult to get the timing of monetary policy just right?

a. Congress must approve all monetary policy changes and this takes time.

b. It takes time to collect accurate data on the current state of the economy.

c. The President must approve monetary policy changes and this takes time.

d. All of the answers are correct.

5. What does it mean to say that the Fed has "overshot" with its use of policy?

a. The Fed shifted the AD curve too much.

b. The Fed asked for more policy than Congress would approve.

c. The Fed caused the Solow growth curve to shift to the right.

d. The Fed shifted the SRAS too much.

6. If the Fed overshoots, what will be the effect?

a. The economy will have a higher than desirable inflation rate, and a growth rate that is high but unsustainable in the long run.

b. The economy will experience disinflation.

c. The economy will fall into recession.

d. Stagflation will occur.

7. If the Fed doesn't shift the AD curve out enough, what will be the effect?

   a. Interest rates will be too low.

   b. Growth will be below the Solow rate.

   c. Unemployment will be too low.

   d. Inflation will be too high.

8. If the Fed makes lots of mistakes with monetary policy, what will be the result?

   a. more business cycle volatility

   b. less GDP volatility

   c. more price stability

   d. All of the answers are correct.

9. If the economy is hit by a negative real shock and the Fed tries to boost growth, what effect will monetary policy have?

   a. It will cause higher unemployment.

   b. It will cause higher inflation.

   c. It will cause higher interest rates.

   d. All of the answers are correct.

10. If monetary policy intended to stabilize the economy mostly leads to higher inflation and not to more output, that means the recession is most likely caused by a

    a. negative demand shock.

    b. positive demand shock.

    c. negative real shock.

    d. positive real shock.

11. If the economy is hit by a negative real shock and the Fed tries to reduce inflation, what will be the effect of monetary policy?

    a. It will reduce growth further.

    b. It will cause higher unemployment.

    c. It will delay recovery from recession.

    d. All of the answers are correct.

12. If the Fed wishes to reduce the inflation rate in the economy, it would need to

    a. increase money growth.

    b. decrease money growth.

    c. decrease interest rates.

    d. encourage more bank lending.

13. A policy to reduce inflation presents a dilemma for the Fed because

    a. the President will rarely support such a policy.

    b. it will cause the economy to overheat and grow faster than the Solow rate.

    c. it will reduce the economy's growth rate and possibly cause a recession.

    d. None of the answers is correct.

14. The Fed's "credibility" is important when it tries to reduce inflation because

　a. Congress rarely believes the Fed is serious about reducing inflation.

　b. "expected" inflation must decline in order for the policy to be successful.

　c. inflation will increase before it begins to decline.

　d. All of the answers are correct.

15. The Fed rarely tries to deflate asset price bubbles because

　a. it is hard to know when a bubble has formed until it is too late.

　b. it is hard to target monetary policy to affect specific markets.

　c. using monetary policy to burst bubbles would negatively affect the entire economy.

　d. All of the answers are correct.

Homework Quiz

1. Monetary policy is carried out by

　a. the President.

　b. Congress and the President.

　c. the Treasury.

　d. the Federal Reserve.

2. Which of the following would be an appropriate monetary policy following a positive demand shock that increases the economy's growth rate above the Solow rate?

　a. a decrease in money growth

　b. an increase in money growth

　c. an increase in taxes

　d. a decrease in government spending

3. Which of the following makes it difficult to get the timing of monetary policy just right?

　a. The Treasury is often slow to carry out monetary policy changes.

　b. Congressional and presidential approval of policy changes is often slow.

　c. It takes 6–18 months for policy changes to affect the economy.

　d. All of the answers are correct.

4. A potential problem with Fed "overshooting" is

　a. recession.

　b. higher inflation.

　c. high unemployment.

　d. All of the answers are correct.

5. A problem with using monetary policy in response to a negative real shock is
   a. the policy has only a limited effect on growth.
   b. the policy causes higher inflation.
   c. the policy may cause inflation expectations to increase.
   d. All of the answers are correct.

6. A dilemma the Fed faces with the use of monetary policy is that
   a. increasing growth causes higher interest rates.
   b. decreasing unemployment causes higher interest rates.
   c. reducing inflation causes slower growth (and possibly a recession).
   d. reducing growth causes higher inflation.

7. A policy to reduce inflation is called
   a. a disinflation policy.
   b. expansionary policy.
   c. fiscal policy.
   d. foreign exchange intervention.

8. In order to achieve a sustainable reduction in inflation
   a. interest rates must be increased.
   b. money growth must be increased.
   c. the Solow growth rate must increase.
   d. inflation expectations must decline.

9. In order to reduce inflation expectations, the Fed must
   a. decrease interest rates.
   b. increase bank lending.
   c. have a credible policy.
   d. focus on preventing a recession in the economy.

10. Which of the following makes it difficult to get monetary policy just right?
    a. It takes time to get accurate data on the current state of the economy.
    b. The Fed's control of the money supply is incomplete.
    c. Monetary policy's impact on the AD curve is uncertain and it takes time.
    d. All of the answers are correct.

Answer Key

Answers to Self-Practice Questions

1. Timing and precision problems make it difficult to get monetary policy just right. First, the Fed must make decisions using incomplete and delayed data. Second, several aspects of monetary policy are uncertain. The Fed's control of the money supply is uncertain. Its control of the AD curve is uncertain. And, it takes time for policy to ultimately shift the AD curve and impact the economy.

   Topic: Monetary Policy: The Best Case

2. In the following graph, the economy is operating above its Solow rate at point *a*. The economy might be described as "overheated" at this point. Contractionary policy (a decrease in money growth) would be needed to get the economy back to its Solow rate. Such a policy would decrease AD and the economy would move to point *b* in the graph (assuming the policy is just right).

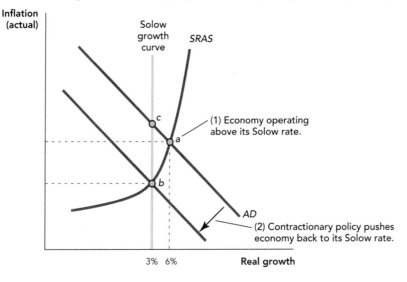

   Topic: Monetary Policy: The Best Case

3. Expansionary policy (an increase in money growth) would be appropriate here. The graph that follows shows how this policy could move the economy from point *b* following the negative demand shock back to the Solow growth rate at point *a* if the policy is just right. However, uncertainty could cause "too much" or "too little" policy. This could cause the policy to overshoot or undershoot the Solow growth rate.

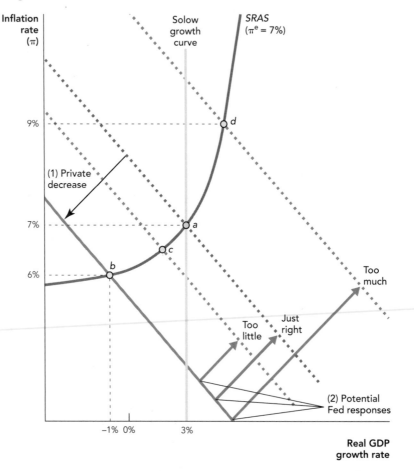

Topic: Monetary Policy: The Best Case

4. Expectations are important because an increase in expected inflation causes a leftward shift of the SRAS curve and a rise in actual inflation. This is important for monetary policy because of the Fed's desire to keep inflation low. Credibility means the Fed is committed to keeping inflation low and is willing to use policy to achieve this goal. A credible policy keeps expected inflation from rising, thus keeping actual inflation lower.

Topic: Reversing Course and Engineering a Decrease in AD

5. A negative real shock could push the economy in recession and causes higher inflation, as shown by the move from point *a* to point *b* in the following graph. If the Fed uses policy (an increase in money growth), AD shifts to the right and the economy moves to point *c*. This has limited ability to increase growth and causes even higher inflation. If the Fed decided instead to keep inflation low, a contractionary policy (a decrease in money growth) would be needed. This would shift AD to the left from point *b*. The result would be lower inflation but also a more severe recession (this is not shown in the following graph. See Figure 16.3 in the text for an illustration of the low-inflation policy.

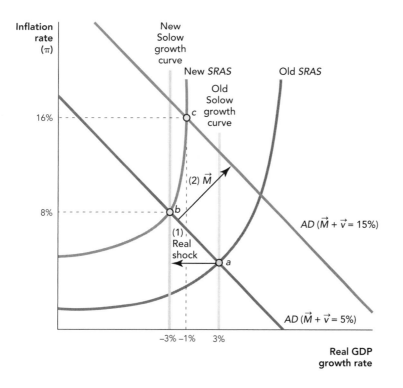

Topic: The Negative Real Shock Dilemma

6. The use of policy in this case helps the Fed achieve its goal of keeping inflation low. See the graph in question 2's answer on p. 229. The move from *a* to *b* lowers inflation.

Topic: Reversing Course and Engineering a Decrease in AD

7. If the Fed does not use policy, inflation remains elevated at point *a* in the graph for the answer to question 2. What's worse, if inflation expectations subsequently rise, SRAS will shift left and inflation will rise even further as the economy moves to point *c* in the graph.

Topic: Reversing Course and Engineering a Decrease in AD

8. There are two basic problems with using monetary policy to deflate asset price bubbles. First, it is hard to recognize when a bubble is forming. After all, if everyone knew it was a bubble, it would not continue to form or would deflate on its own. Therefore, it is hard to recognize when such a policy is needed until it's too late. Second, it is hard to use monetary policy to pinpoint specific markets like housing. Monetary policy impacts the broader economy. So, using contractionary policy to deflate a bubble in a specific market—even if successful—would come at the cost of slower growth across the entire economy.

Topic: Dealing with Asset Price Bubbles

9. A disinflation policy is a policy to reduce inflation in the economy. It presents a dilemma for the Fed because it requires contractionary monetary policy (a decrease in money growth), which can push the economy into recession.

Topic: Reversing Course and Engineering a Decrease in AD

10. The initial equilibrium is shown as point *a* in the following graph. To reduce inflation, the Fed will need to use contractionary policy (a decrease in money growth). This will shift AD to the left and the economy will move to point *b*, where inflation is lower but the economy is in recession. If the Fed sticks to its disinflation policy (that is, if the policy is credible and the Fed does NOT shift AD back to the right to end the recession), expected inflation will decrease and SRAS will shift down and to the right. This will move the economy to point *c*. Another, similar dose of contractionary policy will be required to lower inflation further, but it will require yet another recession (at point *d*) and further decreases in expected inflation to reach 1 percent inflation (at point *e*). The Fed's dilemma is that reducing inflation will require a policy that causes a recession.

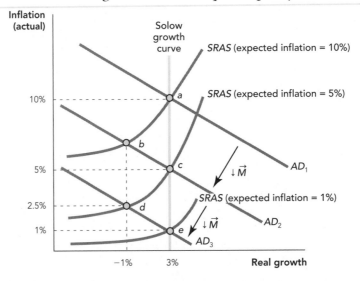

Topic: Reversing Course and Engineering a Decrease in AD

Answers to Multiple-Choice Questions

1. a, Topic: Monetary Ppolicy: The Best Case

2. b, Topic: Monetary Policy: The Best Case

3. d, Topic: Monetary Policy: The Best Case

4. b, Topic: Monetary Policy: The Best Case

5. a, Topic: Monetary Policy: The Best Case

6. a, Topic: Monetary Policy: The Best Case

7. b, Topic: Monetary Policy: The Best Case

8. a, Topic: Rules vs. Discretion

9. b, Topic: Monetary Policy: The Best Case

10. c, Topic: The Negative Real Shock Dilemma

11. d, Topic: The Negative Real Shock Dilemma

12. b, Topic: Reversing Course and Engineering a Decrease in AD

13. c, Topic: Reversing Course and Engineering a Decrease in AD

14. b, Topic: Reversing Course and Engineering a Decrease in AD

15. d, Topic: Dealing with Asset Price Bubbles

17 (34)

The Federal Budget: Taxes and Spending

Learning Objectives

In this chapter, you will learn:

> Some basic facts about the federal government's budget process
> The major sources of federal tax revenue
> The major sources of federal spending
> The difference between budget deficits and the national debt

Summary

The primary purpose of this chapter is to provide an introduction to the federal government's budget—the revenues collected by the government and what it spends those funds on. Before getting to those details, it is useful to provide some basic facts about the government's budget process.

The Federal Government's Budget Process

The first point to understand about the government's budget process is that changes in taxes and government spending literally require an act of Congress—that is, they must be passed into law, which requires passage by both the Senate and House of Representatives and the signature of the President. The specific tax and spending plan for a given fiscal year—running from October 1 of a given year to September 30 of the next year—is referred to as the government's *budget*.

The process of determining the government's budget for a given fiscal year usually begins the preceding January or February, when the President presents a budget proposal to Congress. The budget proposal contains details on the President's desired level of federal spending (how much to spend, and on what) and tax collections (how much to collect, and from whom). The House and Senate begin deliberations on a "budget bill" with specific tax and spending laws. These deliberations usually continue through the summer months. Ultimately, the goal is to end up with a bill that will pass both houses of Congress and that the President will sign into law before October 1. In recent years, however, no budget has been passed and a series of "continuing resolutions" has been used to fund government operations.

Major Sources of Government Revenue

As of 2010, the government collected about $2.2 trillion in tax revenue. About 90% of that revenue comes from the individual income tax, Social Security taxes, Medicare taxes, and the corporate income tax. Figure 17.1 in the text provides a breakdown of federal tax receipts. A few key details about each of the major sources of government revenue are provided here.

The *individual income tax* is the largest source of government revenue, accounting for 43% of total revenue in 2010. This tax is paid by individuals based on their income. The income tax is a **progressive tax**, meaning people with higher incomes face a higher **marginal tax rate**. The marginal tax rate is the tax rate paid on an additional dollar of income. Figure 17.2 in the text shows the marginal tax rate at different income levels for the typical taxpayer in 2010.

The **average tax rate** is defined as the total tax payment divided by total income. The average tax rate, also shown in Figure 17.2, is less than the marginal tax rate because an individual does not pay their marginal tax rate on all of their income. For example, someone with a $50,000 income would pay the 10 percent tax rate on the first $16,750 of their income and the 15 percent rate on the remainder of their income. The income tax is further complicated by various *exemptions* and *deductions* that allow individuals to avoid taxes altogether on part of their income. Exemptions allow an individual to avoid taxes on part of their income for certain behavior—such as having children. Deductions allow individuals to avoid taxes on part of their income for certain expenses they incur—such as paying interest on home mortgage loans. Exemptions and deductions also allow an individual to reduce their average tax rate below their marginal tax rate.

Table 17.1 in the text highlights the progressive nature of the individual income tax. Effective tax rates ranged from 4.3 percent for the bottom 20 percent of income earners, on average, to 25.5 percent for the top 20 percent in 2005. Because of this, the majority of government tax revenue is paid by the highest income earners. For example, the top 20 percent of earners paid 68.7 percent of all taxes. In fact, the top 1 percent of earners alone paid 27.6 percent of all taxes.

Social Security and Medicare taxes are the second-largest source of funding for the federal government, accounting for 40 percent of tax collections in 2010. These taxes are tied to specific programs that provide retirement and medical benefits, primarily to the elderly. The Social Security tax is 12.4 percent of earnings while the Medicare tax is 2.9 percent. In practice, half of these taxes is paid by the employee and half by the employer (with the self-employed paying both halves themselves). In reality, even the employers' share is largely paid by the employee in the form of lower wages.

The *corporate income tax* comes in a distant third in terms of providing government tax revenue, accounting for only 7.2 percent of tax collections in 2010. In general, the corporate income tax rate is 35 percent, although clever accounting can effectively reduce this rate significantly.

Major Sources of Government Spending

Government spending was over $3.7 trillion in 2010. About 80 percent of that spending was directed to the following programs:

> Social Security

> national defense

> Medicare and Medicaid

> unemployment and welfare programs

> interest on the national debt

Figure 17.3 in the text provides the details. Some key facts about the major spending programs are provided here.

Social Security accounted for 19 percent of total government spending in 2010. This program pays benefits to the elderly. Benefits are paid on a "pay as you go" basis, meaning the current elderly are paid from taxes paid by current workers. In the early years of the program, benefits were very generous. This was mainly because there were more workers paying into the program than benefits recipients in the early years. But the program has become less generous over time as the elderly population has increased relative to the working-age population. This demographic problem has become more acute as the baby-boom generation enters retirement age. The program is also less generous to higher income earners than lower income earners. Indeed, the program will generally provide a net *loss* to medium and higher income earners who retire in the future (see Table 17.2 in the text for details). Thus, Social Security is also a welfare program.

Defense spending also accounted for 19 percent of total government spending in 2010. As Table 17.3 in the text indicates, the U.S. spends more on defense by far than any other country in the world.

Medicare and Medicaid reimburse the elderly and poor for a large portion of their medical expenses. Together the two programs accounted for 19.9 percent of total spending in 2010 (separately, Medicare was 12 percent of total spending and Medicaid was 7.9 percent). A disturbing trend is that if medical costs continue to rise at current rates, these programs will make up an even larger share of the federal budget in the future.

Unemployment and welfare programs accounted for 15 percent of spending in the 2010 federal budget. This figure is larger than normal because of the high unemployment rate following the recent recession. In 2007, this category accounted for 9.5 percent of federal spending.

Interest on the national debt accounted for 5 percent of federal spending in 2010. Despite a large run-up in debt since the recent recession, this figure is down from 9.1 percent in 2007 due to historically low interest rates. An increase in interest rates would cause this item to take an even larger share of the federal budget in the future unless debt levels can be sufficiently reduced.

Budget Deficits and the National Debt

The government's budget **deficit** is the difference between its spending and tax revenue in a given year. More specifically, a deficit occurs when spending *exceeds* tax collections. For example, using the revenue and spending numbers for 2010 discussed above, the government's budget deficit for 2010 would be about $1.5 trillion (= $3.7 trillion in spending minus $2.2 trillion in revenue). The term "deficit" has become the default in discussions of the government's budget because the government almost always runs a deficit. But another possibility exists. The government is said to run a *surplus* if its tax revenue exceeds its spending. Since 1960, there have been only five years in which a budget surplus occurred—1969 and 1997 to 2000. This can be seen in Figure 17.5 in the text.

When the government runs a deficit, it must *borrow* to make up the shortfall (just as you must borrow if your spending exceeds your income). The government borrows by issuing bonds (recall the discussion of bonds in Chapter 9). Thus, each year the government runs a deficit that deficit represents new borrowing by the government. The total amount of outstanding borrowing by the government throughout its history is known as the **national debt**. This means that another year's deficit represents an addition to the national debt. We can therefore think of the national debt as the *accumulation* over time and the deficit as the *annual increase* in the national debt for a given year. Notice that a budget *surplus*, if used to pay off existing debt, would represent a *decrease* in the national debt.

The national debt is measured by the outstanding stock of government bonds—which stood at about $14 trillion as of mid-2011. A large portion of this debt is actually held by various branches of the government, so the **national debt held by the public** is often used as the relevant measure. This measure includes any debt held by anyone outside of the U.S. government—which was about $9 trillion as of mid-2011. To put the size of the national debt into perspective, it is often compared to the level of income in the U.S. economy that is measured by GDP. The so-called debt-to-GDP ratio is currently over 60 percent (= $9 trillion in public debt divided by GDP of $14 trillion). Figure 17.4 in the text shows the history of the debt-to-GDP ratio in the U.S.

To reduce the national debt, surpluses are required instead of deficits. However, the debt-to-GDP ratio can be reduced by slowing the growth of the national debt to a rate lower than the growth in GDP. Slowing the growth of the debt will require much smaller deficits than have been observed recently. Unfortunately, smaller deficits will not come easily. A number of factors are contributing to larger deficits in the future. Chief among these are an aging population that will increase spending in Social Security, Medicare, and Medicaid programs—and these are programs that already account for a significant share of the government's budget, thus leaving little room for cuts elsewhere in the budget. Furthermore, making changes in these programs to rein in costs has been politically unpopular. For these reasons, smaller deficits will likely require a painful combination of tax increases and spending cuts in the future.

Key Terms

marginal tax rate the tax rate paid on an additional dollar of income.

average tax rate the total tax payment divided by total income.

alternative minimum tax (AMT) a separate income tax code that began to operate in 1969 to prevent the rich from not paying income taxes.

progressive tax a tax that imposes higher tax rates on people with higher incomes.

flat tax a tax that imposes constant tax rate on all taxpayers, regardless of income.

regressive tax a tax that imposes higher tax rates on people with lower incomes.

deficit the annual difference between federal spending and revenues.

debt total amount of outstanding borrowing by the government throughout its history.

national debt held by the public all federal debt held outside the United States government.

Traps, Hints, and Reminders

> Remember that the *marginal* tax rate is the rate you would pay if you earned an additional dollar of income. Your marginal tax rate will depend on how much income you have already earned (that is, which "tax bracket" you are in). The *average* tax rate is your total tax bill divided by your income. The average tax rate will be less than your marginal rate because (1) you pay the lower marginal rate on income in the lower tax bracket(s) and (2) various exemptions and deductions allow you to avoid paying taxes on certain parts of your income.

> In thinking about who pays a tax, it is important to remember a lesson from microeconomics: the government doesn't dictate who ultimately pays a tax. For example, the government says the employer must pay half of the employee's Social Security tax. In reality, the employee pays this tax because the employee's wage is lower than it would be without the tax. Similarly, the government says firms must pay the corporate income tax. In reality, consumers pay the tax because the firm's prices are higher than they would be without the tax.

> Remember that the Social Security program is set up as a "pay as you go" system, which means that there is no account in which the money you pay into the system is stored until you retire. Today's retirees are paid from the contributions of today's workers. This arrangement is a key part of the underlying problems with the future of the program. As the population ages, there will be fewer workers to pay for the benefits of a growing number of retirees.

> Remember that the vast majority of government spending is accounted for by just a few large government programs—Social Security, national defense, Medicare, and Medicaid. A relatively small share of spending is for what most people think of as traditional welfare programs.

> A government budget *deficit* occurs when government spending exceeds tax revenue. A budget *surplus* occurs when revenue exceeds spending. Deficits and surpluses are measured over a *one-year* period.

> The *national debt* is the total accumulation of outstanding debt incurred by the government over *its entire history*. Deficits cause an *increase* in the national debt and surpluses cause a *decrease* (if used to pay off existing debt).

Self-Practice Questions

1. What are the three largest sources of the U.S. tax revenue?

2. Gary has an income of $20,000 from his job. Suppose the tax rate on the first $10,000 of income is 10 percent (with the first $2,000 of income exempt from taxes) and the rate on all income above $10,000 is 15 percent. What is Gary's marginal tax rate, his total tax bill, and his average tax rate?

3. What factors explain why your average tax rate is less than your marginal tax rate?

4. What does it mean to say the United States has a "progressive" tax system?

5. What does it mean to say that the Social Security system is a "pay as you go" system? What problem does this pose for the future of the Social Security program in the United States?

6. Why might we say that corporations don't really pay the corporate income tax?

7. What are the five largest areas of U.S. government spending?

8. What is the difference between deficits and the national debt? How are they related?

9. What is required to reduce the size of the national debt? Can the debt-to-GDP ratio be reduced without a decrease in the size of the national debt?

10. Why are future reductions in the national debt and the debt-to-GDP ratio going to be difficult to achieve?

Multiple-Choice Questions

1. In 2010, government spending accounted for about _____ of GDP.
   a. 2.5 percent
   b. 18 percent
   c. 25 percent
   d. 50 percent

2. In order from largest to smallest, what are the largest sources of U.S. tax revenue?
   a. individual income tax, corporate income tax, and Social Security/Medicare taxes
   b. individual income tax, Social Security/Medicare taxes, and corporate income tax
   c. corporate income tax, excise taxes, and Social Security/Medicare taxes
   d. corporate income taxes, Social Security/Medicare taxes, tariffs

3. The individual income tax in the United States is an example of a _____ tax.

a. flat

b. consumption

c. regressive

d. progressive

4. The Social Security and Medicare program is funded from

a. the Social Security and Medicare taxes paid by workers.

b. a tax on retirees.

c. the individual income tax.

d. an excise tax on alcohol, cigarettes, and gasoline.

5. If you must pay a tax rate of 25 percent on an additional dollar of income, then 25 percent is your

a. flat tax rate.

b. average tax rate.

c. marginal tax rate.

d. progressive tax rate.

6. Your average tax rate can be less than your marginal tax rate if

a. the income tax system is progressive.

b. you qualify for some exemptions.

c. you qualify for some deductions.

d. All of the answers are correct.

7. Not counting deductions, what is the lowest marginal tax rate for the U.S. income tax?

a. 1 percent

b. 10 percent

c. 57 percent

d. 90 percent

8. If you have an income of $67,000 so far this year, your marginal tax rate is 15%. How much would you pay on the next dollar that you earn?

a. nothing

b. the full dollar

c. less than 15 percent, because the average tax rate would be less than the marginal rate

d. $0.15

9. The average tax rate is
   a. the tax rate paid on an additional dollar of income.
   b. the total tax payment divided by total income.
   c. the total amount of taxes paid by U.S. citizens divided by the total population.
   d. the total amount of taxes paid by U.S. citizens divided by the total population *and* Social Security taxes divided by the population under age 65.

10. If you earned $43,000 last year and paid a total of $5,500 in taxes after all of your deductions, what is your average tax rate?
    a. 10 percent
    b. 12.8 percent
    c. 25 percent
    d. 91 percent

11. The share of the Social Security tax ultimately paid by an employee is
    a. 100 percent because each employee is responsible for paying all of his/her Social Security tax.
    b. less than half, because most of it is paid by the employer as a benefit of employment.
    c. exactly half.
    d. more than half because most of the employer's share is paid by the employee through lower wages.

12. For every dollar of earnings up to $108,600 annually, _____ is paid into the Social Security program.
    a. 2.9 percent
    b. 12.4 percent
    c. 19 percent
    d. 35 percent

13. The corporate income tax rate in the U.S. (not counting deductions and credits) is
    a. zero.
    b. 10 percent.
    c. 15 percent.
    d. 35 percent.

14. In the United States in 2005, the top 20 percent of income earners paid about _____ of total federal tax revenue.
    a. 12 percent
    b. 25 percent
    c. 40 percent
    d. 69 percent

15. What are the four *biggest* areas of federal government spending?

a. unemployment insurance, welfare, foreign aid, and interest on debt

b. welfare, aid to foreign governments, transportation, interest on debt

c. Social Security, welfare, defense, and aid to foreign governments

d. Social Security, defense, Medicare, and Medicaid

16. Which of the following is the way that Social Security works?

a. Social Security taxes are deposited into the general fund and then benefits are allocated as the government sees fit.

b. Each person has a special account with his or her Social Security taxes invested in nontaxable municipal bonds.

c. Each person has a special account with his or her Social Security taxes deposited to earn interest.

d. Each person has a special account with his or her Social Security taxes invested in stocks.

17. How big was the interest on the U.S. national debt as of 2010?

a. 1 percent of the federal budget

b. 10 percent of the federal budget

c. over 60 percent of the federal budget

d. 5 percent of the federal budget

18. As of 2010, the debt-to-GDP ratio (based on debt held by the public) was about:

a. 10 percent.

b. 25 percent.

c. 60 percent.

d. 108 percent.

19. Running a budget deficit implies

a. the government is spending more than it collects in taxes.

b. the government must issue new bonds to cover the deficit.

c. an increase in the national debt.

d. All of the answers are correct.

20. Reducing the size of the national debt can be accomplished by

a. running budget surpluses.

b. reducing the interest rate on the national debt.

c. reducing the size of budget deficits.

d. All of the answers are correcte.

Homework Quiz

1. The single largest source of U.S. tax revenue is

a. Social Security and Medicare taxes.

b. personal income taxes.

c. corporate income taxes.

d. capital gains taxes.

2. Suppose you have income of $50,000, which puts you in the 15 percent tax bracket and you have a total tax bill (after deductions and exemptions) of $6,000. In this case, your average tax rate would be

a. 15 percent.

b. 8.3 percent.

c. 12 percent.

d. 3 percent.

3. The Social Security program in the U.S. is run as a _____ system.

a. earned income tax credit

b. alternative minimum tax

c. pay as you go

d. fully funded

4. In a flat tax system with no deductions and no exemptions

a. the average tax rate will be less than the marginal rate.

b. the average tax rate and marginal tax rate will be equal.

c. the average tax rate will be more than the marginal rate.

d. the average tax rate will be zero regardless of the marginal rate.

5. If your marginal tax rate is 25 percent and your average tax rate is 15 percent, an additional dollar of income will increase your tax bill by

a. 25 cents.

b. 15 cents.

c. 40 cents.

d. Answer cannot be determined without knowing deductions and exemptions

6. If you pay $20,000 in taxes and your income is $100,000 for a given year so that you are in the 25 percent tax bracket, then

a. your average tax rate is 25 percent.

b. your marginal tax rate is 20 percent.

c. your average tax rate is 20 percent.

d. both your average and marginal tax rate is 25 percent.

7. Which of the following federal spending programs was the *smallest* in 2010?

   a. Social Security

   b. Medicare and Medicaid combined

   c. national defense

   d. unemployment and welfare programs

8. Which of the following is a true statement about deficits and the national debt?

   a. The deficit and the national debt are the same thing.

   b. The deficit and the national debt are the same thing unless the government is running a surplus.

   c. The deficit is an accumulation over time and the national debt is an annual total.

   d. The deficit is an annual total and the national debt is an accumulation over time.

9. As of 2010, the national debt held by the public was about

   a. $1.5 trillion.

   b. $9 trillion.

   c. $14 trillion.

   d. $19 trillion.

10. Which of the following problems makes it difficult to reduce the national debt in the future?

   a. The elderly are becoming an increasing share of the population.

   b. Health care costs are rising rapidly.

   c. Social Security, Medicare, and Medicaid already account for a large share of federal spending.

   d. All of the answers are correct.

Answer Key

Answers to Self-Practice Questions

1. The three largest sources of U.S. tax revenue are: the individual income tax, Social Security and Medicare taxes, and the corporate income tax.

   Topic: Tax Revenues

2. Gary's marginal tax rate is 15 percent since any additional income he earns will be taxed at that rate. With the $2,000 exemption, Gary will pay $800 (= 0.1 × $8,000) in taxes on the first $10,000 of income and $1,500 (= 0.15 × $10,000) in taxes on the second $10,000 of income. Thus, Gary's total tax bill is $2,300. His average tax rate is $2,300/$20,000 = 0.115 or 11.5 percent.

   Topic: The Individual Income Tax

3. The marginal tax rate will be higher than the average tax rate because marginal rates (the rate on an additional dollar of earning) increase as you earn more income. However, you pay a lower marginal rate on any lower "brackets" of income you earn. Since you don't pay your marginal rate on all of your income (unless you are in the lowest tax bracket), your average rate will be less than your marginal rate. In addition, any exemptions or deductions that you qualify for will allow you to avoid paying taxes on part of your income.

   Topic: The Individual Income Tax

4. A "progressive" tax system means that marginal tax rates increase as you earn more income. This causes people with higher incomes to pay more taxes.

   Topic: The Individual Income Tax

5. The "pay as you go" system means that taxes paid by current workers are used immediately to pay the benefits of current retirees. In other words, taxes paid by a worker are not saved in an account until the worker retires. This becomes a problem as the population ages, because there are fewer workers paying into the system and more retirees collecting benefits.

   Topic: Social Security

6. Tax law say that corporations must pay the corporate income tax, but in reality the tax is ultimately paid by the corporation's customers (through higher prices for its products), the corporation's employees (through lower wages), and the owners of the corporation (through lower profits).

   Topic: The Corporate Income Tax

7. The five largest areas of U.S. government spending are: Social Security, national defense, Medicare, unemployment and welfare programs, and Medicaid.

   Topic: Spending

8. The deficit refers to the annual difference between government spending and tax revenues (assuming spending exceeds revenues). The national debt is the total accumulation of outstanding borrowing by the government over its entire history. They are related because deficits, which require additional borrowing, cause the national debt to increase.

   Topic: The National Debt, Interest on the National Debt, and Deficits

9. Reducing the size of the national debt will require government budget surpluses (with surpluses used to pay off existing debt). The debt-to-GDP ratio can be reduced without a decrease in the size of the national debt, provided that GDP grows faster than the national debt. One key to slowing the growth of the national debt is smaller deficits.

Topic: The National Debt, Interest on the National Debt, and Deficits

10. Reducing the size of the national debt and the debt-to-GDP ratio will require surpluses or at least significantly smaller deficits in the future. There are several factors contributing to larger deficits in the future: (1) an aging population that will increase costs in the Social Security, Medicare, and Medicaid programs; (2) a trend of increasing health care costs; (3) the size of Social Security, Medicare, and Medicaid together already makes up a significant share of the government's budget; (4) the nature of these programs makes it difficult to reduce costs; and (5) an increase in interest rates could significantly increase interest payments on the existing debt. For these reasons, running smaller deficits or surpluses in the future is likely to require painful tax increases or spending cuts or some combination of the two.

Topic: Will the U.S. Government Go Bankrupt?

Answers to Multiple-Choice Questions

1. c, Topic: Introduction

2. b, Topic: Tax Revenues

3. d, Topic: The Bottom Line on the Distribution of Federal Taxes

4. a, Topic: Social Security and Medicare Taxes

5. c, Topic: The Individual Income Tax

6. d, Topic: The Individual Income Tax

7. b, Topic: The Individual Income Tax

8. d, Topic: The Individual Income Tax

9. b, Topic: The Individual Income Tax

10. b, Topic: The Individual Income Tax

11. d, Topic: Social Security and Medicare Taxes

12. b, Topic: Social Security and Medicare Taxes

13. d, Topic: The Corporate Income Tax

14. d, Topic: The Bottom Line on the Distribution of Federal Taxes

15. d, Topic: Spending

16. a, Topic: Social Security

17. d, Topic: The National Debt, Interest on the National Debt, and Deficits

18. c, Topic: The National Debt, Interest on the National Debt, and Deficits

19. d, Topic: The National Debt, Interest on the National Debt, and Deficits

20. a, Topic: The National Debt, Interest on the National Debt, and Deficits

18 (35)

Fiscal Policy

Learning Objectives

In this chapter, you will learn:

> How fiscal policy works in the "best-case" scenario
> About some issues that limit the effectiveness of fiscal policy
> About the relationship between fiscal policy and government debt
> When fiscal policy is most likely to be effective

Summary

This chapter is about fiscal policy, which involves changes in government spending and taxes. Along with monetary policy (discussed in Chapter 16), fiscal policy is used by the government to stabilize business cycle fluctuations. Since changes in taxes and government spending involve the government's budget, fiscal policy is carried out by Congress and the President (see details on the government's budget process in Chapter 17). We begin with a discussion of how fiscal policy works in the best-case scenario and then turn to some problems with the use of fiscal policy.

Fiscal Policy in the Best-Case Scenario

The best-case scenario for fiscal policy is demonstrated in Figure 18.1 in the text. The figure shows the economy in recession at point *b* following a decrease in AD caused by a decrease in consumption growth. Expansionary fiscal policy in the form of an increase in government spending shifts the AD curve back to the right to pull the economy out of recession and restore growth at the Solow rate at point *a*. Note that the objective of using policy is to get the economy back to its Solow growth rate more quickly than waiting for the economy to recover on its own.

There is an additional effect of fiscal policy in the best-case scenario. In particular, the increase in government spending will generate more private spending so that fiscal policy's impact on AD will be greater than the increase in government spending alone. This secondary increase in private spending is known as the **multiplier effect**. The multiplier effect makes fiscal policy easier for the government to carry out, because it means the increase in government spending needed to bring about recovery need not be as large as the initial decrease in consumption that caused the recession. This is illustrated in Figure 18.2 in the text.

The multiplier effect occurs when the initial increase in spending by the government shows up as an increase in income for the recipients of that spending, who in turn increase their spending. Their increase in spending then represents an increase in income to those who receive it, and they increase their spending. And so on down the line the cycle continues, with each round of increased spending increasing income and, then, spending again.

In summary, it is important to note the following points about the best-case use of fiscal policy: (1) the recession must be caused by a demand shock; (2) the demand shock must be largely the result of a decrease in consumption. These conditions set the stage for understanding the limits of fiscal policy, which we will discuss next.

The Limits of Fiscal Policy

There are four issues that limit fiscal policy's effectiveness in terms of stimulating the economy in the short run:

1. "Crowding out" may sharply reduce the impact of fiscal policy.

2. The amount of spending required to provide adequate stimulus may be very large.

3. It can be difficult to get the timing of fiscal stimulus just right.

4. Fiscal policy does not work well in response to "real" shocks.

Let's discuss each of these issues in turn.

Crowding Out

Crowding out refers to decreases in private-sector (nongovernment) spending that result from the use of expansionary fiscal policy. Crowding out occurs because fiscal policy must ultimately be paid for by the private sector—either through higher current taxes paid by the private sector or borrowing from the private sector (which implies higher taxes in the future). Crowding out is a problem for fiscal policy because it reduces the size of the expansionary shift in AD provided by policy.

To examine the effects of crowding out more carefully, consider three alternative expansionary fiscal policies:

1. A *tax-financed increase in government spending* means an increase in government spending is paid for by raising current taxes on the private sector. Higher taxes on the private sec-

tor mean less money available for spending there. Thus, the increase in government spend-ing "crowds out" private sector spending (primarily spending by consumers in this case). As a result, the net increase in aggregate spending will be less than the initial increase in gov-ernment spending, and causes a smaller shift in the AD curve from the policy.

2. A *deficit-financed increase in government spending* means an increase in government spending is paid for by borrowing. Governments borrow by issuing bonds, but some-one must buy these bonds (that is, someone must be willing to loan funds to the gov-ernment). When the private sector buys government bonds, it means fewer funds available for private investment. Thus, the increase in government borrowing "crowds out" private investment spending (recall that "investment" here refers to spending by businesses on new plants, equipment, etc.). In addition, the increase in government borrowing causes bond prices to fall and interest rates to rise (see the discussion in Chapter 9). Higher interest rates cause further declines in investment spending by busi-nesses and more saving (less spending) by consumers (this effect is illustrated in Figure 18.3 in the text). So once again, crowding out implies the net increase in aggregate spending will be less than the initial increase in government spending, and causes a smaller shift in the AD curve from the policy.

3. A *tax cut with no change in government spending* means more money available for spending in the private sector. It is tempting to think there is no crowding out in this scenario, but unfortunately this is not the case. The tax cut will generally result in more government borrowing since cutting taxes without changing spending will increase the government's budget deficit. The increase in government debt will imply higher future taxes, since the debt will have to be paid off at some point. To the extent that people are patient and forward-looking, they will plan for the future tax increases by saving more (spending less) today. So again, we have a "crowding out" effect. In the extreme case where people are *perfectly* forward-looking, they *fully* anticipate higher future taxes and save the *entire* tax cut so there is *no* expansionary effect from the pol-icy. This extreme response—based on the view that current tax cuts are *equivalent* to future tax increases—is called the **Ricardian equivalence** hypothesis.

In summary, crowding out reduces the potential stimulative impact of fiscal policy. In Figure 18.1, this implies a smaller shift in the AD curve from a given increase in government spending or tax cut. Note also that the crowding out effect is just the op-posite of the multiplier effect shown in Figure 18.2. Indeed, if the multiplier effect is relatively small and crowding out is relatively large, the net shift in AD could be less than what is implied by the increase in government spending alone. Figure 18.4 (35.4) in the text summarizes the paths of crowding out.

One additional comment about crowding out is noteworthy. Crowding out is based on the idea that government spending or borrowing replaces private spending that would have occurred had the government not used policy. As a result, the amount of crowding out is likely to be smaller when private consumers and businesses are *not* will-ing to spend on their own. This means that fiscal policy is likely to be more effective in stimulating the economy when the private sector is generally unwilling to spend.

A Drop in the Bucket

The second factor limiting the effectiveness of fiscal policy is that it is difficult for the government to spend enough money to have an appreciable effect on the aggregate economy. This is simply a result of the sheer size of the economy, which implies that even large amounts of spending can have only a minor impact at the aggregate level. Large increases in spending become even more problematic when budget deficits and the national debt reach burdensome levels.

Timing Problems

Getting the timing right is a problem with fiscal policy just as it was with monetary policy (as discussed in Chapter 16). Carrying out fiscal policy involves various lags associated with the decision-making, implementation, and effectiveness of the policy.

In particular, there are five lags associaated with fiscal policy:

1. Recognition lag: the time required to identify when the economy is in recession.

2. Legislative lag: the time required for Congress to propose and pass a budget plan into law.

3. Implementation lag: the time required for various government agencies to implement the plan.

4. Effectiveness lag: the time required for the policy to impact the economy.

5. Evaluation and adjustment lag: the time required to evaluate whether the plan has worked and whether adjustments are needed.

The recognition lag is the same as discussed with monetary policy in Chapter 16. The legislative and implementation lags are particularly problematic in the case of fiscal policy—more so than with monetary policy—since budgetary changes require Congress to act. The effectiveness lag, on the other hand, is likely to be shorter with fiscal policy than with monetary policy since increases in government spending are a more direct route to stimulating AD than are monetary changes. In general, these lags are important since the objective of fiscal policy is to *speed* the economy's recovery during a recession. Ill-timed policies may exaggerate rather than stabilize business cycle fluctuations (this possibility was illustrated for the case of monetary policy in Chapter 16 of this study guide).

Fiscal Policy and Real Shocks

The fourth limitation of fiscal policy is that it generally is not effective in dealing with real shocks. Figure 18.5 demonstrates this in the text. In the figure, a real shock shifts the Solow growth curve to the left, pushing the economy into recession at a growth rate of -3 percent. Fiscal policy, in turn, shifts AD to the right. But note that the increase in AD largely results in higher inflation rather than increased growth. Intuitively, this result occurs because the real shock has reduced productivity in the economy. Less productive firms are forced to respond to the increase in demand in large part by raising prices since they are unable to increase output by very much.

An additional problem with a real shock is that crowding out is likely to be larger than with demand shocks. This is because the real shock implies that the problem in the economy is not a lack of spending, but rather a decline in productivity. Recall that more crowding out is likely to occur when consumers are generally willing to spend on their own. More extensive crowding out implies that the impact of fiscal policy will be limited.

Fiscal Policy and Government Debt

Another aspect of fiscal policy involves the financing of government spending. For example, an increase in government spending or a tax cut (expansionary fiscal policy) will cause the government's budget position to worsen—that is, it will move the government's budget more toward a deficit or it will worsen any deficit that already exists. Government deficits require the government to borrow, which they do by issuing bonds (again, see discussion of these budget details in Chapter 17). Therefore, expansionary fiscal policy causes larger deficits and a rising national debt.

The relationship between fiscal policy and government deficits and the national debt can cause a dilemma for policymakers if government debt reaches burdensome levels. This is because the policy required to reduce the deficit and the national debt would necessarily be a cut in spending and/or an increase in taxes. The dilemma is that this contractionary policy would negatively affect real growth in the economy. When anxiety over government debt occurs during times of economic weakness or recession (as it often does), the policy required to address the debt issues can cause economic conditions to deteriorate even further.

In summary, it is impossible to separate fiscal policy changes from changes in the government's budget position and the national debt; all of these issues are interconnected. The text discusses some implications of these relationships using examples from Argentina and Mexico (see "When Fiscal Policy Might Make Matters Worse").

When Is Fiscal Policy Most Likely to Be Effective?

The discussion throughout this chapter identifies the circumstances under which fiscal policy is most likely to be effective:

1. When the economy is in critical need of a short-run boost, such as during a severe recession, crisis, or natural disaster—even at the expense of longer-term implications (such as the effects on the national debt).

2. When the problem is a deficiency in demand rather than a real shock—so that policy can generate growth rather than inflation.

3. When there is a general unwillingness to spend in the private sector—thus reducing the effect of crowding out in limiting the effectiveness of policy.

Key Terms

fiscal policy federal government policy on taxes, spending, and borrowing that is designed to influence business fluctuations

multiplier effect the additional increase in AD caused when expansionary fiscal policy increases income and thus consumer spending

crowding out the decrease in private spending that occurs when government increases spending

Ricardian equivalence what occurs when people see that lower taxes today mean higher taxes in the future; so instead of spending their tax cut, they save it to pay future taxes. When Ricardian equivalence holds, a tax cut doesn't increase aggregate demand even in the short run

automatic stabilizers changes in fiscal policy that stimulate AD in a recession without the need for explicit action by policymakers

Traps, Hints, and Reminders

> Remember, fiscal policy involves changes in government spending *or* changes in taxes *or* a combination of both.

> Once again, this chapter makes extensive use of AD-AS graphs. So, it is important that you are familiar with the use of the AD-AS model introduced in Chapter 13.

> Many of the graphs in this chapter are similar to those that show monetary policy in Chapter 16. This is because both monetary and fiscal policy work by shifting the AD curve and also because both types of policy are used to get the economy back to its Solow rate (before the economy recovers on its own).

> Note that the terms "expansionary" and "contractionary" are used to describe the direction of fiscal policy. *Expansionary* fiscal policy (an increase in government spending or cut in taxes) shifts AD to the *right* while *contractionary* fiscal policy (a decrease in government spending or increase in taxes) shifts AD to the *left*.

> Remember that the multiplier effect and crowding out are both secondary effects that can occur following the use of fiscal policy. However, these two effects are exact *opposites* from each other. The multiplier effect involves an *increase* in private spending following expansionary fiscal policy while crowding out involves a *decrease* in private spending following the same policy.

> Remember that the multiplier effect is likely to be larger and crowding out smaller when consumer spending is low, there is a general unwillingness to spend in the economy, or the economy is operating far below its Solow rate. On the other hand, when the economy is operating near its Solow rate, the multiplier effect is likely to be relatively small and crowding out relatively large.

> The Ricardian equivalence hypothesis may sound complicated but its implications for policy are simple: it implies that a tax cut (with no change in government spending) will have *no effect* on the economy. This is because consumers respond to the tax cut (which is an expansionary fiscal policy) by saving, not spending. With no change in spending, there is no stimulative effect of the fiscal policy.

> A more advanced point: Ricardian equivalence is explained for the case of a tax cut (with no change in government spending) in the text. In this case, the tax cut has *no effect* on the economy. Ricardian equivalence also applies for the case of an increase in government spending. In this case, Ricardian equivalence implies that a *tax-financed* increase in government spending is *equivalent* to a *deficit-financed* increase in government spending. This is because, under

Ricardian equivalence, consumers are forward-looking and save more in anticipation of higher future taxes implied by deficit-financing. In other words, Ricardian equivalence means that current taxes and future taxes (implied by current deficits) are *equivalent*.

Self-Practice Questions

1. What conditions are important for fiscal policy to occur in the best-case scenario?

2. What are the four problems with fiscal policy?

3. What are the five lags associated with fiscal policy?

4. How does the multiplier effect affect the use of fiscal policy?

5. Consider the graph in Figure 18.1 in the text. How would the crowding out effect be shown in this graph? What does this imply about the use of fiscal policy?

6. Imagine that the crowding out effect is larger than the multiplier effect. What does this imply about the effectiveness of fiscal policy shown in Figure 18.2?

7. What is Ricardian equivalence? What does it imply about the use of fiscal policy?

8. How does the effectiveness of fiscal policy depend on what initially causes a recession?

9. Explain the dilemma policymakers face when government deficits and the national debt reach burdensome levels?

10. When is fiscal policy most likely to succeed?

Multiple-Choice Questions

1. Fiscal policy shifts which of the following curves in the AD-AS model?
   a. aggregate demand curve
   b. Solow growth curve
   c. short-run aggregate supply curve
   d. All of the answers are correct.

2. In the best-case scenario for fiscal policy, recessions are caused by a fall in ____, and a recovery can be achieved by using fiscal policy to increase ____.
   a. $\vec{C}$; $\vec{I}$
   b. $\vec{C}$; $\vec{G}$
   c. $\overrightarrow{NX}$; $\vec{G}$
   d. $\overrightarrow{NX}$; $\vec{C}$

3. When fiscal policy shifts the AD curve by more than the initial increase in government spending, that is known as the

    a. multiplier effect.

    b. secondary effect.

    c. crowding out effect.

    d. drop in the bucket effect.

4. Which of the following answers lists the four limits to fiscal policy?

    a. crowding out, multiplier effect, gains from trade, real shocks instead of demand shocks

    b. crowding out, real shocks instead of demand shocks, timing issues, and bond financing

    c. crowding out, drop in the bucket, externalities, monetary policy

    d. crowding out, drop in the bucket, timing issues, and real shocks instead of demand shocks

5. If $\vec{G}$ increases by 5 percent and AD shifts a total of 3 percent, then the economy has experienced

    a. a crowding out effect that outweighs the multiplier effect.

    b. timing issues.

    c. a multiplier effect that outweighs the crowding out effect.

    d. the drop in the bucket effect.

6. Which of the following would be an appropriate fiscal policy during a recession?

    a. an increase in taxes

    b. an increase in money growth

    c. an increase in government spending growth

    d. All of the answers are correct.

7. If the economy is operating at its Solow growth rate and the government engages in $100 million worth of fiscal policy, which of the following is likely to be true?

    a. The multiplier effect is likely to be larger than the crowding out effect.

    b. The crowding out effect is likely to be larger than the multiplier effect.

    c. Both the multiplier effect and crowding out are likely to be large.

    d. Both the multiplier effect and crowding out are likely to be small.

8. According to the crowding out effect, an increase in $\vec{G}$ financed through bond sales will decrease _____.

    a. $\vec{C}$

    b. $\vec{I}$

    c. $\vec{M}$

    d. both $\vec{C}$ and $\vec{I}$.

9. If the government is currently running a budget deficit and there is an increase in government spending without an increase in current taxes, then

   a. the government will have to issue bonds.

   b. the government's budget deficit will increase.

   c. the national debt will increase.

   d. All of the answers are correct.

10. A tax cut would be an example of

    a. contractionary fiscal policy.

    b. contractionary monetary policy.

    c. expansionary fiscal policy.

    d. expansionary monetary policy.

11. The crowding out effect means that increases in government spending

    a. are offset by higher inflation.

    b. are offset by higher budget deficits.

    c. cause a decrease in private spending.

    d. cause an increase in private spending.

12. If government gives a one-time tax rebate to stimulate the economy (with no change in government spending) and consumers save MOST (but not all) of the rebate, then the policy will cause

    a. a large shift in AD to the right.

    b. a small shift in AD to the right.

    c. a shift in AD to the left.

    d. no shift in AD.

13. Ricardian equivalence is an extreme form of

    a. crowding out.

    b. the multiplier effect.

    c. a timing issue.

    d. a real shock.

14. President Obama's $780 billion stimulus in 2008 amounted to about 2 percent of GDP in the three years after the plan was passed. This is an example of

    a. crowding out.

    b. the multiplier effect.

    c. a real shock.

    d. the drop in the bucket effect.

15. Policymakers face a dilemma when trying to reduce government deficits and the national debt because the policy that is needed causes

 a. slower growth in the economy and possibly a recession.

 b. higher inflation.

 c. an overheated economy.

 d. real shocks.

16. According to the Ricardian equivalence hypothesis, a tax cut (with no change in government spending) will be

 a. fully saved by consumers.

 b. fully spent by consumers.

 c. partly saved and partly spent by consumers.

 d. voluntarily sent back to the government to pay off the national debt.

17. What is the effect of fiscal policy when there has been a negative real shock?

 a. a large increase in GDP growth

 b. a small increase in GDP growth

 c. an overheated economy

 d. deflation

18. Suppose fiscal policy is used during a recession that is caused by a negative real shock. What is the likely effect on inflation?

 a. Fiscal policy causes the same amount of inflation regardless of whether a recession is caused by a demand shock or a real shock.

 b. There will be more inflation when fiscal policy is used with a real shock than with a demand shock.

 c. There will be more inflation when fiscal policy is used with a demand shock than with a real shock.

 d. Fiscal policy leads to deflation not inflation.

19. Which of the following scenarios would imply that fiscal policy might be successful?

 a. The country has a real shock and the national debt is already 200 percent of GDP.

 b. The country has a real shock and government is running a budget surplus.

 c. The country has a negative demand shock and unemployment is quite high.

 d. The country has a positive demand shock.

20. Which of the following problems could cause fiscal policy to make business cycle fluctuations worse, not better?

 a. recognition lag

 b. legislative lag

 c. implementation lag

 d. All of the answers are correct.

Homework Quiz

1. Fiscal policy is carried out by
   a. the Fed.
   b. the Treasury Department.
   c. the legislative branch of government (Congress and the President).
   d. the Expansionary Policy Agency (EPA).

2. If the growth rate of government spending increases by 2 percent and causes a net shift in AD of 3 percent, then
   a. timing issues must be present.
   b. there must be no crowding out.
   c. the crowding out effect must outweigh the multiplier effect.
   d. the multiplier effect must outweigh the crowding out effect.

3. Which of the following would be an example of expansionary fiscal policy?
   a. a decrease in taxes
   b. an increase in money growth
   c. a decrease in government spending
   d. All of the answers are correct.

4. If the economy is operating well below its Solow growth rate and the government engages in $500 billion worth of fiscal stimulus, which of the following is likely to be true?
   a. The crowding out effect is likely to be larger than the multiplier effect.
   b. The multiplier effect is likely to be larger than the crowding out effect.
   c. Both crowding out and the multiplier effect are likely to be large.
   d. Both crowding out and the multiplier effect are likely to be small.

5. As a result of the crowding out effect, an increase in government spending financed by a current tax increase will decrease:
   a. consumption growth.
   b. investment growth.
   c. money supply growth.
   d. velocity growth.

6. The multiplier effect implies that an increase in government spending will:
   a. increase private spending.
   b. decrease private spending.
   c. cause a positive real shock.
   d. cause smaller budget deficits.

7. The appropriate policy to reduce government budget deficits and the national debt would be:

a. contractionary monetary policy.

b. expansionary monetary policy.

c. contractionary fiscal policy.

d. expansionary fiscal policy.

8. According to the Ricardian equivalence hypothesis, a tax cut (with no change in government spending) would

a. cause a large shift in AD to the right.

b. cause a small shift in AD to the right.

c. cause a shift in AD to the left.

d. cause no shift in AD.

9. When fiscal policy is used in response to a real shock

a. the multiplier effect is likely to be large.

b. the crowding out effect is likely to be large.

c. the crowding out effect is likely to be small.

d. the economy is likely to overheat.

10. Which of the following circumstances would make it more likely that fiscal policy would be effective in fighting a recession?

a. The recession is caused by a real shock.

b. A decline in consumer confidence has decreased consumer spending.

c. Congress is in gridlock and cannot pass a budget bill.

d. The national debt has surpassed 200 percent of GDP.

Answer Key

Answers to Self-Practice Questions

1. In the best-case scenario, fiscal policy is used in response to a recession caused by a demand shock that results from a decrease in consumer spending. In the best case, fiscal policy encourages more private spending through the multiplier effect and the negative impact of crowding out is small. In addition, the timing problems caused by various lags that affect fiscal policy will be insignificant in the best-case scenario (perhaps because the recession is relatively severe).

   Topic: Fiscal Policy: The Best Case

2. The four problems with fiscal policy are: (1) crowding out (the idea that government spending replaces private spending); (2) a drop in the bucket (the idea that government stimulus is small relative to the size of the economy); (3) getting the timing of policy just right (the idea that the economy may recover before policy takes effect); and (4) real shocks (the idea that policy is largely ineffective in response to real shocks).

   Topic: The Limits to Fiscal Policy

3. The five lags associated with fiscal policy are: (1) recognition lag (it takes time to identify when the economy is in recession); (2) legislative lag (it takes time for Congress to pass a stimulus plan); (3) implementation lag (it takes time for various government agencies to implement the stimulus plan); (4) effectiveness lag (it takes time for the stimulus plan to impact the economy); and (5) evaluation and adjustment lag (it takes time to determine whether the plan has worked and to make adjustments).

   Topic: A Matter of Timing

4. The multiplier effect makes it easier to use fiscal policy. It means that a small increase in government spending can have a larger impact on the economy.

   Topic: Fiscal Policy: The Best Case

5. Figure 18.1 in the text shows the increase in AD caused by an increase in government spending. Crowding out would be shown in this graph by a secondary shift in AD back to the left. This is because crowding out implies a decrease in private spending that results from the use of expansionary fiscal policy. The implication is that fiscal policy provides less stimulus than is suggested by the use of policy alone.

   Topic: Crowding Out

6. Crowding out adds an additional shift of the AD curve back to the left in Figure 18.2 of the text. This is because crowding out is just the opposite of the multiplier effect. If crowding out is larger than the multiplier effect, the net effect of fiscal policy would be even less than suggested by the initial increase in government spending (and shift in AD) shown in Figure 18.2.

   Topic: Fiscal Policy: The Best Case; Crowding Out

7. Ricardian equivalence is an extreme case of crowding out. As such, Ricardian equivalence limits the effectiveness of fiscal policy. In the case of a tax cut (with no change in government spending), the crowding out is so severe that there is *no* stimulus whatsoever from the policy. This is because the entire tax cut is saved, with no increase in spending. Without any new spending, there is no stimulus.

   Topic: A Special Case of Crowding Out: Ricardian Equivalence

8. Fiscal policy is more likely to be effective when the recession is caused by a demand shock rather than a real shock. In response to a real shock, fiscal policy has only a limited effect on growth and causes a larger increase in inflation.

   Topic: Fiscal Policy Does Not Work Well to Combat Real Shocks

9. If policymakers decide to reduce budget deficits and the national debt, a contractionary policy will be required. The dilemma is that contractionary policy will reduce growth in the economy. So policymakers will be forced to choose between two bad options: accepting high deficit and debt levels or reducing them with a policy that weakens the economy.

   Topic: When Fiscal Policy Might Make Matters Worse

10. In general, there are three conditions that make it more likely that fiscal policy will succeed: (1) when the economy is in severe need of short-run stimulus; (2) when there is a deficiency in demand rather than a real shock; and (3) when there is a general unwillingness to spend in the private sector. Note that this is really just another way of asking question 1.

    Topic: So When Is Fiscal Policy a Good Idea?

Answers to Multiple-Choice Questions

1. a, Topic: Fiscal Policy: The Best Case

2. b, Topic: Fiscal Policy: The Best Case

3. a, Topic: The Multiplier

4. d, Topic: The Limits to Fiscal Policy

5. a, Topic: Crowding Out

6. c, Topic: Fiscal Policy: The Best Case

7. b, Topic: Crowding Out

8. d, Topic: Crowding Out

9. d, Topic: When Fiscal Policy Might Make Matters Worse

10. c, Topic: Government Spending versus Tax Cuts as Expansionary Fiscal Policy

11. c, Topic: Crowding Out

12. b, Topic: A Special Case of Crowding Out: Ricardian Equivalence

13. a, Topic: Crowding Out

14. d, Topic: A Drop in the Bucket: Can Government Spend Enough to Stimulate Aggregate Demand?

15. a, Topic: When Fiscal Policy Might Make Matters Worse

16. a, Topic: A Special Case of Crowding Out: Ricardian Equivalence

17. b, Topic: Fiscal Policy Does Not Work Well to Combat Real Shocks

18. b, Topic: Fiscal Policy Does Not Work Well to Combat Real Shocks

19. c, Topic: So When Is Fiscal Policy a Good Idea?

20. d, Topic: A Matter of Timing

19 (9)

International Trade

Learning Objectives

In this chapter, we continue the study of exchange begun in Chapter 2. Topics covered are:

> Analyzing Trade with Supply and Demand

> The Costs of Protectionism

> Arguments against International Trade

Summary

The economics of trade does not vary, whether it is between two parties within a country, or two parties in different countries. Trade takes place when both sides expect to gain. There are, however, political issues associated with trade between two parties in different countries.

Gains from free trade can be seen graphically in Figure 19.1, where $5 and 100 units are the equilibrium price and quantity if there is no trade.

With no trade, consumer surplus is area A, producer surplus is area $B + F$, and total surplus is area $A + B + F$. Once this market is opened up for free trade, then consumers can buy at the world price of $1. Then, consumer surplus is $A + B + C + E$, producer surplus is F, and total surplus is $A + B + C + E + F$. Thus, total surplus has grown by area $C + E$ or there are gains from trade of $C + E$.

Conversely, we can see what happens if the government imposes some type of protection on this market. **Protectionism** is an economic policy of restraining trade

Figure 19.1

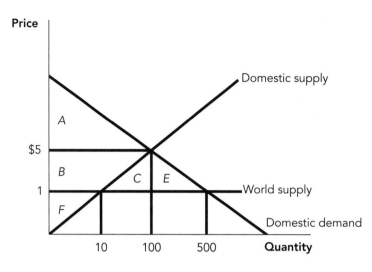

through quotas, tariffs, or other regulations that burden foreign producers but not domestic producers. A **trade quota** is a quantity restriction by which imports greater than the quota amount are forbidden. A **tariff** is a tax on imports.

In Figure 19.1, if the government imposed a quota or tariff large enough that none of the good was imported and price returned to the no-trade equilibrium, where domestic supply equals domestic demand, there will be lost gains from trade. As in the no-trade situation just discussed, consumer surplus is area A, producer surplus is area $B + F$, and total surplus is $A + B + F$. The gains from opening up the market to free trade, area $C + E$, are lost due to the protection. Area E is a consumption loss due to domestic consumers losing consumption they formerly had. Area C is an efficiency loss due to relatively inefficient domestic producers replacing relatively efficient foreign producers in supplying this good to the domestic market.

We can also model the effects of a tariff by using supply and demand analysis. Figure 19.2 shows what happens when a tariff is imposed on a free trade situation similar to that shown in Figure 19.1.

Figure 19.2

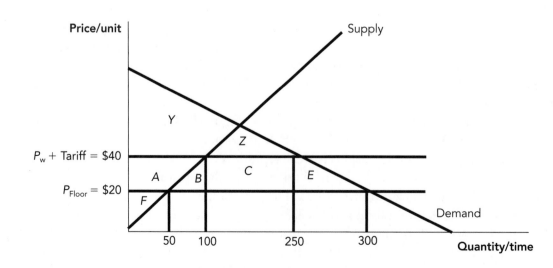

In Figure 19.2, with domestic free trade at the world price of $20, domestic production is 50 units and domestic consumption is 300 units. This means that imports are 250 units, with free trade. Consumer surplus is $Y + Z + A + B + C + E$, while producer surplus is F. Total surplus is $Y + Z + A + B + C + E + F$, with free trade.

Again in Figure 19.2, if a $20 per unit tariff is adopted, raising the domestic price from the world price of $20 to $40, then domestic production rises to 100 units, domestic consumption falls to 250 units, and imports fall to 150 units. Also due to the tariff, consumer surplus falls to $Y + Z$, while producer surplus rises to $C + H$. Government revenue is area C, the amount of imports, i.e., $250 - 100 = 150$, times the amount of the tariff of $20. Notice that the area of government revenue in Figure 19.2 equals $3,000. This means that total surplus after the tariff is area $Y + Z + A + C + F$. Notice that missing are areas $B + E$ from total surplus, with free trade. That makes $B + E$ the deadweight welfare loss due to the tariff.

With protection, the good is no longer sold by suppliers with the lowest costs. Since there are lost gains from trade with the protection, the sum of consumer plus producer surplus is no longer maximized.

Protectionism, in general, raises the price of an imported good by reducing supply in the domestic market. This leads to an increase in price of the domestic substitutes for the foreign good, also, since the supply of the good, domestic plus foreign, will be reduced.

Other issues are associated with international trade. One concern is the effect on wages. Wages depend on productivity and encouraging workers to move to relatively productive industries. International trade between two countries can cause wages in both countries to rise. With international trade, jobs are lost in some industries, but jobs grow in other industries. Keeping jobs via protectionism is very expensive; retraining displaced workers or somehow compensating workers who lost their jobs would be a better policy. Child labor is related to the income of the people of a country, as is free trade. So free trade, rather than restrictions on free trade, is the better policy to reduce child labor around the world. Some people argue for protection of certain strategic or national defense industries. Every industry will argue that it is strategic or important for national defense, and, if protected, will eventually become inefficient due to reduced competition.

Decreases in transportation costs, integration of world markets, and increased speed of communication have made the world seem smaller. This trend is sometimes called *globalization*. Some people think this is new or bad, but the world has only recently become as globalized as it was prior to World War I. To give up globalization is to give up the gains from international trade.

Key Terms

protectionism the economic policy of restraining trade through quotas, tariffs, or other regulations that burden foreign producers but not domestic producers

trade quota a restriction on the quantity of goods that can be imported—imports greater than the quota amount are forbidden or heavily taxed

tariff a tax on imports

Traps, Hints, and Reminders

Trade takes place, whether it occurs between individuals in a country or individuals in different countries, when both individuals expect to benefit.

A tariff is simply a tax; so it has many of the effects on a market that any other tax would.

Homework Quiz

1. Among the winners with a tariff on cars are
   a. domestic producers of cars.
   b. domestic consumers of cars.
   c. the economy as a whole.
   d. All of the answers are correct.

Figure 19.3

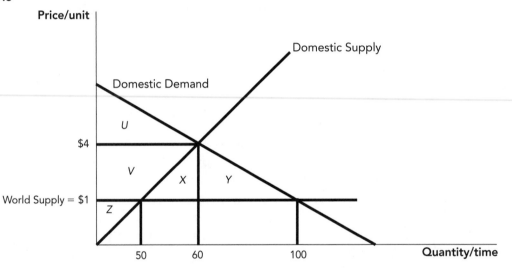

2. In Figure 19.3, with no international trade, consumer surplus is area
   a. U.
   b. $U + V + X + Z$.
   c. $V + Z$.
   d. Z.

3. In Figure 19.3, with no international trade, producer surplus is area
   a. U.
   b. $U + V + X + Y$.
   c. $V + Z$.
   d. Z.

4. In Figure 19.3, with no international trade, the total of producer and consumer surplus is

  a. U.

  b. $U + V + X + Y$.

  c. $V + Z$.

  d. Z.

5. In Figure 19.3, with international trade, imports are

  a. 20 units.

  b. 40 units.

  c. 80 units.

  d. 100 units.

6. In Figure 19.3, with international trade, consumer surplus is area

  a. U.

  b. $U + V + X + Y$.

  c. $X + Y$.

  d. Z.

7. In Figure 19.3, with international trade, producer surplus is area

  a. U.

  b. $U + V + X + Y$.

  c. $X + Y$.

  d. Z.

8. In Figure 19.3, with international trade, total surplus is

  a. U.

  b. $U + V + X + Y$.

  c. $X + Y$.

  d. Z.

9. In Figure 19.3, the gain from international trade is area

  a. U.

  b. $U + V + X + Y$.

  c. $X + Y$.

  d. Z.

10. In Figure 19.3, due to international trade, consumers

  a. gain V.

  b. lose V.

  c. gain $V + X + Y$.

  d. lose $V + X + Y$.

11. In Figure 19.3, due to international trade, producers

   a. gain V.

   b. lose V.

   c. gain $V + X + Y$.

   d. lose $V + X + Y$.

12. In Figure 19.3, if the market was protected to such an extent that all international trade stopped, then the deadweight loss would be

   a. $3.

   b. $60.

   c. $120.

   d. $240.

13. A tax on imports is called

   a. a comparative advantage.

   b. a tariff.

   c. an absolute advantage.

   d. a quota.

14. A restriction on the amount of imports to less than it would be with free trade is called

   a. a comparative advantage.

   b. a tariff.

   c. an absolute advantage.

   d. a trade quota.

15. According to the textbook, an argument made in favor of protection is that

   a. it increases total surplus

   b. it makes society better off.

   c. we need to protect some industries for national security reasons.

   d. All of the answers are correct.

Self-Practice Questions

1. Among the winners with a free trade on cars are

   a. domestic consumers of cars.

   b. the domestic government.

   c. the domestic economy as a whole.

   d. All of the answers are correct.

Figure 19.4

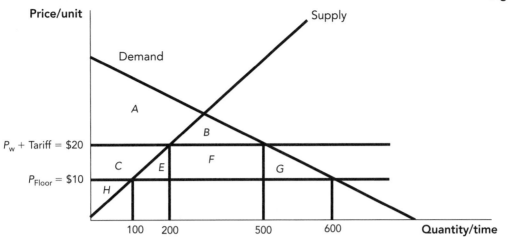

2. In Figure 19.4, with free international trade, consumer surplus is area

a. $A + B$.

b. $A + B + C + E + F + G$.

c. $C + H$.

d. H.

3. In Figure 19.4, with free international trade, producer surplus is area

a. $A + B$.

b. $A + B + C + E + F + G$.

c. $C + H$.

d. H.

4. In Figure 19.4, with free international trade, the total of producer and consumer surplus is area

a. $A + B + C$.

b. $A + B + C + E + F + G + H$.

c. $A + C + H$.

d. H.

5. In Figure 19.4, with free international trade, imports are

a. 100 units.

b. 300 units.

c. 500 units.

d. None of the answers are correct.

6. In Figure 19.4, with the tariff, consumer surplus is area

a. $A + B$.

b. $A + B + C + E + F + G$.

c. $C + H$.

d. H.

7. In Figure 19.4, with the tariff, producer surplus is area
   a. *A + B.*
   b. *A + B + C + E + F + G.*
   c. *C + H.*
   d. *H.*

8. In Figure 19.4, with the tariff, tariff revenue is area
   a. *A + B.*
   b. *F.*
   c. *E + G.*
   d. *H.*

9. In Figure 19.4, with the tariff, trade total surplus is
   a. *A + B.*
   b. *A + B + C + E + F + G.*
   c. *A + B + C + F + H.*
   d. *H.*

10. In Figure 19.4, the net loss from the tariff is area
    a. *A + B.*
    b. *F.*
    c. *E + G.*
    d. *H.*

11. In Figure 19.4, due to the tariff, trade consumers
    a. gain *C.*
    b. lose *C.*
    c. gain *C + E + F + G.*
    d. lose *C + E + F + G.*

12. In Figure 19.4, due to international trade, producers
    a. gain *C.*
    b. lose *C.*
    c. gain *C + E + F +G.*
    d. lose *C + E + F + G.*

13. In Figure 19.4, the government revenue from the tariff is
    a. $10.
    b. $1,000.
    c. $3,000.
    d. $5,000.

14. Free trade

    a. hurts the economy.

    b. increases total surplus.

    c. reduces imports.

    d. makes the people of a country worse off.

15. According to the textbook, an argument made in favor of protectionism is

    a. it increases total surplus

    b. it makes society better off.

    c. a country needs to protect its key industries.

    d. All of the answers are correct.

Answers to Self-Practice Questions

1. c, Topic: Analyzing Trade with Supply and Demand

2. b, Topic: Analyzing Trade with Supply and Demand

3. d, Topic: Analyzing Trade with Supply and Demand

4. b, Topic: Analyzing Trade with Supply and Demand

5. c, Topic: Analyzing Trade with Supply and Demand

6. a, Topic: The Costs of Protectionism

7. c, Topic: The Costs of Protectionism

8. b, Topic: The Costs of Protectionism

9. c, Topic: The Costs of Protectionism

10. c, Topic: The Costs of Protectionism

11. d, Topic: The Costs of Protectionism

12. a, Topic: The Costs of Protectionism

13. c, Topic: The Costs of Protectionism

14. b, Topic: Analyzing Trade with Supply and Demand

15. c, Topic: Arguments Against International Trade

20 (36)

International Finance

Learning Objectives

In this chapter, you will learn:

> How the balance of trade and balance of payments between nations are related
> What a country's balance of payments implies for its domestic saving and investment
> What exchange rates are and how they are determined
> How monetary and fiscal policies affect exchange rates and, in turn, how exchange rates affect policy outcomes

Summary

This chapter is about the financial interactions that occur between international trading partners—and the implications of these interactions for macroeconomic performance. The discussion is organized into four broad topics: the balance of payments; implications for domestic saving and investment; exchange rates; and implications for monetary and fiscal policy. We will address each topic in turn.

The Balance of Payments

To begin, it is useful to recognize that there are two types of interactions that can occur between trading partners: (1) the trade of goods and services and (2) the trade of assets (or capital). The trade of goods and services was discussed in Chapter 2. Much of the discussion in this chapter refers to the trade of capital, which is a direct consequence of the trade of goods and services.

Recall that the flow of goods and services between countries is measured by *net exports*, which is defined as *exports* minus *imports*. This is the "*NX*" term in the familiar GDP = C + I + G + NX equation. If a country's exports exceed its imports so that NX > 0, a **trade surplus** is said to occur. On the other hand, if imports exceed exports to make NX < 0, a **trade deficit** occurs.

The Case of Overall Balanced Trade

To understand the flow of assets between countries, it is important to recognize that every trade of goods and services in one direction requires a trade of assets in the opposite direction. Consider the example in Figure A. The United States exports goods and services to China. As payment for these exports, earnings of dollars flow into the United States. These earnings are equal to the value of the exports. The United States also imports goods and services from China. The spending to pay for these imports is a flow of dollars out of the United States that is equal to the value of the imports. Notice that if there is *balanced* trade of goods and services between the United States and China—that is, if exports equal imports so that NX = 0—the flow of assets (dollars) between the two countries will also be balanced.

Figure A

But what if trade is not balanced between the two countries? Suppose the United States imports more from China than it exports to China, so that the United States is running a trade deficit (NX < 0) with China. This would imply that spending on imports exceeds earnings from exports, so that there is a *net outflow* of dollars from the United States. Is this trade deficit—and the accompanying outflow of assets—a problem for the United States? Before answering this question, consider this. The arrangement between the United States and China in the diagram above is much like your relationship with your grocer. Unless you work in or supply produce to the grocery store where you usually shop, you will run a trade deficit with your grocer because you buy (import) more goods from the store than you sell (export) to the store. There is also a net outflow of dollars from you to the store. Is this a problem?

You probably do not regard the trade deficit you run with your grocer as a problem. One reason you don't view it as a problem is that you benefit from trade with the grocer. But also, you may recognize that you run trade *surpluses* with other trading partners that offset the trade deficit with the grocer. To illustrate this possibility, consider Figure B where a new trading partner—specifically, your employer—is introduced.

The two circles on the right represent you and your grocer. The arrows between these circles show the trade deficit and net outflow of dollars between you and your grocer. The new circle on the left shows your relationship with your employer. You run a trade *surplus* with your employer because you export more labor services to your employer than you import from her. Earnings from your employer implied by this trade surplus represent a net *inflow* of dollars for you. So, if you have *overall balanced*

Figure B

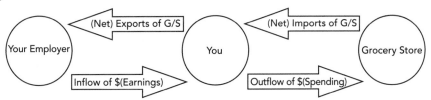

Balanced Trade Between You, the Grocery Store, and your Employer
(Balanced Trade Implies a Balanced Capital Flow—No Borrowing or Lending)

trade with both trading partners—that is, if (net) exports to your employer are equal to (net) imports from your grocer—the inflow of earnings from your employer will equal the outflow of spending to the grocery store. In this way, a trade *surplus* with one trading partner can be used to offset a trade *deficit* with another trading partner to achieve overall balanced trade.

Returning to the international trade context, the same result applies to the relationship between the United States and all of its trading partners. Running a trade surplus with some trading partners can be used to offset trade deficits with other trading partners (such as China). In other words, if overall trade balance (with all trading partners) is achieved, then the flow of assets must also balance. This is illustrated in Figure C (which is the same diagram as Figure B except that the names have been changed to countries).

Figure C

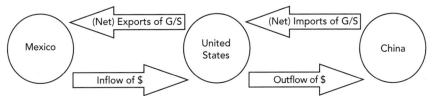

Balanced Trade Between United States and Rest of World
(Balanced Trade Implies a Balanced Capital Flow—No Borrowing or Lending)

Note that running trade deficits with some trading partners and surpluses with others is a natural result of trade. It is a natural result of comparative advantage to export more to those who buy the products and services we specialize in and import more from those who produce the things we do not produce ourselves (see Chapter 2 for a discussion of comparative advantage and specialization). To have balanced trade with every *individual* trading partner essentially requires a "barter" system (and achieving this balance with every individual trading partner is one of the disadvantages of such a system).

The Case of Overall Unbalanced Trade

The more interesting and difficult question is what the case of *unbalanced* trade with the rest of the world implies. Is it a problem if the U.S. trade deficit with China is *not* offset by trade surpluses with its other trading partners? To consider this possibility, let's turn to Figure D. Suppose trade with Mexico ends so there is no longer a trade surplus to offset the trade deficit with China. In other words, there is no longer a net inflow of funds from Mexico to finance the net outflow of funds to China. (In the analogy with individual trade, this is equivalent to saying that you quit working for your employer and no longer have the earnings required to continue spending at the grocery store.) The balance of payments requires the trade deficit with China (and the outflow of funds it implies) to be offset by an inflow of funds from somewhere. Generally speaking, the required inflow of funds must come from "borrowing" from abroad. (Intuitively, the term "borrowing" is used here because it is the only way a country or an individual's spending can exceed its earnings.) As shown in Figure D, borrowing from abroad provides the inflow of funds required to achieve balance of payments.

Figure D

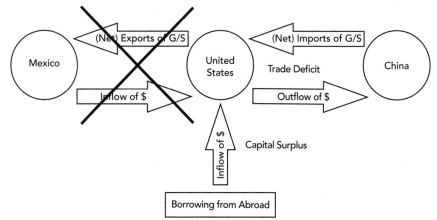

Unbalanced Trade Between United States and Rest of World
(A Trade Deficit Implies a Capital Surplus)

The inflow of funds required to offset a trade deficit is called a *capital inflow* or **capital surplus**. There are three possible sources of such a capital surplus:

1. Taking on debt (borrowing)

2. Selling previously acquired assets

3. Drawing down cash reserves

Likewise, a trade surplus would require an offsetting *capital outflow* or **capital deficit** to achieve balance of payments. A capital deficit can result from:

1. Paying off debt

2. Buying assets

3. Building up cash reserves

The case of a trade surplus and the required capital deficit is illustrated in Figure E. In this case, rather than "borrowing" from abroad, the United States is generally viewed as "lending" abroad to achieve the required capital outflow.

In the official language of international finance, a country's international balance of payments is described by the following accounting identity:

Current account = Capital account + Change in official reserves.

Each of these terms can now be understood. The **current account** describes all transactions that are "closed" in the current period—transactions that do not require any future transactions to be settled. Officially, three items make up the current account:

1. The balance of trade (net exports of goods and services)

2. Net income from capital held abroad (such as interest and dividends)

3. Net transfer payments (such as foreign aid)

Figure E

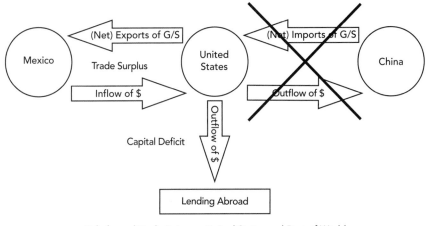

Unbalanced Trade Between United States and Rest of World
(A Trade Surplus Implies a Capital Deficit)

In the example of balanced trade with all trading partners (Figure C), only the current account is involved and all trade flows are balanced so that no offsetting action is required on the other side of the balance of payments identity.

The **capital account** involves the transfers of assets or capital required to offset surpluses or deficits in the current account. In general, three items make up the capital account:

1. foreign direct investment (FDI), which refers to the construction of *new* factories or other tangible assets in the domestic country

2. portfolio investment, which refers to the foreign purchase and transfer of ownership of *existing* domestic assets such as stocks, bonds, or other asset claims

3. other investment, such as the movement of a bank account across international borders

Take care to note that each of the items in the capital account *on net* can represent either an inflow or outflow of capital into or out of the domestic country. For example, the United States can receive more or less FDI from abroad than it provides in foreign countries. In the previous examples (Figures D and E), the capital surplus and deficit represent a change in the capital account to balance the position of the current account that results from the trade deficit or surplus on the left-hand side.

The last item in the balance of payments relationship is *changes in official reserves*. This refers primarily to changes in official holdings of *foreign* currency by domestic governments, although other foreign assets such as gold are also officially included.

Saving, Investment, and Capital Flows

So what does all of this tell us about the international perspective? It tells us that the U.S. trade deficit with China might not be offset by trade surpluses with other trading partners, so that the United States is running a trade deficit with the rest of the world. This is, in fact, currently the case. The balance of payments identity tells us that the United States must finance this trade deficit with a net capital inflow from the rest of the world. Such a net capital inflow implies that the United States is essentially borrowing from the rest of the world to help finance its investment at home. In other words, domestic saving is insufficient to finance domestic investment so the short-fall must be made up by foreign investment.

The relationship between domestic saving, investment, and international capital flows can be seen by looking at the national spending identity (first introduced in Chapter 5):

$$Y = C + I + G + NX.$$

Recall that Y is GDP, C is consumption spending, I is investment (or business spending), G is government purchases, and NX is net exports. Rearranging terms provides:

$$Y - C - G = I + NX.$$

The expression on the left-hand side, $Y - C - G$, is called *national saving*. It represents the difference between income and spending by consumers and the government in the aggregate economy. If we use S to denote national saving, we can express the national spending identity as follows:

$$S = I + NX.$$

This result says that national saving in an economy must equal investment plus net exports. This means that S and I need not be equal in an open economy (that is, an economy that engages in trade), and that any surplus (shortage) of domestic saving above (below) domestic investment must flow out to (in from) other countries. The net flow of saving into or out of the economy is represented by the NX term, which can be positive or negative. That is, if $NX > 0$ (the economy runs a trade surplus), there must be a net capital outflow (because domestic saving exceeds domestic investment). On the other hand, if $NX < 0$ (the economy runs a trade deficit), there must be a net capital inflow (because domestic saving is less than domestic investment).

Thus, the relationship between a country's trade balance, its national saving, and its capital flow can be summarized as follows:

Trade deficit $(NX < 0) \rightarrow$ Saving $<$ Investment
$\rightarrow$ Net capital inflow (Capital surplus)

Balanced trade $(NX = 0) \rightarrow$ Saving $=$ Investment $\rightarrow$ Balanced capital flow

Trade surplus $(NX > 0) \rightarrow$ Saving $>$ Investment
$\rightarrow$ Net capital outflow (Capital deficit)

So, is the U.S. trade deficit with the rest of the world a problem? Most economists would argue that it is not a problem, taking the view that the trade deficit implies investors around the world are willing to invest in the United States. This allows investment to continue in spite of low saving at home. And this is a good thing, because more investment means more productivity and more economic growth at home. A less optimistic view would be that the trade deficit implies the United States is saving too little. Note, however, that the trade deficit is a symptom of insufficient saving rather than the cause of it. This suggests the focus should be on addressing the low saving problem rather than the trade deficit itself. The potential problem is that a country cannot run trade deficits indefinitely into the future. Trade surpluses must eventually occur to "pay back" the foreign investors who provide the net capital inflow.

Exchange Rates

Since international trade involves transactions between trading partners that use different currencies, there is a need to exchange currency from one country for currency from another country. The **exchange rate** is the price of one currency in terms of another currency. Exchange rates are determined by the relative forces of supply and demand for the currencies involved.

The supply and demand for the Japanese yen is shown in Figure 20.2 in the text. The graph shows the market for yen with the exchange rate measured in "dollars per yen" on the vertical axis and the quantity of yen on the horizontal axis. If the dollar-per-yen exchange rate rises along the vertical axis, it means the yen is stronger (an **appreciation** of the yen has occurred) and the dollar is weaker (a **depreciation** of the dollar has occurred). The demand curve for yen slopes downward because a higher price (exchange rate) for yen is associated with a lower quantity of yen demanded. The supply curve for yen slopes upward because a higher exchange rate is associated with a higher quantity of yen supplied. Equilibrium in the market for yen occurs where the demand and supply curves intersect, thus determining the equilibrium dollar per yen exchange rate and the equilibrium quantity of yen exchanged in the market.

It is important to know the factors that will shift the demand and supply curves in foreign exchange markets.

Shifts in the demand for a currency are caused by:

1. changes in the demand for a country's exports

2. changes in the favorability of a country for foreign investment (for example, a change in interest rates in a country)

3. changes in the desirability of a currency for foreign reserve holdings

In general, *increases* in each of these factors will *increase* the demand for a country's currency. Such an increase in demand for yen is shown in Figure 20.3 in the text.

Shifts in the supply of a currency are caused by monetary policy actions (increases and decreases in the money supply) by the central bank of a country. Increases in supply will cause the currency to weaken while decreases in supply will cause it to strengthen. The effects of an increase and decrease in the supply of dollars by the Fed are shown in Figures 20.4 and 20.5 in the text.

While supply and demand analysis is useful for understanding exchange rate movements over relatively short periods of time, it does not fully explain how the values of various currencies are aligned over the long run. Economists use the **purchasing power parity (PPP) theorem** to explain how exchange rates are determined over the long run. The PPP theory states that *the real purchasing power of a currency should be the same whether that currency is spent at home or converted into another currency and spent abroad.*

All of the exchange rates we have discussed so far—like the ones in the supply and demand graphs shown in the text—are **nominal exchange rates** that show the rate at which *currency* from one country exchanges for *currency* from another country. The **real exchange rate** is the rate at which *goods and services* from one country exchange for *goods and services* from another country. To calculate the real exchange rate, you must know the nominal exchange rate and the prices of goods and services in the two countries.

For example, the real exchange rate (r) between the United States and Japan can be calculated using the formula:

$$r = e \times (P^{US}/P^{Japan})$$

where e is the nominal exchange rate expressed as yen per dollar, P^{US} is the U.S. price of goods and services, and P^{Japan} is the price of goods and services in Japan. The real exchange rate calculated using this formula is expressed in units of Japanese goods and services per unit of U.S. goods and services. To illustrate, suppose the price of an order of sushi is \$6 in the United States and ¥240 in Japan. If the nominal exchange rate is 120 yen per dollar (or $e =$ ¥120/\$1), then the real exchange rate can be calculated as:

$$r = ¥120/\$1 \times \$6/¥240 = 720/240 = 3/1$$

or 3:1 (stated as 3 orders of Japanese sushi per order of U.S. sushi).

The key to understanding the PPP theory is to recognize that the theory is used to explain how the *nominal* exchange rate is determined, but that the theory is based on a statement about the *real* exchange rate. Specifically, the theory states that the real exchange rate between two countries should be 1:1. This is what it means for "purchasing power" to be the same (that is, for "parity" to occur) across countries. To achieve this 1:1 real exchange rate, it is the nominal exchange rate, and possibly also the prices of the goods involved, that must adjust.

In general, the PPP theory is based on the **law of one price**, which states that if trade is free then identical goods should sell for about the same price in all locations around the world. For example, suppose sushi sells for \$6 an order in the United States and ¥240 in Japan. The law of one price would require that the nominal exchange rate adjust to 40 yen per dollar to achieve purchasing power parity; that is, to achieve a 1:1 real exchange rate. As you can see from this example, the nominal exchange rate predicted by the PPP theory is:

$$e = P^{Japan}/P^{US} = ¥240/\$6 = ¥40/\$1$$

As you may quickly recognize, a problem with this sushi example is that it is difficult to imagine how **arbitrage**—that is, buying sushi in Japan and selling it in the United States to profit from the price difference—could occur with a highly perishable product like sushi. In other words, the sushi would likely spoil unless it was shipped overnight at a very high cost, and even then it would be nothing like fresh sushi. This illustrates one of the reasons why the law of one price, and therefore the PPP theory, is only approximately true. This reason and some others are provided:

1. transportation costs

2. the fact that some goods cannot be shipped at all

3. tariffs and quotas

Because of these problems, we only expect prices in different locations to equalize to the point that it is no longer profitable for arbitrage to occur. The larger the transportation costs or trade restrictions (tariffs and quotas), the larger the gap is between prices in different locations. For goods that cannot be shipped at all, large price disparities will persist. In general, the PPP theory will provide a less accurate approximation of nominal exchange rates in economies that have limited port access (high transportation costs) and high trade barriers (tariffs and quotas).

In a final note about exchange rates, the text discusses a number of different regimes that are used by countries to manage the value of their currency. A **floating exchange rate** regime is one in which exchange rates are determined by market forces. There are a number of alternatives to a floating exchange rate. **Dollarization** occurs when a country uses the U.S. dollar as its own currency. **Fixed or pegged exchange rates** occur when a country makes a rigid promise to maintain a specified exchange rate between its currency and other currencies. A **dirty or managed float** means the country is willing to allow the exchange rate to fluctuate within certain bounds.

Monetary and Fiscal Policy, Exchange Rates, and the Balance of Trade

The basic framework for understanding how international affairs influence monetary and fiscal policy outcomes was established in previous chapters using the AD-AS framework (see Chapter 13 for details on the AD-AS model). From the AD-AS model, we already know that a change in net exports will shift the AD curve. So, we must determine whether policy actions have an effect on net exports. It turns out that policy does affect net exports and the key to this effect is policy's impact on exchange rates.

More specifically, there are two separate effects that are important here:

1. the impact of monetary and fiscal policy on exchange rates.

2. the impact of exchange rates, in turn, on exports, AD, and the ultimate policy outcome.

For monetary policy, the connection between policy actions and exchange rates is simple. Monetary policy involves changes in the supply of money which, in turn, affect exchange rates. Specifically, an expansionary monetary policy in the United States that increases the supply of dollars will cause the value of the dollar to depreciate, and vice versa. This exchange rate effect will, in turn, impact net exports in a way that *exaggerates* the shift of the AD curve implied by the inital policy action. For example, expansionary monetary policy will initially shift AD to the right, and then an increase in net exports that results from the depreciation of the domestic currency will shift the AD curve still further to the right.

This is because a depreciation of the dollar makes U.S. exports less expensive abroad and imports more expensive in the United States, thus increasing exports and decreasing imports, so that net exports increase as suggested. In the short run, this magnifies the expansionary effect of the policy. In the long run, higher inflation. Figure 20.6 in the text illustrates these effects.

In the case of fiscal policy, the connection between policy actions and exchange rates results from the policy's effect on interest rates. An expansionary fiscal policy increases the budget deficit and increases interest rates (see Chapters 9 and 18 for details). The increase in interest rates, in turn, increases the demand for the domestic currency causing the value of the domestic currency to appreciate (see the list of factors that shift the demand for a currency earlier in this chapter). This appreciation of the currency will affect net exports. This is because an appreciation makes domestic goods more expensive for foreigners and foreign goods less expensive at home, thus decreasing net exports. This exchange rate effect *limits* the expansionary impact of the policy, as the decline in net exports brought about by the appreciation of the domestic currency reduces the size of the rightward shift in AD. Note that this adds another limiting factor to the list of limits to fiscal policy discussed in Chapter 18.

Key Terms

trade deficit the deficit that occurs when the value of a country's imports exceeds the value of its exports

trade surplus the surplus that occurs when the value of a country's exports exceeds the value of its imports

balance of payments a yearly summary of all the economic transactions between residents of one country and residents of the rest of the world

capital surplus the surplus that occurs when the inflow of a country's foreign capital is greater than the outflow of domestic capital to other nations

current account the sum of the balance of trade, net income on capital held abroad, and net transfer payments

capital account this measures changes in foreign ownership of domestic assets including financial assets like stocks and bonds as well as physical assets

exchange rate the price of one currency in terms of another currency

appreciation an increase in the price of one currency in terms of another currency

depreciation a decrease in the price of a currency in terms of another currency

nominal exchange rate the rate at which you can exchange one currency for another

real exchange rate the rate at which you can exchange the goods and services of one country for the goods and services of another

purchasing power parity (PPP) theorem the idea that the real purchasing power of a money should be the same, whether it is spent at home or converted into another currency and spent abroad

law of one price the result that if trade were free, then identical goods should sell for about the same price throughout the world

floating exchange rate a regime in which a country allows its exchange rate to be determined primarily by market forces

fixed or pegged exchange rate a regime in which a country's government or central bank has promised to convert its currency into another currency at a fixed rate

dollarization what occurs when a foreign country uses the U.S. dollar as its currency

dirty or managed float a regime in which a country's currency value is not pegged but government intervenes extensively in the market to keep the value within a certain range

Traps, Hints, and Reminders

> A lot of information and a lot of new vocabulary are introduced in this chapter. This material also involves topics that students often find to be difficult. Be sure to devote enough time to learn these concepts.

> Remember that the balance of payments is really just an accounting relationship that involves the flow of funds that results from the trade of goods and services between countries. It often helps if you think of your personal trade with, for example, the local grocery store. If you run a "trade deficit" with the grocery store but don't have a job to provide the funds needed to support that deficit, you must borrow (or engage in one of the other activities that fall in the category of a capital surplus) to get the capital inflow required to achieve balance of payments. In this way, a capital surplus is offsetting your trade deficit.

> Don't lose sight of the big result from the whole "balance of payments" discussion: when a country has unbalanced trade with the rest of the world (that is, a trade deficit or a trade surplus), there *must* be an offsetting capital flow to achieve balance of payments. In the case of a trade deficit, there must be a capital surplus (inflow). For a trade surplus, there must be a capital deficit (outflow). The trade imbalance shows up on the "current account" side of the balance of payments identity and the capital flow shows up on the capital account side.

> In Figure D, note that "borrowing from abroad," which provides the needed capital surplus, can actually be the result of either (1) taking on debt (that is, actually borrowing); (2) selling assets; or (3) drawing down cash reserves. Likewise, the "lending abroad" in Figure E that provides the needed capital deficit can come from either (1) paying off debt; (2) buying assets; or (3) building up cash reserves. The "borrowing" and "lending" terms are used generally to provide an understanding of where funds are coming from or going.

> Many problems involving foreign exchange markets (and exchange rates) involve basic supply and demand analysis. It is important to familiarize yourself with shifting supply and demand curves to work these problems. As always with these types of graphical problems, practice makes perfect!

> Students are often confused by exchange rates because every exchange rate can be quoted in two different ways. For example, in talking about the exchange rate between dollars and yen, we can use the dollar-per-yen exchange rate or the yen-per-dollar exchange rate. The two are reciprocals of one another. For example, if the yen-per-dollar exchange rate is 1/2, then the dollar-per-yen exchange rate is 2/1 or 2. Spending some time looking at the exchange rates shown in Table 20.1 may be helpful here.

> Make sure you understand how movements in exchange rates affect the currencies involved. For example, an increase in the yen-to-dollar exchange rate implies a *strengthening* (or *appreciation*) of the dollar and a *weakening* (or *depreciation*) of the yen, and vice versa. If the dollar-per-yen exchange rate increases, it implies the opposite effect on the two currencies (an appreciation of the yen and depreciation of the dollar).

> When calculating the *real* exchange rate, make sure you use the correct nominal exchange rate in the calculation. For example, the formula provided requires the yen-per-dollar exchange rate, not the dollar-per-yen exchange rate. Using the wrong one will give the wrong answer.

> Be sure to express the units correctly when you calculate a real exchange rate. Using the formula provided, the result will be expressed as "units of foreign good per unit of U.S. good." Note that the real exchange rate is always expressed in units of goods, not currency.

Self-Practice Questions

1. What is the difference between a *trade* surplus and a *capital* surplus? Is it possible to have both a trade surplus and a capital surplus?

2. What are the sources of a capital surplus? A capital deficit? How does a capital surplus or deficit show up in the official balance of payments accounts?

3. Why is gold more likely to sell for the same price regardless of location than are haircuts?

4. Would you worry about a trade deficit with one country? Why or why not? How would a trade deficit with the rest of the world be different?

5. Explain how an "exchange rate effect" enhances the effectiveness of expansionary monetary policy but limits the effectiveness of expansionary fiscal policy.

6. If the United States becomes a worse place to invest, what will happen to the current and capital accounts?

7. A pound of Parmesan cheese costs $8.50 in the United States and 12.50 euros in Italy. If the nominal exchange rate is 0.7279 euros per U.S. dollar, what is the *real* exchange rate? What would *nominal* exchange rate to be in order to achieve purchasing power parity in this example?

Multiple-Choice Questions

1. If China sells more goods to Germany than Germany sells to China, then China has a _____ with Germany.
   a. comparative advantage
   b. trade surplus
   c. trade deficit
   d. current account balance

2. If more foreign investment flows into the United Kingdom than it invests abroad, then the United Kingdom has a
   a. capital surplus.
   b. trade surplus.
   c. capital deficit.
   d. current account balance.

3. The yearly summary of all economic transactions between residents of one country and residents of the rest of the world is the
   a. capital account.
   b. current account.
   c. trade balance.
   d. balance of payments.

4. What are the sources of the *investments* part of the capital account?
   a. foreign direct investment, portfolio investment, and other investments (such as moving bank deposits)
   b. foreign direct investment, portfolio investment, and foreign reserve transfers
   c. foreign direct investment, portfolio investment, and gold transfers
   d. foreign direct investment, foreign aid, and bank investment

5. If your country has a trade imbalance that is not being balanced by on offsetting capital account imbalance, that implies that the balance is being made up where?
   a. changes in official reserves
   b. printing money
   c. current account imbalance
   d. inflation

6. If your country has a trade deficit, then which of the following is probably in surplus?
   a. capital account
   b. current account
   c. gold transfers
   d. official reserves

7. If the French think that the United States is a better place to invest than France, then the United States is likely to have _____ with France.

    a. a trade surplus

    b. a capital account surplus

    c. a capital account deficit

    d. decreasing bank reserves

Use the following table (from July 12, 2009) for questions 8–11.

Currency Last Trade	US $	Yen	Euro	Can $	UK £	AU $	Swiss Franc
1 US $	—	92.5850	0.7179	1.1638	0.6197	1.2858	1.0867
1 Yen	0.0108	—	0.0078	0.0126	0.0067	0.0139	0.0117
1 Euro	1.3930	128.9664	—	1.6211	0.8632	1.7911	1.5137
1 Can $	0.8593	79.5540	0.6169	—	0.5325	1.1048	0.9338
1 UK £	1.6137	149.4029	1.1585	1.8780	—	2.0749	1.7536
1 AU $	0.7777	72.0058	0.5583	0.9051	0.4820	—	0.8452
1 Swiss Franc	0.9202	85.1983	0.6606	1.0709	0.5703	1.1832	—

8. Which of the following currencies is most valuable?

    a. 1 US $

    b. 1 Yen

    c. 1 UK £

    d. 1 Euro

9. If an American wants to buy 20 Swiss Francs with U.S. dollars, how many dollars does she need?

    a. 92.02

    b. 18.40

    c. 37.34

    d. 9.20

10. How many Australian dollars (rounded) are required to purchase 1 Canadian dollar?

    a. 1

    b. 1.10

    c. 0.90

    d. 0.72

11. If a haircut costs $20 in the United States and 27.17 Swiss Francs in Switzerland, what is the *real* exchange rate between Switzerland and the United States?

    a. 1.0867

    b. 0.9202

    c. 1.3585

    d. 0.7999

12. An increase in a country's exports will

    a. increase demand for that country's currency and increase the value of its currency.

    b. increase demand for that country's currency and decrease the value of its currency.

    c. decrease demand for that country's currency and increase the value of its currency.

    d. decrease demand for that country's currency and decrease the value of its currency.

13. If a country becomes more desirable as a place to invest, then its currency will

    a. appreciate.

    b. depreciate.

    c. be unaffected.

    d. experience inflation.

14. If a country's central bank increases the supply of its currency, then its currency will

    a. appreciate.

    b. depreciate.

    c. be unaffected.

    d. It is unclear from this example what will happen.

15. If a Big Mac costs $2.89 in the United States and 260 yen in Japan, then the nominal exchange rate predicted by the PPP theory is:

    a. 0.01 yen per dollar.

    b. 751.4 yen per dollar.

    c. 751.4 dollars per yen.

    d. 89.97 yen per dollar.

16. Which of the following would you expect to most closely fulfill the law of one price?

    a. 1 gallon of oil

    b. a shave at the barber

    c. cement

    d. an apartment

17. When a country allows its currency to change value at the whims of the market, this is known as

a. dollarization.

b. floating exchange rates.

c. a dirty or managed float.

d. fixed or pegged rates.

Homework Quiz

1. If Canada invests more abroad than other countries invest in Canada, then Canada has a

a. capital surplus.

b. trade surplus.

c. trade deficit.

d. current account balance.

2. A capital account surplus implies a

a. trade surplus.

b. net capital outflow.

c. net capital inflow.

d. current account surplus.

3. If a country runs a trade surplus and has no changes in official reserves, then it has a

a. current account surplus.

b. capital account surplus.

c. capital account deficit.

d. both a and c are correct.

4. Which of the following would be included in the capital account?

a. foreign direct investment

b. portfolio investment

c. movements of bank deposits across international borders

d. All of the answers are correct.

5. If the yen-per-dollar exchange rate declines from 100 yen per dollar to 90 yen per dollar, then

a. the dollar has depreciated.

b. the dollar has appreciated.

c. the yen has depreciated.

d. deflation has occurred.

6. If countries around the world stop using the U.S. dollar as their official reserve currency, then the

   a. demand for dollars would decrease and the dollar would appreciate.

   b. demand for dollars would decrease and the dollar would depreciate.

   c. demand for dollars would increase and the dollar would appreciate.

   d. demand for dollars would increase and the dollar would depreciate.

7. Expansionary monetary policy by the Fed is likely to cause the U.S. dollar to

   a. appreciate.

   b. depreciate.

   c. remain unaffected in value.

   d. There is not enough information to determine the answer.

8. If the same bottle of Australian wine costs AU$24.80 in Australia and $16.99 in the United States, then the nominal exchange rate predicted by the PPP theory would be

   a. AU$0.6851 per U.S. dollar.

   b. AU$421.352 per U.S. dollar.

   c. AU$1.4597 per U.S. dollar.

   d. $421.352 per Australian dollar.

9. Which of the following may prevent the actual exchange rate from being exactly what the PPP theory predicts?

   a. trade restrictions between countries

   b. high transportation costs

   c. inability to trade the good at all

   d. All of the answers are correct.

10. The use of expansionary fiscal policy may cause which of the following?

   a. an increase in domestic interest rates

   b. an appreciation of the domestic currency

   c. a decline in domestic exports

   d. All of the answers are correct.

Answer Key

Self-Practice Questions

1. A trade surplus says that your country has exported more goods and services to other countries than it has imported from other countries. In other words, $NX > 0$ in your country. A capital surplus says that other countries have provided more financial assets to your country than you have sent to other countries. In other words, there is a net capital inflow in your country. It is not possible to have a trade surplus and a capital surplus at the same time. A trade surplus must be offset by a capital deficit for balance of payments to occur.

Topic: The Balance of Payments

2. The possible sources for a capital surplus are: (1) taking on debt (borrowing); (2) selling assets; and (3) drawing down cash reserves. The possible sources for a capital deficit are just the opposite: (1) paying off debt; (2) buying assets; and (3) building up cash reserves. These items appear in the balance of payments through the capital account (as either FDI, portfolio investment, or other investment) or changes in foreign currency reserves (in other words, as items on the right-hand side of the balance of payments identity).

Topic: The Balance of Payments

3. Gold is more likely to sell for the same price regardless of location (a result of the law of one price) than haircuts because you can easily ship gold. You can't easily ship haircuts. If the price of gold is cheap in one country, entrepreneurs will go to that country and buy gold to ship to other locations. This arbitrage will have the effect of equalizing gold prices in different locations.

Topic: The Purchasing Power Parity Theorem

4. A trade deficit with one country is generally not a problem because it can be offset by trade surpluses with other countries. It is common to run trade deficits with some trading partners and trade surpluses with others because of normal trade patterns. A trade deficit with the rest of the world, however, must be offset by a capital inflow (or capital surplus) from the rest of the world. This means that foreign investors are providing capital for investment at home. While such a capital inflow is good because it allows for investment to continue in spite of low saving at home, such "borrowing" can't go on forever. Eventually, a trade surplus must occur to "pay back" the inflow of capital.

Topic: The U.S. Trade Deficit and Your Trade Deficit; The Balance of Payments

5. Both monetary and fiscal policy have an effect on exchange rates. For expansionary monetary policy, this effect occurs because an increase in the money supply will cause a depreciation of the currency. This depreciation makes exports more attractive for foreigners and imports less attractive at home. The result is an increase in net exports that increases AD more than the initial increase in the money supply, thus enhancing the effect of policy. For expansionary fiscal policy, the exchange rate effect occurs because higher deficits increase interest rates and

cause the currency to appreciate. This appreciation decreases net exports and shifts AD back to the left, thus partially offsetting the initial shift caused by the policy.

Topic: How Monetary and Fiscal Policy Affect Exchange Rates and How Exchange Rates Affect Aggregate Demand

6. If the United States becomes a worse place to invest, the demand for the U.S. dollar will decrease, causing a depreciation of the dollar. This makes U.S. exports more attractive to foreigners, thus improving the U.S. trade balance (that is, our current account will be less of a deficit). Accordingly, there will be less foreign investment in the United States, which will cause the capital account to be less of a surplus.

Topic: Two Sides, One Coin

7. Real exchange rate = nominal Euro-per-dollar exchange rate × (U.S. Price/ Italian Price) = 0.7279 × (8.50/12.50) = 0.4949 or approximately 1/2:1. In other words, approximately 1/2 pound of Italian cheese per pound of U.S. cheese. To achieve purchasing power parity (that is, in order for the real exchange rate to be 1:1), the nominal exchange rate would need to be 1.47 euros per dollar (= Italian price/U.S. price = 12.5 euros/$8.50).

Topic: Exchange Rate Determination in the Long Run

Answers to Multiple-Choice Questions

1. b, Topic: The U.S. Trade Deficit and Your Trade Deficit
2. a, Topic: The Balance of Payments
3. d, Topic: The Balance of Payments
4. a, Topic: The Balance of Payments
5. a, Topic: The Balance of Payments
6. a, Topic: The Balance of Payments
7. b, Topic: The Balance of Payments
8. c, Topic: What Are Exchange Rates?
9. b, Topic: What Are Exchange Rates?
10. b, Topic: What Are Exchange Rates?
11. d, Topic: What Are Exchange Rates?
12. a, Topic: Exchange Rate Determination in the Short Run
13. a, Topic: Exchange Rate Determination in the Short Run
14. b, Topic: Exchange Rate Determination in the Short Run
15. d, Topic: Exchange Rate Determination in the Long Run
16. a, Topic: Exchange Rate Determination in the Long Run
17. b, Topic: Fixed vs. Floating Exchange Rates

21 (19)

Political Economy and Public Choice

Learning Objectives

This chapter covers political economy and public choice. The topics discussed include:

> Voters and the Incentive to Be Ignorant

> Special Interests and the Incentive to Be Informed

> One Formula for Political Success: Diffuse Costs, Concentrated Benefits

> Voter Myopia and the Political Business Cycles

> Two Cheers for Democracy

Summary

This chapter begins by asking why mainstream economics is often ignored in the political realm. The authors offer three possibilities: politicians are right to ignore economic analysis; the possibility that mainstream economists are just wrong about economics; or the voting public and politicians have incentives that encourage them to ignore economics.

The first bad incentive comes from the fact that each voter knows that his or her vote is unlikely to decide a particular election. So voters individually decide not to become as informed as they might about various issues. Or voters individually decide to remain rationally ignorant. **Rational ignorance** is when the benefits from acquiring more information are less than the costs.

Rational ignorance matters because if voters are ignorant, then it is hard for them to make informed choices about what policies to support. Also, voters who are rationally ignorant will often make decisions for irrational reasons. Finally, rational ignorance matters because not everyone is rationally ignorant, and those who are not may have an advantage in getting the policies that benefit them at the expense of taxpayers as a whole.

A *special interest group* is a small group of people with a common interest. A special interest group can have an incentive to be informed. Any benefit a small group receives is spread over fewer people (a small percentage) than the voting public as a whole. Also, the benefits a special interest group can achieve for its members may, on a per member basis, be more, even much more, than the share of taxes per member that will be needed to support the government's providing the benefit.

The book discusses the U.S. sugar industry and its benefits from a government imposed quota on sugar imports. Sugar interests also donate to members of both political parties that are on the Senate Agriculture Committee who vote on the quota. In this case, sugar producers are rationally informed, since they each gain large benefits from the sugar quota and voters are rationally ignorant, since the sugar quota, costs them a cent or a few cents on any particular product that contains sugar.

The sugar example is a case of *concentrated benefits* and *diffused costs*. Concentrated benefits are benefits that accrue to a few individuals. Diffused costs are costs, like taxes, which are spread out widely, for example, like taxes, which fall on all taxpayers. Concentrated benefits and diffused costs provide an opportunity for a special interest group to get a benefit at the expense of taxpayers; they also provide an incentive to waste resources.

For example, if a policy costs society $500 and would provide a special interest group that pays 2 percent of the total tax bill of society a $400 benefit, then the group will certainly favor and push for this policy. If successful, the special interest group would then get its $400 benefit while paying $10 (or .02 × $500). So, the net gain of the special interest group is $390, that is, $400 − $10. However, society is wasting resources on this policy. It will cost society $500 to provide a $400 benefit, so $100 (or $500 − $400) is wasted. If enough policies are adopted that waste resources, then society members will see their standard of living erode.

A possible macroeconomic case of rational ignorance is that the winner of a United States presidential election can be accurately predicted by the state of the macroeconomy and the length of time the incumbent party has held the White House. This assumption is called the *political business cycle*. Maybe people in the United States who vote for president are myopic and do not consider to what extent the president is responsible for current economic conditions, or maybe the economy is the single critical issue for presidential voters. This voting pattern, of course, has created an incentive for incumbent presidents. They naturally do what they can to make the U.S. economic conditions as favorable as they can when heading into a presidential election, even if economic conditions are only artificially made to appear better. The book gives an example of social security payments being increased before a presidential election, while a tax increase was delayed until the following year. Data also shows that U.S. personal *income* has grown faster in election years than in nonelection years, and the difference is enough that it is likely not due to chance. This movement in U.S. personal income around elections is part of the political business cycle.

Up to this point in the chapter, democracy with rationally ignorant voters, special interest groups, and wasted resources does not look too good. However, when you look around the world, democratic countries are the richest, so they must be doing something right.

The alternative to democracy is often an autocratic government that seeks through control of the press to keep the people uninformed. While voters in democracies may sometimes be rationally ignorant, they are often better informed than people in autocratic societies, where the government controls the press. The evidence is that famines have happened not due to lack of food in a country. Rather, the reason is that the government is not responsive to the public because of a lack of a free press and representative government.

Key Terms

public choice the study of political behavior using the tools of economics

rational ignorance when the benefits of being informed are less than the costs of becoming informed

median voter theorem when voters vote for the policy that is closest to their ideal point on a line, then the ideal point of the median voter will beat any other policy in a majority rule election

Traps, Hints, and Reminders

Rational ignorance is when a person does not find it worthwhile to acquire information.

Concentrated benefits and diffused costs provide an incentive for special interest groups to be informed and may provide an incentive for the government to waste resources.

Homework Quiz

1. It is rational to remain ignorant when the costs of information are
   a. positive.
   b. negative.
   c. greater than the benefits from the information.
   d. less than the benefits from the information.

2. Among the problems created by rational ignorance is
   a. that information is more costly.
   b. that voters may decide based on irrational criteria.
   c. that old economic ideas that have been shown to be wrong.
   d. microeconomics.

3. Special interest groups can get gains for their members if
   a. benefits and costs are concentrated.
   b. benefits and costs are diffuse.
   c. benefits are concentrated and costs are diffuse.
   d. benefits are diffuse and costs are concentrated.

Use Scenario 1 to answer Questions 4 through 7.

Scenario 1

A. The interest group pays 5 percent of all taxes.

B. The interest group can get a $500 benefit from the government.

C. The policy benefit given the interest group costs the government $700.

4. In Scenario 1, the part of the benefit cost paid by members of the special interest group is

   a. $35.

   b. $465.

   c. $500.

   d. $700.

5. In Scenario 1, the net benefit to the members of the special interest group is

   a. $35.

   b. $465.

   c. $500.

   d. $700.

6. In Scenario 1, the net benefit to society is

   a. −$200 (minus $200).

   b. $35.

   c. $665.

   d. $700.

7. If the government in Scenario 1 adopts this policy, it will be

   a. maximizing societal happiness.

   b. wasting resources.

   c. rationally ignorant.

   d. maximizing GDP.

8. Famines are least likely when the press is

   a. free under a dictator.

   b. government-controlled in a democracy.

   c. free in a democracy.

   d. government-controlled under a dictator.

9. The median voter theorem says that if voters vote for the policy closest to their ideal point, then in a majority rule election

   a. the median policy will beat any other policy.

   b. the ideal point of the median voter will beat any other policy.

   c. the ideal point furthest from the median voter will beat any other policy.

   d. All of the answers are correct.

Self-Practice Questions

1. If the costs of information are greater than the benefits in an area, it is rational to
   a. become informed.
   b. not buy the product in that area.
   c. remain ignorant.
   d. forget the information.

2. When voters use irrational criteria, for example, the physical attractiveness of a candidate, to make a voting decision, it could be due to
   a. informed rationality.
   b. rational certainty.
   c. rational ignorance.
   d. All of the answers are correct.

3. If benefits are concentrated and costs are diffuse, then special interest groups
   a. are ineffective.
   b. can make their members better off at the expense of society as a whole.
   c. will make their members and society as a whole better off.
   d. are illegal.

Use Scenario 1 to answer Questions 4 through 7.

Scenario 1

A. The interest group pays 10 percent of all taxes.
B. The interest group can get a $700 benefit from the government.
C. The policy benefit given the interest group costs the government $1,000.

4. In Scenario 1, the part of the benefit cost paid by members of the special interest group is
   a. $100.
   b. $600.
   c. $700.
   d. $1,000.

5. In Scenario 1, the net benefit to the members of the special interest group is

a. $100.

b. $600.

c. $700.

d. $1,000.

6. In Scenario 1, the net benefit to society is

a. −$300 (minus $300).

b. $100.

c. $600.

d. $900.

7. If the government in Scenario 1 adopts this policy, it will be

a. maximizing societal happiness.

b. making a rationally ignorant decision.

c. rewarding an interest group at the expense of the rest of society.

d. maximizing GDP.

8. Famines are most likely when the press is

a. free under a dictator.

b. government-controlled in a democracy.

c. free in a democracy.

d. government-controlled under a dictator.

9. Democracies have a good record in

a. not killing their own citizens.

b. supporting property rights.

c. economic growth.

d. All of the answers are correct.

10. Special interest groups seek situations that have

a. concentrated costs.

b. diffused costs.

c. diffused benefits.

d. All of the answers are correct.

Answers to Self-Practice Questions

1. c, Topic: Voters and the Incentive to Be Ignorant

2. c, Topic: Voters and the Incentive to Be Ignorant

3. b, Topic: Special Interests and the Incentive to Be Informed

4. a, Topic: One Formula for Political Success: Diffuse Costs, Concentrated Benefits

5. b, Topic: One Formula for Political Success: Diffuse Costs, Concentrated Benefits

6. a, Topic: One Formula for Political Success: Diffuse Costs, Concentrated Benefits

7. c, Topic: One Formula for Political Success: Diffuse Costs, Concentrated Benefits

8. d, Topic: Two Cheers for Democracy

9. d, Topic: Two Cheers for Democracy

10. b, Topic: Two Cheers for Democracy